Hedge Funds
FOR
DUMMIES®

by Ann C. Logue

BICENTENNIAL
1807
WILEY
2007
BICENTENNIAL

Wiley Publishing, Inc.

Hedge Funds For Dummies®

Published by
Wiley Publishing, Inc.
111 River St.
Hoboken, NJ 07030-5774
www.wiley.com

WILEY

About the Author

Ann C. Logue is a freelance writer and consulting analyst. She has written for *Barron's*, the *New York Times*, *Newsweek Japan*, *Compliance Week*, and the *International Monetary Fund*. She's a lecturer at the Liautaud Graduate School of Business at the University of Illinois at Chicago. Her current career follows 12 years of experience as an investment analyst. She has a BA from Northwestern University, an MBA from the University of Chicago, and she holds the Chartered Financial Analyst designation.

Dedication

To Rik and Andrew, for their love and support.

Author's Acknowledgments

So many wonderful people helped me with this book! I talked to many hedge fund managers and others in the investment business, including Cliff Asness, Catherine Cooper, Beth Cotner, Nancy Fallon-Houle, Marshall Greenwald, Steve Gregornik, Anil Joshi of NuFact, Russ Kuhns, Alecia Licata of the CFA Institute, Dan Orlow, Tino Sellitto, Lisa Springer, Ryan Tagal at Morningstar, Scott Takemoto, and Gary Tilkin and Kelly Quintanilla at Global Forex Trading. I also talked to a handful of other hedge fund managers who asked to remain anonymous; they know who they are, and I hope they also know how much I appreciate their help. The CFA Society of Chicago put on a great conference entitled "New Considerations in the Quest for Alpha", which took place in the middle of writing this book and gave me some valuable insights. I'm grateful to the volunteers and presenters who made the day so productive for me.

I want to thank a few friends who helped give me direction on writing this and who pointed me to friends of theirs who work in the hedge-fund business. Bev Bennett, Lisa Duffy, Mary Richardson Graham, and Erik Sherman all were wonderful help. I also need to acknowledge Jennie Phipps, the proprietor of Freelance Success (www.freelancesuccess.com), one of the best resources out there for professional writers.

As for the mechanics of putting together the book, Natalie Harris, Stacy Kennedy, and Josh Dials of Wiley were fabulous to work with. Their patience and good humor got me through a tough schedule. Marcia Layton-Turner gets kudos for introducing me to her agent, Marilyn Allen, who became my agent and made the book possible.

Thanks, everyone!

Publisher's Acknowledgments

We're proud of this book; please send us your comments through our Dummies online registration form located at www.dummies.com/register/.

Some of the people who helped bring this book to market include the following:

Acquisitions, Editorial, and Media Development

Project Editor: Natalie Faye Harris

Acquisitions Editor: Stacy Kennedy

Assistant Editor: Courtney Allen

Copy Editor: Josh Dials

Editorial Program Coordinator: Hanna K. Scott

Technical Editor: Russell Rhoads

Editorial Manager: Christine Beck

Editorial Assistants: Erin Calligan, David Lutton

Cartoons: Rich Tennant
(www.the5thwave.com)

Composition Services

Project Coordinator: Adrienne Martinez

Layout and Graphics: Claudia Bell, Carl Byers, Lavonne Cook, Barry Offringa, Laura Pence, Julie Trippetti

Proofreaders: Jessica Kramer, Christy Pingleton, Christine Sabooni

Indexer: Techbooks

Publishing and Editorial for Consumer Dummies

> **Diane Graves Steele,** Vice President and Publisher, Consumer Dummies

> **Joyce Pepple,** Acquisitions Director, Consumer Dummies

> **Kristin A. Cocks,** Product Development Director, Consumer Dummies

> **Michael Spring,** Vice President and Publisher, Travel

> **Kelly Regan,** Editorial Director, Travel

Publishing for Technology Dummies

> **Andy Cummings,** Vice President and Publisher, Dummies Technology/General User

Composition Services

> **Gerry Fahey,** Vice President of Production Services

> **Debbie Stailey,** Director of Composition Services

Contents at a Glance

Table of Contents

Part IV: Special Considerations Regarding Hedge Funds 255

Introduction

∙∙

You've seen the headlines in the financial press. You've heard the rumors about mythical investment funds that make money no matter what happens in the market. And you want a part of that action.

I have to be upfront: Hedge funds aren't newfangled mutual funds, and they aren't for everyone. They're private partnerships that pursue high finance. If you don't mind a little risk, you can net some high returns for your portfolio. However, you have to meet strict limits put in place by the Securities and Exchange Commission — namely that you have a net worth of at least $1 million or an annual income of $200,000 ($300,000 with a spouse). Most hedge-fund investors are institutions, like pensions, foundations, and endowments; if you work for an institution, you definitely need to know about hedge funds. I also have to let you in on a little secret: Not all hedge fund mangers are performing financial alchemy. Many of the techniques they use are available to any investor who wants to increase return relative to the amount of risk taken.

Hedge Funds For Dummies tells you what you need to know, whether you want to research an investment in hedge funds for yourself or for a pension, an endowment, or a foundation. I also give you information about investment theories and practices that apply to other types of investments so you can expand your portfolio. Even if you decide that hedge funds aren't for you, you can increase the return and reduce the risk in your portfolio by using some of the same techniques that hedge fund managers use. After all, not everything fund managers do requires a PhD in applied finance, and not everything in the world of investing is expensive, difficult, and inaccessible.

About This Book

First, let me tell you what this book is not: It is not a textbook, and it is not a guide for professional investors. You can find several of those books on the market already, and they are fabulous in their own right. But they can be dry, and they assume that readers have plenty of underlying knowledge.

This book is designed to be simple. It assumes that you don't know much about hedge funds, but that you're a smart person who needs or wants to know about them. I require no calculus or statistics prerequisite; I just give you straightforward explanations of what you need to know to understand how hedge funds are structured, the different investment styles that hedge fund managers use, and how you can check out a fund before you invest.

And if you still want to read the textbooks, I list a few in the Appendix.

Conventions Used in This Book

I'll start with the basics. I put important words that I define in *italic* font. I often **bold** the key words of bulleted or numbered lists to bring the important ideas to your attention. And I place all Web addresses in `monofont` for easy access.

I've thrown some investment theory into this book. You don't need to know this information to invest in hedge funds, but I think it's helpful to know what people are thinking when they set up a portfolio. I also make an effort to introduce you to some technical terms that will come up in the investment world. I don't want you to be caught short in a meeting where a fund manager talks about generating alpha through a multifactorial arbitrage model that includes behavioral parameters. Many hedge fund managers are MBAs or even PhDs, and two notorious ones have Nobel Prizes. Folks in the business really do talk this way! (To alert you to these topics, I often place them under Technical Stuff icons; see the section "Icons Used in This Book.")

During printing of this book, some of the Web addresses may have broken across two lines of text. If you come across such an address, rest assured that I haven't put in any extra characters (such as hyphens) to indicate the break. When using a broken Web address, type in exactly what you see on the page, pretending as though the line break doesn't exist.

What You're Not to Read

I include sidebars in the book that you don't need to read in order to follow the chapter text. With that stated, though, I do encourage you to go back and read through the material when you have the time. Many of the sidebars contain practice examples that help you get a better idea of how some of the investment concepts work.

You can also skip the text marked with a Technical Stuff icon, but see the previous section for an explanation of why you may not want to skim over this material.

Foolish Assumptions

The format of this masterpiece requires me to make some assumptions about you, the reader. I assume that you're someone who needs to know a lot about hedge funds in a short period of time. You may be a staff member or director at a large pension, foundation, or endowment fund, and you may need to invest in hedge funds in order to do your job well, even if you aren't a financial person. I assume that you're someone who has plenty of money to invest (whether it's yours or not) and who could benefit from the risk-reduction strategies that many hedge funds use. Maybe you've inherited your money, earned it as an athlete or performer, gained it when you sold a company, or otherwise came into a nice portfolio without a strong investment background.

I also assume that you have some understanding of the basics of investing — that you know what mutual funds and brokerage accounts are, for example. If you don't feel comfortable with the basic information, you should check out *Investing For Dummies* or *Mutual Funds For Dummies,* both by Eric Tyson. (Calculus and statistics may not be prerequisites, but that doesn't mean I don't have any!)

No matter your situation or motives, my goal is to give you information so that you can ask smart questions, do careful research, and handle your money in order to meet *your* goals.

And if you don't have a lot of money, I want you to discover plenty of information from this book so that you'll have it at the ready someday. For now, you can structure your portfolio to minimize risk and maximize return with the tools that I provide in this book. You can find more strategies than you may know.

How This Book Is Organized

Hedge Funds For Dummies is sorted into parts so that you can find what you need to know quickly. The following sections break down the structure of this book.

Part I: What Is a Hedge Fund, Anyway?

The first part describes what hedge funds are, explains how managers structure them, and gives you a little history on their development. It also covers the nuts and bolts of SEC regulation and the process of buying into a hedge fund. Go here for the basics.

Part II: Determining Whether Hedge Funds Are Right for You

In this part, I cover many investment considerations — including your time horizon, your liquidity needs, taxes, and other special needs you may have — in order to help you figure out if you should be in a hedge fund. If you decide against it, the information here may give you some ideas on other ways you can invest your money. All investors face a list of goals for their money as well as a series of constraints that they must meet. The art of investing is balancing your investment objectives with constraints so that your money works the way you need it to.

Part III: Setting Up Your Hedge Fund Investment Strategy

Part III is the fun part — an overview of the many different ways that a hedge fund manager can generate a big return while keeping investment risk under control. Fund managers can buy and sell, take big risks, or rely on arbitrage; become shareholder activists or trade anonymously; or speculate on interest rates, currencies, or pork bellies.

This part also covers ways you can evaluate a hedge fund's risk-adjusted performance. You've probably heard of a handful of headline-grabbing hedge-fund scams, and you can find plenty of investors who have learned the hard way just how much risk their hedge funds had.

Part IV: Special Considerations Regarding Hedge Funds

Part IV covers some additional information that you need to know, including alternatives to hedge funds for smaller investors. It also tells you how to get help with your investment and how to check out the background of the fund and fund manager before you invest. My goal is to help you do the right thing with your money, and this section helps you make the decisions that will achieve this goal.

Part V: The Part of Tens

In this *For Dummies*-only part, you get to enjoy some top 10 lists. I present 10 reasons to invest in hedge funds, 10 reasons to avoid them, and 10 myths about the hedge-fund business. I also include an Appendix full of references so that you can get more information if you desire.

Icons Used in This Book

You'll see five icons scattered around the margins of the text. Each icon points to information you should know or may find interesting about hedge funds. They go as follows:

This icon notes something you should keep in mind about hedge-fund investing. It may refer to something I've already covered in the book, or it may highlight something you need to know for future investing decisions.

Tip information tells you how to invest a little better, a little smarter, a little more efficiently. The information can help you ask better questions of your hedge fund manager or make smarter moves with your money.

I've included nothing in this book that can cause death or bodily harm, as far as I can figure out, but plenty of things in the world of hedge funds can cause you to make expensive mistakes. These points help you avoid big problems.

I put the boring (but sometimes helpful) academic stuff here. I even throw in a few equations. By reading this material, you get the detailed information behind the investment theories, some interesting trivia, or some background information.

Where to Go from Here

Well, open up the book and get going! Allow me to give you some ideas. You may want to start with Chapter 1 if you know nothing about hedge funds so you can get a good sense of what I'm talking about. If you need to set up your investment objectives, look at Chapters 7, 8, and 9. If you want to know what hedge fund managers are doing with your money, turn to Chapters 10 through 13. And if you're about to buy into a hedge fund, go straight to Chapter 18 so that you can start your due diligence.

If you aren't a big enough investor for hedge funds but hope to be some day, start with Chapters 5, 6, and 9 to discover more about structuring portfolios. Chapter 16 can help you meet your investment objectives as a small investor.

Part I

What Is a Hedge Fund, Anyway?

The 5th Wave   By Rich Tennant

"Consultants and brokers? Leverage? Market efficiency?
I say we stick the money in the ground like always, and
then we feed this guy to the sharks."

In this part . . .

You read about hedge funds in the financial press. You hear about their ability to generate good returns in all market cycles. And you wonder — just what is this investment? In this part, you find out. Part I covers definitions and descriptions you hear in the hedge fund world, offers the basics on just how much regulatory oversight hedge funds have, and lets you know how to buy into a hedge fund.

Chapter 1

What People Talk About When They Talk About Hedge Funds

*I*s a hedge fund a surefire way to expand your wealth or a scam that will surely rip you off? Is it a newfangled mutual fund or a scheme for raiding corporations and ripping off hard-working employees? You see hedge funds in the news all the time, but it's hard to know exactly what they are. That's because, at its essence, a hedge fund is a bit of a mystery. A *hedge fund* is a lightly regulated investment partnership that invests in a range of securities in an attempt to increase expected return while reducing risk. And that can mean just about anything.

Some of the smartest money managers on Wall Street have started their own hedge funds, attracted by the freedom to manage money as they see fit while raking in good money for themselves and their investors in the process. Hedge fund managers today take on the roles of risk managers, investment bankers, venture capitalists, and currency speculators, and they affect discussions in boardrooms at brokerage firms, corporations, and central banks all over the world.

In this chapter, I cover the basic vocabulary and structure of hedge funds. Having this knowledge helps you understand hedge funds so that you can figure out what you need to know in order to make the best decisions with your money. Also, I clarify what a hedge fund is and what it isn't, which is important because you come across a lot of myth and misinformation out there. The information you find here serves as a springboard for the topics I introduce throughout the rest of the book, so get ready to dive in.

Defining Hedge Funds (Or Should I Say Explaining Hedge Funds?)

Here's the first thing you should know about hedge funds: They have no clear identity or definition. In the investment world, "I run a hedge fund" has the same meaning as "I'm a consultant" in the rest of the business world. The speaker may be managing money and making millions, or she may want a socially acceptable reason for not having a real job. The person who really manages money may go about her business in any number of ways, from highly conservative investing to wildly aggressive risk taking. She may be beating the market handily, or she may be barely squeaking by.

I'm not trying to say that the term "hedge fund" means nothing. Here's the short answer: A *hedge fund* is a lightly regulated investment partnership that uses a range of investment techniques and invests in a wide array of assets to generate a higher return for a given level of risk than what's expected of normal investments. In many cases, but hardly all, hedge funds are managed to generate a consistent level of return, regardless of what the market does. Before I get to the longer, more complicated explanation of hedge funds, however, it helps to know exactly what hedging is.

Hedging: The heart of the hedge-fund matter

Hedging means reducing risk, which is what many hedge funds are designed to do. Maybe you've hedged a risky bet with a friend before by making a conservative bet on the side. But a hedge fund manager doesn't reduce risk by investing in conservative assets. Although risk is usually a function of return (the higher the risk, the higher the return), a hedge fund manager has ways to reduce risk without cutting into investment income. She can look for ways to get rid of some risks while taking on others with an expected good return, often by using sophisticated techniques. For example, a fund manager can take stock-market risk out of the fund's portfolio by selling stock index futures (see Chapter 5). Or she can increase her return from a relatively low-risk investment by borrowing money, known as *leveraging* (see Chapter 11). If you're interested in investing in hedge funds, you need to know how the fund managers are making money.

Risk remains, no matter the hedge-fund strategy, however. Some hedge funds generate extraordinary returns for their investors, but some don't. In 2005, the Credit Suisse/Tremont Hedge Fund Index — a leading measure of hedge-fund performance (www.hedgeindex.com/hedgeindex/en/default.aspx) — reported that the average hedge-fund return for the year was 7.61 percent. The NASDAQ Composite Index (www.nasdaq.com) returned only 1.37 percent for the same period, but the Morgan Stanley Capital International World Index (www.mscibarra.com) was up 10.02 percent. The amount of potential return makes hedge funds more than worthwhile in the minds of many accredited and qualified investors (see Chapter 2 for more on hedge-fund requirements).

In 2005, 9,000 hedge funds managed a total of $1 trillion dollars, according to Hedge Fund Research, a firm that tracks the hedge-fund industry (www.hedgefundresearch.com). In 2005, therefore, the average fund had $111 million in assets. Given the industry's standard fee structure, in which managers charge at least 1 or 2 percent of assets (see Chapter 2), the typical fund generated $1.1 to $2.2 million on the year for the fund manager.

Return is a function of risk. The challenge for the hedge fund manager is to eliminate some risk while gaining return on investments — not a simple task, which is why hedge fund managers get paid handsomely if they succeed. (For more on risk and return, check out Chapter 6.)

Identifying hedge funds: The long explanation

Okay, I'll go ahead and start covering the gory details of hedge funds. A *hedge fund* is a private partnership that operates with little to no SEC regulation (see Chapter 3). A hedge fund differs from so-called "real money" — traditional investment accounts like mutual funds, pensions, and endowments — because it has more freedom to pursue different investment strategies. In some cases, these unique strategies can lead to huge gains while the traditional market measures languish. The following sections dig deeper into the characteristics of hedge funds, as well as the bonuses that come with funds and the possibility of bias in the reported performances of funds.

Little to no regulatory oversight

Hedge funds don't have to register with the U.S. Securities and Exchange Commission (SEC). The funds and their managers also aren't required to register with the National Association of Securities Dealers (NASD) or the Commodity Futures Trading Commission, the major self-regulatory bodies in the investment business. However, many funds register with these bodies anyway, choosing to give investors peace of mind and many protections otherwise not afforded to them (not including protection from losing money, of course). Whether registered or not, hedge funds can't commit fraud, engage in insider trading, or otherwise violate the laws of the land.

In order to stay free of the yoke of strict regulation, hedge funds agree to accept money only from accredited or qualified investors. *Accredited investors* are individuals with a net worth of at least $1 million or an annual income of $200,000 ($300,000 for a married couple; see Chapter 2 for more information). *Qualified investors* are individuals, trust accounts, or institutional funds with at least $5 million in investable assets.

The reason for the high-net-worth requirement is that regulators believe people with plenty of money generally understand investment risks and returns better than the average person, and accredited investors can afford to lose money if their investments don't work out. In order to avoid the appearance of improper marketing to unqualified investors, hedge funds tend to stay away from Web sites, and some don't even have listed telephone numbers. You have to prove your accredited status before you can see offering documents from a fund or find out more about a fund's investment style.

Aggressive investment strategies

In order to post a higher return for a given level of risk than otherwise expected (see Chapter 6, which covers risk calculation in much detail), a hedge fund manager has to do things differently than a traditional money manager. This fact is where a hedge fund's relative lack of regulatory oversight becomes important: A hedge fund manager has a broad array of investment techniques at his disposal that aren't feasible for a tightly regulated investor.

Here are a few investment techniques that I cover in great detail in this book:

- ✔ **Short-selling (Chapter 11):** Hedge fund managers buy securities that they think will go up in price. If they spot securities that are likely to go down in price, they borrow them from investors who own them and then sell the securities in an attempt to buy them back at lower prices in order to repay the loans.

✔ **Leverage (Chapter 11):** Hedge funds borrow plenty of money in order to increase return — a technique that can also increase risk. The fund has to repay the loan, regardless of how the investment works out.

The use of leverage is a key difference between hedge funds and other types of investments. Most hedge funds rely on leverage to increase their returns relative to the amount of money that they have in their accounts. Because of the risk that comes with the strategy, funds often use leverage only for low-risk investment strategies in order to increase return without taking on undue risk.

✔ **The Buffet Line:** Okay, so I made this one up. But hedge fund managers do have a wide range of investment options. They don't have to lock in to stocks and bonds only. They buy and sell securities from around the world, invest in private deals, trade commodities, and speculate in derivatives. They have flexibility that traditional asset managers only dream about. (See Chapters 10 through 13 for more information on the many options.)

Manager bonuses for performance

Another factor that distinguishes a hedge fund from a mutual fund, individual account, or other type of investment portfolio is the fund manager's compensation. Many hedge funds are structured under the so-called *2 and 20* arrangement, meaning that the fund manager receives an annual fee equal to 2 percent of the assets in the fund and an additional bonus equal to 20 percent of the year's profits.

The performance fee is a key factor that separates hedge funds from other types of investments. U.S. Securities and Exchange Commission regulations forbid mutual funds, for example, from charging performance fees. You may find that the percentages differ from the 2 and 20 formula when you start investigating prospective funds, but the management fee plus bonus structure rarely changes.

The hedge fund manager receives a bonus only if the fund makes money. Many investors love that the fund manager's fortunes are tied to theirs. The downside of this rule? After all the investors pay their fees, the hedge fund's great performance relative to other investments may disappear. For information on fees and their effects on performance, see Chapters 2 and 4.

Biased performance data

What gets investors excited about hedge funds is that the funds seem to have fabulous performances at every turn, no matter what the market does. But the great numbers you see in the papers can be misleading.

Hedge funds are private investment partnerships with little to no regulatory oversight, which means that fund managers don't have to report performance numbers to anyone other than their fund investors. Many hedge fund managers report their numbers to different analytical, consulting, and index firms, but they don't have to. Naturally, the funds most likely to participate in outside performance measurement are the ones most likely to have good performance numbers to report — especially if the fund managers are looking to raise more money.

On the other end of the success spectrum, many hedge funds close shop when things aren't going well. If a fund manager is disappointed about losing his performance bonus (see Chapter 2), he may just shut down the fund, return all his investors' money, and move on to another fund or another project. Hedge Fund Research, a consulting firm that tracks the industry (www. hedgefundresearch.com), estimates that 11.4 percent of hedge funds closed in 2005. After a fund shuts down, it doesn't report its data anymore (if it ever did); poorly performing funds are most likely to close, which means that measures of hedge-fund performance have a bias toward good numbers.

You have to do your homework when buying into a hedge fund. You can't rely on a rating service, and you can't rely on the SEC, as you can with a mutual fund or other registered investment. You have to ask a lot of tough questions about who the fund manager is, what he plans for the fund's strategy, and who will be verifying the performance numbers. (Chapter 18 covers this process, called *due diligence,* in more detail.)

Pledging the secret society: Getting hedge fund information

Some hedge funds are very secretive, and for good reason: If other players in the market know how a fund is making its money, they'll try to use the same techniques, and the unique opportunity for the front-running hedge fund may disappear. Hedge funds aren't required to report their performance, disclose their holdings, or take questions from shareholders.

However, that doesn't mean hedge fund managers refuse to tell you anything. A fund must prepare a partnership agreement or offering memorandum for prospective investors that explains the following:

- ✔ The fund's investment style
- ✔ The fund's structure
- ✔ The fund manager's background

A hedge fund should also undergo an annual audit of holdings and performance and give this report to all fund investors. (The fund manager may require you to sign a nondisclosure agreement as a condition of receiving the information, but the information should be made available nonetheless.) But the hedge fund manager doesn't have to give you regular and detailed information, nor should you expect to receive it. (See Chapter 8 for more on transparency issues.)

Beware the hedge fund that gives investors no information or that refuses to agree to an annual audit — that's a blueprint for fraud. See Chapter 18 for more information on doing your due diligence.

Surveying the History of Hedge Funds

Hedge funds haven't been around forever, but they aren't exactly new, either. Their fortunes have varied with those of the markets, and their structures have evolved with the development of modern financial-management theories and techniques.

Knowing the history of hedge funds will give you a sense of how the modern hedge fund market came to be. You'll understand how some of the myths of funds originated and why some of the practices (like fee structure and secrecy) developed over time. And, the history is interesting. Isn't that reason enough? In this section, I cover some of the highlights and lowlights that have come since the development of the first hedge fund in 1949.

Alfred Winslow Jones and the first hedge fund

Alfred Winslow Jones wrote a book in 1941 that examined the attitudes of residents of Akron, Ohio toward large corporations. The book, *Life, Liberty, and Property: A Story of Conflict and a Measurement of Conflicting Rights,* is still in print by the University of Akron Press. When it came out, the magazine *Fortune* reprinted sections of the book, and Jones eventually joined the magazine's editorial staff. While at *Fortune,* he learned quite a bit about investing, and in 1949, he quit the magazine to form a money-managing firm, A.W. Jones & Co., which is still in business in New York.

At *Fortune,* Jones covered some of the developing theories in modern finance — especially the notion that markets were inherently unpredictable. He was determined to find a way to remove the risk from the market, and the way he found was to buy the shares of stocks expected to go up while selling short the stocks expected to go down. With this strategy, he could remove much of the risk of the market, and his fund would have steady performance year in and year out. I describe this style of investing, sometimes called *long-short investing,* in Chapter 11. And in a twist of fate, *Fortune* first used the term "hedge fund" to describe Jones' fund in a 1966 article.

Alfred Winslow Jones had two other innovations for the modern hedge fund, both of which have overshadowed his investment style:

- ✔ **His analysis of the Investment Company Act of 1940:** In the analysis, he stated that a private-partnership structure can remain unregistered as long as its investors are accredited.

- ✔ **His fee.** He charged his investors 20 percent of the fund's profits. More than 50 years later, few hedge fund managers still hedge the way that Jones did, but almost every manager copies his partnership structure and fee schedule.

1966 to 1972: Moving from hedging to speculating

After Alfred Winslow Jones developed a nice business collecting 20 percent of the profits from his partners by using his hedging strategy, other money managers wondered if they could also set up private partnerships and charge 20 percent while following different investment strategies. The answer? Yes. The name "hedge fund" stuck, but the emerging funds were more speculative than hedged. *Hedging* is the process of reducing risk. *Speculating* is the process of seeking a high return by taking on a greater-than-average amount of risk. Although hedging and speculating are opposing strategies, many hedge funds today use both.

The change in strategy took place partly because the stock market was really strong, so short-selling proved to be a losing game (see Chapter 11). Also, because the stock market was so strong, money managers could make a lot of money by borrowing and buying stock.

And then, in 1972, the bottom dropped out. A stock-market bubble that formed at the end of the 1960s finally and totally burst, leaving hedge fund managers with big losses. Some managers who had borrowed heavily (or leveraged; see Chapter 11) found themselves insolvent. Most of the newly formed hedge funds shut their doors, and the aggressive style of investing fell out of favor for about a decade.

George Soros, Julian Robertson, and hedge-fund infamy

George Soros, who co-founded the Quantum Fund with Jim Rogers, and Julian Robertson, who founded the Tiger Fund, are two legendary names in the hedge-fund business. They both formed their funds in the late 1960s to early 1970s go-go era, managed to hold on through the market collapse that took place in 1972, and then started posting spectacular profits in the 1980s.

Both funds followed a macro strategy, which means they looked to profit from big changes in the global macroeconomy (see Chapter 13). They took bets on changes in interest rates, exchange rates, economic development, and commodities prices. They also used options and futures (see Chapter 5) to improve their returns and manage their risks. (In 1988, George Soros published a book about his unconventional approach to investing, *The Alchemy of Finance* [Wiley].)

Both fund managers achieved icon status of sorts in the 1990s, and then both managers ran into trouble. Soros made huge profits by betting (and investing accordingly) that the currencies of several Asian countries were overvalued. He was right, but the resulting collapse of the currencies led to political unrest in Indonesia and Malaysia and turned Soros into a pariah. Julian Robertson believed that the huge increases in technology stocks were overdone in the 1990s, and he was proven right in 2000, but his performance suffered terribly until then. (Chapter 13 dives into these stories more deeply.)

The rise and fall of Long-Term Capital Management

One infamous hedge fund, Long-Term Capital Management, had spectacular performance year after year until it nearly caused a global financial meltdown in 1998. The history of this firm tells a tale of just how little hedging takes place at some of the biggest and best-performing hedge funds.

The 1960s and 1970s brought about huge changes in the way that people thought about finance and investing. Experts developed several new academic theories (you can read about them in Chapters 6 and 14). Some academics realized that they could earn more by managing money than they could by teaching students how to do it, so they quit their university jobs and started hedge funds.

In 1994, John Meriwether, an experienced bond trader at Solomon Brothers, joined with other traders and two professors, Robert Merton and Myron Scholes, to form a fund. The fund's managers took advantage of relatively small differences in the prices of different bonds. Most of their trades were simple and low-risk, but they used a huge amount of borrowed money (known as *leverage*) to turn their simple trades into unusually large returns. In 1997, Merton and Scholes shared the Nobel Prize in Economics, giving their fund a highly academic aura. People thought the fund was filled with investors who had discovered an unusually low-risk way of generating unusually large returns.

In the summer of 1998, the Russian government defaulted on its bonds, which caused investors to panic and trade their European and Japanese bonds for U.S. government bonds. Long-Term Capital Management bet that the small differences in price between the U.S. bonds and the overseas bonds would disappear; instead, the concern over Russia's problems led to large differences in price that steadily widened. The mistake made it difficult for Long-Term Capital Management's managers to repay the large amounts of money that the fund had borrowed, which put pressure on the investors who had given the loans. The Federal Reserve Bank then organized a restructuring plan with the banks that Long-Term Capital Management dealt with in order to prevent a massive financial catastrophe. In total, Long-Term Capital Management lost $4.6 billion dollars.

The Yale Endowment: Paying institutional attention to hedge funds

The Yale University Endowment, which operates in the financial and trade press, has $15.2 billion under management as of press time, making it the second-largest college endowment in the world. Its success has driven most of the institutional interest in hedge funds, and institutional interest has created all the demand in the market. The performance of the Yale Endowment is considered a milestone.

It has long kept 25 percent of its assets in hedge funds, and in this avenue, it performs the best out of all the major university endowments. The fund's manager, David Swensen, earned a doctorate in finance at Yale and worked on Wall Street before joining Yale's staff in 1985. Once on board, he decided to diversify the university's money into holdings other than stocks and bonds, adding investments in private equity, oil, timberland, and hedge funds.

Management members at other endowments and foundations have long looked at Yale's performance with green-eyed envy. They've witnessed one of the richest colleges get richer, in part due to hedge-fund investing, and they want to do the same. By 2005, the National Association of College and University Business Officers reported that 8.7 percent of all college-endowment money was invested in hedge funds, up from 1.8 percent in 1996. And, in 2005, 21.7 percent of the money in endowments larger than $1 billion was invested in hedge funds.

Generating Alpha

Hedge fund managers all talk about alpha. Their goal is to generate alpha, because alpha is what makes them special. But what the heck is it? Unfortunately, alpha is one of those things that everyone in the business talks about but no one really explains.

Alpha is a term in the Modern (Markowitz) Portfolio Theory (MPT), which I explain in Chapter 6. The theory is a way of explaining how an investment generates its return. The equation used to describe the theory contains four terms:

- The risk-free rate of return
- The premium over the risk-free rate that you get for investing in the market
- Beta
- Alpha

Beta is the sensitivity of an investment to the market, and *alpha* is the return over and above the market rate that results from the manager's skill or other factors. If a hedge fund hedges out all its market risk, its return comes entirely from alpha.

People aren't always thinking of the Modern (Markowitz) Portfolio Theory when they use alpha. Instead, many people use it as shorthand for whatever a fund does that's special. In basic terms, alpha is the value that the hedge fund manager adds.

In theory, alpha doesn't exist, and if it does exist, it's as likely to be negative (where the fund manager's lack of skill hurts the fund's return) as positive. In practice, some people can generate returns over and above what's expected by the risk that they take, but it isn't that common, and it isn't easy to do.

Introducing Basic Types of Hedge Funds

Despite the ambiguities involved in describing hedge funds, which I outline in detail at the beginning of this chapter, you can sort them into two basic categories: absolute-return funds and directional funds. I look at the differences between the two in the following sections.

Because hedge funds are small, private partnerships, I can't recommend any funds or fund families to you. And because hedge fund managers can use a wide range of strategies to meet their risk and return goals (see the chapters of Part III), I can't tell you that any one strategy will be appropriate for any one type of investment. That's the downside of being a sophisticated, accredited investor: You have to do a lot of work on your own!

Absolute-return funds

Sometimes called a "non-directional fund," an *absolute-return fund* is designed to generate a steady return no matter what the market is doing. Alfred Winslow Jones managed his pioneering hedge fund with this goal, although the long-short strategy (see Chapter 11) that he used was just one of several methods that snagged him consistent returns (see the section "Alfred Winslow Jones and the first hedge fund").

Although absolute-return funds are close to the true spirit of the original hedge fund, some consultants and fund managers prefer to stick with the label absolute-return fund rather than "hedge fund." The thought is that hedge funds are too wild and aggressive, and absolute-return funds are designed to be slow and steady. In truth, the label is just a matter of personal preference.

An absolute-return strategy is most appropriate for a conservative investor who wants low risk and is willing to give up some return in exchange. (See Chapter 9 for more information on structuring your portfolio.) Hedge fund managers can use many different investment tools within an absolute-return strategy, a few of which I present in Part III of this book.

Some say that absolute-return funds generate a bond-like return, because like bonds, absolute-return funds have relatively steady but relatively low returns. The return target on an absolute-return fund is usually higher than the long-term rate of return on bonds, though. A typical absolute-return fund target is 8 percent to 10 percent, which is above the long-term rate of return on bonds and below the long-term rate of return on stock.

Directional funds

Directional funds are hedge funds that don't hedge — at least not fully (see the section "Hedging: The heart of the hedge-fund matter" for more on hedging). Managers of directional funds maintain some exposure to the market, but they try to get higher-than-expected returns for the amount of risk that they take. Because directional funds maintain some exposure to the stock market, they're said to have a *stock-like return.* A fund's returns may not be steady from year to year, but they're likely to be higher over the long run than the returns on an absolute-return fund.

Directional funds are the glamorous funds that grab headlines for posting double or triple returns compared to those of the stock market. The fund managers may not do much hedging, but they have the numbers that get potential investors excited about hedge funds.

A directional strategy is most appropriate for aggressive investors willing to take some risk in exchange for potentially higher returns. (See Chapter 9 for more information on structuring your portfolio.)

Meeting the People in Your Hedge Fund Neighborhood

Many different people work for, with, and around hedge funds. The following sections give you a little who's who so you understand the roles of the people you may come into contact with and of people who play a large role in your hedge fund.

Managers: Hedging for you

The person who organizes the hedge fund and oversees its investment process is the *fund manager* — often called the *portfolio manager* or even PM for short. The fund manager may make all the investment decisions, handling all the trades and research himself, or he may opt to oversee a staff of people who give him advice. (See Chapter 2 for more information on hedge fund managers.) A fund manager who relies on other people to work his magic usually has two important types of employees:

✔ **Traders:** The traders are the people who execute the buy-and-sell decisions. They sit in front of computer screens, connected to other traders all over the world, and they punch in commands and yell in the phones.

Traders need to act quickly as news events happen. They have to be alert to the information that comes across their screens, because they're the people who make things happen with the fund.

✔ **Analysts:** Traders operate in real time, seeing what's happening in the market and reacting to all occurrences; analysts take a longer view of the world. They crunch the numbers that companies and governments report, ask the necessary questions, and make projections about the future value of securities.

Lawyers: Following the rules

Although hedge funds face little to no regulation, they have to follow a lot of rules in order to maintain that status. Hedge funds need lawyers to help them navigate the regulation exemptions and other compliance responsibilities they face (see Chapter 3), and hedge fund investors need lawyers to ensure that the partnership agreements are in order (see Chapter 2) and to assist with due diligence (see Chapter 18).

Consultants: Studying funds and advising investors

Because big dollars are involved, many hedge fund investors work closely with outside consultants to advise them on their investment decisions. Hedge fund managers also work with consultants — both to find accredited investors through marketing and to make sure that they're meeting their investors' needs. (For more information on working with a consultant, see Chapter 17.)

A consultant can take a fee from an investor or from a hedge fund, but not from both. That way, the consultant stays clear of any conflicts of interest.

Advising investors

A key role for consultants is helping investors make sound investment decisions. Staff members who oversee large institutional accounts — like pensions, foundations, or endowments — rely heavily on outside advisors to ensure that they act appropriately, because these types of accounts hinge on the best interests of those who benefit from the money. (See Chapters 8 and 10 for more on this responsibility.)

Consultants not only ensure that investors follow the law, but also advise investors on the proper structure of their portfolios in order to help them meet their investment objectives. A consultant analyzes how the investor divides the money among stocks, bonds, and other assets and then recommends alternative allocations that may result in less risk, higher return, or both (see Chapter 9 for more on asset allocation).

Monitoring performance

Investment consultants track the performance of their clients, of course, but they also build relationships with hedge fund managers and collect data on the risk, return, and investment styles of different funds and fund managers. They use the information they collect to advise their clients on investment alternatives. Because you can find only a few central repositories for hedge-fund performance information, and because hedge funds don't have to make their return data public, this is an important service. (See Chapter 14 for more info on evaluating performance.)

Marketing fund managers

Many hedge funds are small organizations. In some cases, the fund managers work alone. These funds have a small number of investors, and they may not allow their investors to take money out for a year or two, so they don't need to do constant marketing. It rarely makes sense for a hedge fund to have a dedicated marketing person on staff.

But that doesn't mean hedge funds don't need to find other investors. When the fund is new or when current investors want to withdraw their money, marketing becomes important. To help find new investors, many hedge funds work with consultants, who bring together investors looking for suitable hedge funds and hedge funds looking for suitable investors.

Paying Fees in a Hedge Fund

Hedge funds are expensive, for a variety of reasons. If a fund manager figures out a way to get an increased return for a given level of risk, he deserves to be paid for the value he creates. And, one reason hedge funds have become so popular is that money managers want to keep the money that they earn instead of getting bonuses only after they meet big corporate overhead. Face it — a good trader would rather keep his gains than share them with an overpaid CEO who doesn't know a teenie from a tick. (Chapters 2 and 4 contain more information on paying fees, but here I cover the basics.)

A *teenie* is ¹⁄₁₆ of a dollar. A *tick* is a price change. If the next trade takes a security up in price, it's an *uptick;* if it takes the security down, it's a *downtick.* In the olden days, when everything traded in eighths or teenies, ticks were printed on strips of paper called *ticker tape.* If a person did something notable, like win a World Series or land on the moon, he or she would receive a parade, and everyone at the brokerage firms would open their windows and throw out their used ticker tape (hence, ticker-tape parade).

Almost all hedge fund managers receive two types of fees: management fees and performance fees. More than anything else, this business model, not the investment style, distinguishes hedge funds from other types of investments.

Managing management fees

A *management fee* is a fee that the fund manager receives each year for running the money in the fund. Usually set at 1 percent to 2 percent of assets in a fund, the management fee covers certain operating expenses, salaries for the fund manager and staff, and other costs of doing business. The fund pays other expenses in addition to the management fee, such as trading commissions and interest.

For example, say a hedge fund has $100,000,000 in assets. It charges a 2-percent management fee, which is $2,000,000. The fund has an additional $1,750,000 in trading expenses and interest. The fund investors have to pay fees from the assets whether the fund makes money or bombs.

If the fund's management fee is too low, the fund manager won't be able to run the business effectively or hire the necessary staff. If the fee is too high, the fund manager will make such a nice living that he or she will have little incentive to pursue a performance bonus.

Shelling out your percentage of performance fees

Most hedge funds take a percentage of the profits as a *performance fee* — also called the *incentive fee* or sometimes the *carry.* The industry standard is 20 percent, although some funds take a bigger cut and some take less. You need to read the offering documents you receive from a fund to find out what the fund charges and whether the fund's potential performance justifies the fee.

If the fund loses money, the fund manager gets no performance fee. In most funds, the fund managers can't collect performance fees after losing years until the funds' assets return to their previous high levels, sometimes called the *high-water marks*. You can find a detailed explanation of how these fees work in Chapter 2.

The performance fee means that the fund manager's incentives are closely aligned with those of the fund's investors. As folks on Wall Street say, hedge fund managers eat what they kill. The big problem with the performance fee is that if a fund has a negative year, the fund manager has an incentive to close the fund and start over instead of losing the performance fee. And every fund will have a bad year once in a while.

In many cases, a hedge fund's outstanding performance disappears after the performance fee hits the manager's pocket. You may find that you're paying a lot of money and dealing with many complications to be in a hedge fund when you could get the same net return through a different type of investment, like a mutual fund.

Chapter 2

Examining How Hedge Funds Are Structured

*Y*ou may have heard that a hedge fund is just a mutual fund with better performance, but hedge funds have some characteristics that make them very different from other investment vehicles. For instance, hedge funds don't necessarily have better performance than mutual funds, but they do have higher fees. In this chapter, I cover some of the fine points about the structure of hedge funds that you need to know before you make any commitments. For example, in order to give hedge fund managers the flexibility to pursue aggressive and offbeat investment strategies, the funds themselves have a rigid approach to their investors. Purchase and sale restrictions tend to be high, and the fees associated with the funds tend to be great.

And even if you decide that hedge funds aren't right for you after you read this book, you can still benefit from some of the strategies used in other investment vehicles such as mutual funds and pooled accounts. I cover mutual funds that have some hedge-fund characteristics in Chapters 15 and 16; I cover other accounts, which, like hedge funds, are for wealthy investors but that have some big differences, in this chapter.

Exploring the Uneven Relationships between Fund Partners

Most hedge funds are structured as lightly regulated (if at all) investment partnerships (see Chapter 1 for more on this definition), but that doesn't mean that the partners within a fund are equal. Some partners stand on higher ground than others, and the structure of the fund affects the liability that investors may take on. If you're not familiar with hedge-fund partnerships, read on to find out more. If you buy into a hedge fund, you enter into a partnership, and you need to know what rights and obligations you have — especially if something goes wrong.

General partners: Controlling the fund

A hedge fund's *general partners* are the founders and money managers of the fund. These people have the following responsibilities:

- Form the fund
- Control the fund's investment strategy
- Collect the fees charged
- Pay the bills
- Distribute the bonuses

In exchange for their control, general partners take on unlimited liability in the fund, which means that their personal assets are at stake if the fund's liabilities exceed its assets. Many general partners own their stakes through S corporations or other structures that shield their personal assets.

Under the Internal Revenue code, an *S corporation* is an ownership structure for small businesses that under U.S. tax code provides owners with limited liability, meaning that their personal assets are unlikely to be called upon to settle any corporate liabilities. (It isn't the perfect protection, by the way, and a good lawyer can explain all the nuances to you.) An S corporation pays no income tax because all gains and losses of the corporation pass through to the individual shareholders in proportion to their holdings. The shareholders claim the gains and losses on their personal income taxes.

When the general partners launch the fund, they put up the seed money for operations. They rent office space, buy the fund's computers, and hire an administrative staff. The partners have to do much of this work before a single dollar enters the fund or any asset-management fee hits their bank accounts. It's possible to set up a hedge fund for as little as $10,000, depending on how much work the fund manager does and how much the lawyers who advise her charge.

A fund's original general partners may grant the general-partner status to certain key hires or give it as a reward to top-performing employees. Some firms give the partnership in lieu of bonuses, and at other firms, managers expect new partners to write checks to cover their shares of the partnership stake.

When general partners leave a fund, the other general partners buy out their stakes. The money for the buyout may come from different sources:

- From the new investments of any new partners
- From the firm's own account
- From a note given to the former partner, which the fund pays off over time

Limited partners: Investing in the fund

The *limited partners* (often shortened to *limiteds*) of a hedge fund are the people who invest in the fund — yep, I'm talking about you. When investors give their money to the fund manager (a general partner) to invest, they take a stake in the fund as a business. Limited partners can come in many different flavors:

- Individual investors, pension funds, or endowments
- Brokerage firms or investment companies that are sponsoring the fund's general partners
- Other partnerships or corporations formed to make investments in hedge funds (as with a fund of funds; see Chapter 15 for more information on funds of funds)

Limited partnership has its drawbacks. Limited partners pay fees to the general partners for their management services (see the section "Fee, Fi, Fo, Cha Ching! Paying the Fees Associated with Hedge Funds" later in the chapter). They have little or no say in the fund's operations. And the fund may restrict ongoing communication with the general partners to only a few times per year. But, in exchange for these limitations of control, limited partners have limited liability. You can lose only the amount you invest in the fund and no more. If the hedge fund goes belly-up and a landlord comes looking for back rent, he can go after the general partners and their personal assets, but he can't come to the limited partners and ask them for money.

Only Accredited or Qualified Investors Need Apply

Much like going to college, watching romantic comedies, or following NASCAR, hedge funds aren't for everyone. If you don't meet the U.S. Securities and Exchange Commission's definition of an accredited investor (see Chapter 3 for more on the SEC), you can't invest in a hedge fund. And some hedge funds go beyond the SEC requirements, making sure that all investors are qualified purchasers. Hedge funds are risky investment funds that may use unusual strategies or buy exotic assets, and they have to answer to very little regulatory oversight. As the joke goes, when doctors make mistakes, at least they kill their patients. When hedge fund managers make mistakes, they ruin their clients.

In the following sections, I help you identify your investment status and give you some reasons for the SEC requirements. I also present some options available to you if you don't meet the requirements.

Which kind of investor are you?

Federal securities laws provide a great deal of oversight to smaller investors — especially individuals who have little financial expertise but want to benefit from the potential returns that come with mutual funds and stock ownership. Rigid regulations govern mutual fund operations, initial public offerings of securities, and licensing for brokers. However, lawmakers also understand that some investors know the risks they're taking and that these investors can afford to take them. The government allows these folks to invest in securities with much less regulatory oversight: venture capital, private offerings, and hedge funds, to name a few.

Rather than make investors take a test of their financial knowledge, the SEC has set different asset thresholds. The following section covers all the reasons in detail; here, I give you the quick and dirty on the different types of investors.

Accredited investor

An *accredited investor* is an individual who can enter into a hedge fund due to his or her financial standing. An investor is considered accredited if he or she meets any of the following criteria:

- Has a net worth of more than $1 million, owned alone or jointly with a spouse
- Has earned $200,000 in each of the past two years
- Has earned $300,000 in each of the past two years when combined with a spouse
- Has a reasonable expectation of making the same amount in the future

For investment institutions, such as pensions, endowments, and trusts, the primary qualification is having $5 million in assets.

The Securities and Exchange Commission defines the term accredited investor under Rule 501 of Regulation D as follows:

1. A bank, insurance company, registered investment company, business development company, or small business investment company

2. An employee benefit plan, within the meaning of the Employee Retirement Income Security Act — if a bank, insurance company, or registered investment adviser makes the investment decisions or if the plan has total assets in excess of $5 million

3. A charitable organization, corporation, or partnership with assets exceeding $5 million

4. A director, executive officer, or general partner of the company selling the securities

5. A business in which all the equity owners are accredited investors

6. A natural person who has individual net worth, or joint net worth with the person's spouse, that exceeds $1 million at the time of the purchase

7. A natural person with income exceeding $200,000 in each of the two most recent years, or joint income with a spouse exceeding $300,000 for those years, and a reasonable expectation of the same income level in the current year

8. A trust with assets in excess of $5 million — not formed to acquire the securities offered — whose purchases a sophisticated person makes

See Chapter 3 for more information on accreditation and registration.

Qualified purchaser

Many hedge funds set a more stringent standard than the SEC, asking that investors be *qualified purchasers* under their own internal guidelines. Typically, qualified purchasers are individuals with at least $5 million in investable assets. Trusts, endowments, and pensions must have at least $25 million in investable assets. Investors who meet a firm's qualified-purchaser standards are sometimes called *super accredited.*

Funds go above and beyond because of concerns that the accredited-investor definition hasn't been indexed for inflation (it was last revised in 1982, when a dollar was worth more than twice what it's worth today). Many people now meet the definition thanks to appreciation in residential real estate or self-directed retirement savings. An investor may have $1 million in assets, but that doesn't mean he's knowledgeable enough or solvent enough to invest in lightly regulated hedge funds.

Some firms may not set a qualified-purchaser standard, but they set their minimum-investment standards for their limited partners high enough that they may as well have a rule in place. For example, a hedge fund may demand that its new investors put in at least $1 million or $5 million, which eliminates a novice investor who has most of her wealth in her house and her IRA account.

Why do hedge fund investors need to be qualified or accredited?

A million bucks in assets? An income of $200,000 per year? No fair! Not so fast — Paris Hilton is proof that money has nothing to do with sophistication and sound decision-making. Maybe she's the reason the little investor can't be in a hedge fund!

From the hedge fund manager's perspective, he or she has two very practical reasons for requiring investors to be accredited or qualified. The first is that the administrative work that comes with a large number of small accounts is much greater than with a small number of large accounts.

The second reason is a legal matter. No, a fund won't get in trouble if it sells to unaccredited investors; it just can't charge performance fees. Under the Investment Advisers Act of 1940, registered funds can't charge performance fees unless their investors invest at least $750,000 or have a net worth of $1.5 million. Hedge fund managers don't want to lose their big bonuses because small investors clutter their funds (see the section "Fee, Fi, Fo, Cha Ching! Paying the Fees Associated with Hedge Funds" for more on fund fees).

Do funds really check up on you?

What if your net worth is $999,000, and a hedge fund requires that its investors have $1 million in assets? You're so close! Will the fund let you squeak in? It depends. The fund may force you to sign a statement saying that you're accredited and that you meet any other standards the fund has set. It may ask for proof in the form of W2 forms, tax returns, or account statements. Heck, the fund may take your word for it.

In any event, if your investment in the fund doesn't work out, you can't argue that the fund manager took advantage of a little guy like you.

Most funds have a simple way to verify their investors' net worth: They ask for big upfront investments or commitments. You may be able to borrow the money to invest in a hedge fund (using some leveraging of your own; see Chapter 11), but any lender will likely want proof that you can repay your loan, even if the investment goes south.

Do I have alternatives if I don't qualify?

If you don't qualify for a hedge fund as an accredited or qualified investor, you may be tempted to put this book down and pick up a copy of *Frugal Living For Dummies* (by Deborah Taylor-Hough [Wiley]). That's a good and useful book, no matter your income, but don't give up on *Hedge Funds For Dummies* yet. I still have useful information for you! The following sections give you options if you don't qualify for a hedge fund outright.

Using hedge-fund strategies within a small portfolio

Understanding how hedge funds work can help you make better choices among mutual funds or help you balance a large position in your company's stock. Part III of this book outlines many of the strategies that hedge funds use to gain a high return. And if you flip to Chapter 16, you'll see plenty of ideas for using these strategies in a smaller investment portfolio.

Finding mutual funds that use hedge-fund strategies

Some mutual fund companies offer funds designed to capture the benefits of hedge funds within the highly regulated mutual-fund structure. For example, some mutual funds now follow a long-short strategy — they can buy stocks expected to go up and sell short stocks expected to go down. (To *sell short,* a fund manager borrows an asset, sells it, and then buys the asset back at a lower price to repay the original asset lender. The fund makes money if the asset falls in price; see Chapter 11.) Janus and Laudus Rosenberg are among the fund companies that offer these funds. Chapters 15 and 16 cover mutual funds that use hedge-fund techniques in great detail. You can also check out *Mutual Funds For Dummies,* 4th Edition, by Eric Tyson (Wiley), for more general info on mutual funds.

Following the Cash Flow within a Hedge Fund

As counterintuitive as it may sound, cash isn't always good. Cash management is a huge challenge for any investment manager, causing some hedge fund managers to turn down money. They do this because until they can use new funds to buy securities that they expect to appreciate in price, the cash sits in the funds, earning very little interest. That lack of activity quickly puts a drag on the overall performance of the funds. The sad truth is that in some market climates, fund managers simply can't find any good investments that fit their funds' parameters.

In the following sections, I present the strategies that hedge funds use during periods of market inactivity, and I outline the policies that some hedge funds use regarding withdrawals and closings.

Substituting commitments for cash

To give their funds time to put cash to work without diluting performance, many hedge fund managers ask new investors for commitments rather than for cash up front. For example, say an investor wants to invest $5 million. A fund manager asks for a commitment for the entire $5 million, but she takes only $1 million for an initial investment. After she puts the initial money to work by purchasing securities that she expects to appreciate, she goes back to the investor for some or all the remaining $4 million.

If a hedge fund asks for only part of an investment with a commitment to fund the rest at a later date, you have to be ready to write the check. You may decide to have the money sitting in cash, earning a low rate of return, until the hedge fund manager is ready for the money. And the hedge fund gets all the glory of great performance!

The following table shows another numerical example. If a hedge fund manager doesn't see any great investment opportunities, she can increase return by limiting how much money the investor puts in:

Money the investor earmarks for a hedge fund	$5,000,000
Money the fund manager puts work	$4,000,000
Return on that portion	15%
Money kept in cash for lack of good opportunities	$1,000,000
Cash return	2%
Fund manager's return in dollars	$620,000
Fund manager's return in percentages	12%

In this example, the investor's return is the same, but the hedge fund manager gets to report a higher return on her portion:

Money the investor earmarks for a hedge fund	$5,000,000
Amount the fund manager takes	$4,000,000
Return on that portion	15%
Fund manager's return in dollars	$600,000
Fund manager's return in percentages	15%
Amount investor keeps in cash	$1,000,000
Cash return in percentages	2%
Cash return in dollars	$20,000
Investor's total return in cash	$620,000
Investor's total return in percentages	12%

Waiting for withdrawals and distributions

Many hedge funds specialize in complex *illiquid* investments; in other words, it may not be easy for the fund to sell a security and get full price for it. Because of that fact, most hedge funds limit the amount and timing of investment withdrawals. Funds may even require investors to give notice of withdrawals in order to allow the fund manager time to generate cash without disrupting the overall portfolio (see Chapter 7 for more info on this topic).

Some hedge funds go further than limiting withdrawals to once per quarter or once per year — they may not allow investors to withdraw their money for more than two years.

Sometimes, a hedge fund gets so big that the fund manager can't find any more great investments that fit the fund's investment strategy. At that point, he may start returning the fund's money to his investors. Whether they want them or not, the investors get their checks, and they have to find other places to put their money — places that meet their desired risk and return parameters.

A hedge fund's need for cash may not fit yours. The fund may not be able to invest all the money that you want it to; it may not be able to give your money back when you need it; or it may send you a check when you least expect it, hurting your ability to meet your financial goals. This is another reason only accredited investors are allowed in hedge funds. Anyone who depends on cash in a hedge fund for any outside reasons has no business investing in the fund. (See Chapter 7 for more information on hedge fund cash flows and what they mean to your investment needs.)

Regular payment distributions

Many hedge funds make regular distributions to their investors. Once per quarter, or once per year, for example, a fund may send its investors some portion of the fund's earned income (dividends and interest) and capital gains (asset price appreciation).

Although the amount returned to investors may vary greatly each time, the process has some benefits:

- ✔ It helps reduce pressure for withdrawals by allowing investors to get some cash out.
- ✔ It helps the fund manager keep the size of the fund matched to the available investment opportunities in the market, according to the strategy the fund currently follows.
- ✔ It makes it easier for taxable investors to pay the IRS (see Chapter 8 for more information).

Be sure to ask the fund manager about this policy during your initial interview (see Chapter 18).

Extraordinary distributions

Many hedge funds are reluctant to commit to regular schedules for monetary distributions because a commitment would limit their investment flexibility. Instead, these funds choose to make distributions when cash builds up beyond the managers' abilities to put the money to work in suitable investments. A fund manager gets the excess money out by issuing an *extraordinary distribution* to his investors, and then he focuses on investing the remaining funds. The money goes to investors in proportion to the amount that each has invested in the fund.

Extraordinary distributions are called *return of capital* because the fund manager reduces the amount of money that each investor has in the fund. A return of capital can be a quick way to increase performance on a percentage basis by making the overall fund size smaller. As with regular distributions, an extraordinary distribution may be good for the manager, but not always for the investor, who needs to find another investment opportunity that matches his or her desired risk-and-return profile.

A liquidation with no sale: Closing the fund

For one reason or another, hedge funds close all the time. Industry observers estimate that 10 to 15 percent of hedge funds close each year. They may send you a letter in the mail, along with a check for your investment (unless your partnership agreement specifies otherwise), and you have to pack up shop, too. But why?

- ✔ The manager can't find good investment opportunities in the market that match the fund's strategy.

- ✔ Sometimes, a hedge fund gives up after a string of losses — especially when the fund manager doesn't make money anymore.

- ✔ Hedge fund managers sometimes get bored with their work and quit, even if their funds have solid performances. (This doesn't happen often; the money hedge fund managers make can buy a lot of excitement.)

Whatever the reason, the fund manager closes the fund, sells the fund's assets, pays off its liabilities, and distributes whatever's left to the investors.

Fee, Fi, Fo, Cha Ching! Paying the Fees Associated with Hedge Funds

Ever since the first hedge fund, started by Alfred Winslow Jones in the late 1940s, funds have charged investors fees. The norm is a combination of a management fee and a performance fee. Almost all funds formed since Jones's have used a similar structure — a 1- or 2-percent management fee and a 20-percent performance fee — although some funds may charge different rates. In addition, you may have to pay a fee to get into a hedge fund, and the fund may want more when you get out.

Why should you have to pay for all the risk involved with a hedge fund? I can give you a couple reasons besides return. Although a hedge fund manager probably has some of her personal money invested in the fund, she needs cash to pay the fund's operating expenses. She also wants an incentive for the risk she's taking in starting and operating the fund in order to make herself and all her client's money.

In the following sections, I discuss all the fees that drain a bit of money from your bottom line but that give life to the hedge-fund business.

All these fees reduce the return that you receive. If your hedge fund generates a high return, the amount you give will be worth it. If not, being in the fund will just be expensive.

Management fees

A hedge fund can be an expensive business to run. The general partners of the fund have to worry about paying for many areas of the business, including the following:

- ✔ Rent and utility costs of the office space, telephones, computers, pens, paper, and so on
- ✔ The price of research services, specialized software, and brokerage commissions
- ✔ The salaries for the fund managers and staff
- ✔ The lawyers and accountants who track the fund's assets and help it comply with applicable regulations

All these supplies and employees cost money. And who pays for it all? The fund investors.

Most funds charge management fees of about 1 percent to 2 percent of the fund's assets, usually at the end of the fiscal year. Some charge higher fees — especially if they follow strategies that involve expensive research and related expenses, such as shareholder activism (see Chapter 12 for more information on that topic). Other funds keep the fee relatively low by paying only some expenses out of the fee; the funds pay for other bills, especially legal and accounting expenses, directly out of funds assets. You need to find out upfront what management fees a prospective fund charges, what other expenses the fund incurs, and how the fund calculates its fees (see Chapter 18 for more on due diligence).

A hedge fund manager receives a management fee no matter how the fund performs. However, if the fund's assets increase, the fee does, too. Two percent of $60,000,000 is more than 2 percent of $50,000,000, so a 20-percent investment return translates into a 20-percent increase in management fees.

Sales charges

Hedge funds incur expenses throughout the year. They may take their management fees on a periodic basis, like once per quarter or once every six months, but the rate of fee collection may not match the rate at which the bills come in. Some funds may need money up front in order to operate, so they charge upfront *sales charges* — often at the same scale as the management fees (1 percent to 2 percent that comes out of the amount invested). The sales charge allows the fund to cover its expenses and pay its staff until the management fees and performance fees come in.

Performance fees

Hedge fund managers charge *performance fees* as a reward for getting excellent returns for their investors. One of the many appeals of hedge funds is that the managers eat their own cooking, as the saying goes — their incentives are aligned with their investors' goals. If the fund doesn't make money, the fund manager doesn't get paid.

A typical performance fee is 20 percent of the fund's annual profits before fees. Some funds charge a higher rate if performance is above a predetermined benchmark — say, 20 percent on investment returns of up to 50 percent and 35 percent on any returns generated over 50 percent.

Performance fees come with a downside for fund managers: The fund only gets paid if it turns profit, and most funds set what's called a *high water mark*. The fund can only charge a performance fee if the fund's assets return to where they were before the fund started losing money. If it had $10 million in year one and lost 10 percent, making the asset value $9 million, the manager can't charge a performance fee until the assets appreciate back to $10 million. See Table 2-1 for examples of the ebb and flow of performance fees.

Is the high water mark a good thing for investors? It depends. The fund manager pays a penalty for not making money, which is a powerful incentive to manage the fund well. However, the loss of a performance fee for more than a year can be painful to the fund manager. If the fund loses a large amount of money in its bad year, it may take a while for the asset values to recover. Sometimes, a hedge fund manager will disband a fund after a losing year and then launch a new fund instead of losing out on a few years of performance fees. In the investment business, very good years often follow very bad years, so disbanding the fund means that the fund's investors lose out on what could be a year of great performance that would help them recoup their losses.

Table 2-1	How Hedge-Fund Fees Depend on Performance				
	Year 1	**Year 2**	**Year 3**	**Year 4**	**Year 5**
Beginning-of-Year Assets	$50,000,000	$56,800,000	$47,314,400	$56,569,097	$59,850,104
Investment Performance	20%	−15%	22%	10%	15%
Incremental Asset Increase	$10,000,000	$(8,520,000)	$10,409,168	$5,656,910	$8,977,516
Total Asset Value before Fees	$60,000,000	$48,280,000	$57,723,568	$62,226,006	$68,827,620
Management Fee as a Percent of Total Assets	2%	2%	2%	2%	2%
Dollars-for-Management Fee	$1,200,000	$965,600	$1,154,471	$1,244,520	$1,376,552
Performance Fee as a Percent of Incremental Asset Increase	20%	-	-	20%	20%
Dollars-for-Performance Fee	$2,000,000	-	-	$1,131,382	$1,795,503
Proceeds to the Fund Manager (Management Fee + Performance Fee)	$3,200,000	$965,600	$1,154,471	$2,375,902	$3,172,056
Percentage Change		−70%	20%	106%	34%
End-of-Year Assets (Beginning-of-Year Assets + Performance Assets Less Fees)	$56,800,000	$47,314,400	$56,569,097	$59,850,104	$65,655,564
Percentage Change	14%	−17%	20%	6%	10%

Note: At the end of the second year, the fund's assets are below where they ended in the first year. Until the fund's assets recover, the fund manager won't receive a performance fee.

Hedge fund investors may well be ready to accept the crunchy with the smooth, so many want to reduce the fund manager's incentive to disband the fund after a loss. After all, a few years of poor performance may be part and parcel of a great long-term investment strategy. Some funds address this desire of investors by calling for graduated performance fees that may give the fund managers some of the performance-fee money while they climb back up to the high water mark. For example, a fund manager may receive a performance fee of 10 percent of profits until the fund reaches the high-water mark, at which point she gets the full 20 percent of profits thereafter.

Redemption fees

You pay money while you're in the hedge fund, and you may have to pay money to get into the fund in the first place, but at least you're off the hook when you get out, right? Nope! Many hedge funds charge *redemption fees* when their investors withdraw their money. These fees may be another 1 percent to 2 percent of assets. One reason funds charge redemption fees is that they can. Another reason is that they increase the money that the fund manager earns. But I can give you some better reasons, too. Hedge funds want to impress upon their limited partners that investment is a long-term proposition, so they can't get out easily. Also, the general partners have to deal with sales and administrative costs involved with raising the money to meet the redemption.

A hedge fund that charges a redemption fee may waive it if it has held the investment for a certain amount of time, or if you provide a certain amount of notice about when you plan to withdraw the funds.

Commissions

If you employ a broker or consultant to find a suitable hedge fund for you, and this person introduces you to the general partners, he or she will expect to be paid for said services. The consultant may charge you a flat fee, or he or she may take a percentage of the assets invested. To find out more about the function of a consultant and the benefits of the services provided, check out Chapter 17.

Dealing with the Hedge Fund Manager

Many money managers choose to run hedge funds because they don't want all the headaches that come with running big businesses (and because they want a lot of money). The managers dream of sitting in front of trading screens and making investment decisions all day. They want to avoid sitting in meetings, holding the hands of their nervous clients, or making presentations to marketing departments. However, many hedge fund investors want regular contact with the people managing their money, and they want the niceties of notes, golf outings, and occasional dinners. Therefore, many hedge fund managers often hire marketing employees to work with clients so that they can concentrate on running the money. It helps to know a fund manager's policies on meetings and communication, so I cover these topics in the sections that follow.

The partnership agreement you sign will probably discuss what kind of communication the hedge fund manager wants to arrange and how often he'll make contact. See the previous section for more on contract talk.

Making time for meetings

How often you hold meetings with your fund manager depends on the fund you enter and the fund manager's style. After the initial investment meeting, some funds hold quarterly or annual meetings for all their investors. Other fund managers never meet with their investors again. Some fund managers make an effort to say hello whenever investors come to town, and others prefer to be undisturbed.

If you feel like you have to have regular, face-to-face communication with the hedge fund manager you associate with, make sure a manager is amenable to this request before you commit your money.

Communicating with the written word

Your hedge fund manager should offer you a quarterly report on the fund's investment performance to date, giving you a sense of where the returns are relative to the appropriate investment benchmarks and letting you know how the market outlook suits the fund's strategy. (You can read more about performance calculation in Chapter 14.)

You may also want to read through a prospective fund's report archives before you invest to discover more about the fund's investment style and communication philosophy.

Once a year, your fund manager should give you a comprehensive report on the fund's performance, including the total value of the assets under management and the total fees charged. An outside auditor should prepare this report — not the hedge fund manager. Make sure of this before you sign up. You probably won't get a comprehensive list of holdings; it depends on the fund's transparency views (see Chapters 8 and 9). But you should get enough information on industry and asset classes to get a sense of the fund's overall risk-and-return profile, which helps you evaluate how the fund's performance fits your portfolio needs.

Hedge funds are private partnerships. It's reasonable to expect regular performance information, including such risk measures as Value at Risk (see Chapter 14). It isn't reasonable to expect much more. When it comes to how much written communication is allowed from an investor to a fund manager, you have to look at it case by case.

Seeking Alternatives to Hedge Funds

After you discover more information about how hedge funds operate and are structured, you may realize that you don't have the assets or the desire to invest in them right now. Maybe the structure of the whole operation scares you off. That's okay! You have other ways to put the performance and risk-management advantages of hedge funds to work in your portfolio.

Table 2-2 gives you a basic overview of how hedge funds compare to other types of investments; the following sections delve deeper into the topic.

Table 2-2	Comparing Hedge Funds with Other Investment Vehicles					
	Hedge Funds	Mutual Funds	Pooled Accounts	Individual Accounts	Discretionary Accounts	Family Offices
Open to the Public	No	Yes	No	No	Yes	No
Open Only to Accredited Investors	Yes	No	No	No	No	Yes
Buy In at Any Time	No	Yes	No	Yes	Yes	Yes
Cash Out at Any Time	No	Yes	No	Yes	Yes	Yes
Advisor Registered with the SEC	Maybe	Yes	Yes	Yes	No	Maybe
Advisor Licensed as a Broker	Maybe	Maybe	Maybe	Maybe	Yes	Maybe
Charges Management Fees	Yes	Yes	Yes	Yes	No	Yes
Charges Performance Fees	Yes	No	Maybe	Maybe	No	Maybe
Uses Hedging Strategies	Maybe	Maybe	Maybe	Maybe	Maybe	Maybe
Uses Aggressive Investment Strategies	Maybe	Maybe	Maybe	Maybe	Maybe	Maybe
Outperforms the Market	Maybe	Maybe	Maybe	Maybe	Maybe	Maybe

Making mutual funds work for you

A *mutual fund* is a company formed to buy securities and registered with the Securities and Exchange Commission (SEC). Most mutual funds are open-ended, which means they offer shares to the public every day. Anyone with enough money on hand can buy the shares, regardless of net worth or income, and anyone in a mutual fund can cash out the shares at any time.

For a long time, mutual funds couldn't use most options and futures trading strategies (see Chapters 5 and 10 for more on these topics) or techniques such as short-selling or leveraging (see Chapter 11). The regulation that prohibited the strategies, known as the *Short-Short Rule,* was repealed in 1997. However, few mutual funds availed themselves of the new techniques because investors weren't interested at the time. Now that people are more aware of hedge funds, they want mutual-fund alternatives, and the fund companies are delivering.

You can discover more about mutual funds that hedge in Chapters 15 and 16.

Profiting from pooled accounts

If several investors put their money together to invest, the result is a *pooled account.* This account can be small, like an investment club formed by a handful of people who want to discover more about buying stocks, or it can be very large. Some pooled accounts are more or less mutual funds for institutional investors. For example, several churches may pool their endowments under one investment manager. One large nonprofit organization, Commonfund (`www.commonfund.org`), offers several pooled account options for university endowments and other nonprofit organizations.

A hedge fund is a type of pooled account, but it follows more aggressive investment strategies and charges performance fees. Some pooled accounts avoid performance fees so they can attract investors who have more money than a mutual fund can invest efficiently, but who aren't qualified to invest in a hedge fund.

Entering individually managed accounts

A portfolio manager or broker manages an *individually managed account* for a specific account holder. The person managing the account can customize it to your needs, using aggressive strategies or hedging techniques where appropriate. You can structure individually managed accounts in many ways and find many different managers who can run your account.

Individual money manager

A money manager may be willing to take on individual accounts, especially for high-net-worth individuals who want lower fees, more flexibility, and more transparency than may be available with a hedge fund. To a large extent, the money manager operates these accounts like pooled accounts (see the previous section). She may have several individual accounts with a growth strategy, so she buys the same stocks for each of them, for example. But if one of her accounts has a unique tax situation, she can manage the account without affecting any of her other accounts. An individual account manager charges a fee based on the assets held, so she has an incentive to protect her clients' assets. The downside is that the return after fees may not be any better than with any other type of account.

Brokerage discretionary account

Many stockbrokers have a good sense of how to invest, so they may offer to make decisions for some of their clients (or take them up on offers). When they do, they open a *discretionary account,* because the client signs over discretion for the assets to the stockbroker.

This route is generally a bad idea. You pay a stockbroker on commission. The more trades ordered for your account, the more you pay the broker. Some brokers are good and responsible people. Others churn through every asset their clients possess if it means that they take home the maximum possible commission. Don't enter into a discretionary-account agreement lightly.

Family offices

If a family has enough money — especially inherited wealth or money from a business owned by generations of family members — its members may use a *family-office service* to handle the family's financial affairs. These offices often sit in departments of private banks that work with several families. Some families, like the Rockefellers, may be able to justify having an office that works only for them. Typical family offices offer tax- and estate-planning services, bill paying, and education planning. No hedge fund is going to offer these services. The family office may also manage the assets of the family. The family office asset manager may or may not use hedging techniques, depending on the family's needs and circumstances.

Chapter 3

Not Just a Sleeping Aid: Analyzing SEC Registration

In This Chapter

▶ Becoming familiar with SEC registration

▶ Reviewing strategies for SEC exemption

▶ Preparing yourself to invest in a non-registered fund

*B*ecause hedge funds don't have to register with the U.S. Securities and Exchange Commission (SEC), hedge funds can pursue investment strategies that other types of investment pools can't. For example, hedge funds have more freedom to borrow money to increase return, concentrate money into a handful of positions, and invest in assets that can't be easily sold. This freedom also means that hedge fund managers don't have to disclose their investment techniques (which can be good for return [see Chapter 6] but bad for your due diligence [see Chapter 18]), and they're free to change course with the prevailing market winds.

The ability to invest in ways that other types of investments can't is a major part of the hedge-fund appeal. And the major benefit of this perk? The pursuit of higher return for less risk. But without certain regulations, investors face another risk: that the people running their funds aren't who they say they are, and that the funds aren't handling money appropriately.

When hedge funds were the exclusive province of very wealthy individuals and well-endowed institutions, a lack of transparency wasn't a huge concern. Regulators figured that investors could afford to do their own due diligence (and to lose some money). But over the years, hedge funds have increased in popularity with smaller investors. It's all relative, but a million ain't what it used to be. One million in 2005 was only worth $492,942 in 1982, the last time the accredited-investor threshold was raised (see Chapter 2). You may be rich, but are you rich enough to meet the demands of the hedge fund business? That's the issue that regulators grapple with now.

Hedge funds don't have to register with the SEC because they're designed for sophisticated investors: individuals with a net worth of $1 million or an annual income of $200,000 ($300,000 for married couples), and institutions holding assets of $5 million. In 2006, the SEC began requiring some hedge funds to register. Later in the year, a court ruled that the agency didn't have the authority to require such registration. Now the entire requirement is in limbo, and it's unclear what the funds that are already registered will do. Some hedge funds are registered, some are not, and Congress will likely pass legislation reinstating some type of registration requirement. Stay tuned!

So, as an investor, why should you care about SEC registration? For one thing, registration and transparency are ongoing controversies in the hedge-fund industry. The freedom from regulation and disclosure may help funds earn better returns, but it also scares off some investors and allows unscrupulous managers to rip off others. You also need to know the limited protections of registration if you intend to invest in a registered fund, as well as the reasons why a fund may choose to avoid registration. This chapter helps you become familiar with registration so you can make better decisions with your money.

Getting to Know the SEC's Stance on Registration and Regulation

In September 2003, the U.S. Securities and Exchange Commission (SEC) issued a 134-page document discussing hedge funds. In the document, the commission made the following statements: "We are concerned about our inability to examine hedge fund advisers and evaluate the effect of the strategies used in managing hedge funds on our financial market." "We also are concerned about the lack of applicable regulatory measures necessary to ensure that material information to assist investors in making fully informed investment decisions is available."

More recently, regulators have been concerned about the increased popularity of hedge funds and the way that inflation has lowered the relative height of the accredited-investor requirement. They also worry about a few hedge fund scandals that have dotted the newswire, including stories of hedge fund managers who took investors' money and spent it instead of investing for maximum return relative to risk. (I cover some of these stories in Chapter 18; you won't spoil anything if you flip there now.)

The SEC's primary concern is that the original definition of an accredited investor — a person with at least $1 million in assets or a yearly income of $200,000 ($300,000 for a married couple) — hasn't been adjusted for inflation for over 20 years. Between increasing real-estate prices, individually managed retirement accounts, and general increases in asset values across the board, many investors found themselves with enough assets to qualify; however, they didn't necessarily have the investment sophistication nor the resources envisioned when the original criteria were set.

In the following sections, I discuss some of the issues surrounding regulation. As of press time, the issue is up in the air; the SEC's hedge-fund registration program has stopped by court order, but it seems likely that Congress will call for new regulations or registration systems in order to protect investors from unscrupulous operators. Understanding the philosophy and history of regulations will help you evaluate news events to see how they affect your portfolio. And, the information here gives you some good context for due diligence (see Chapter 18).

Examining the SEC's past and current policies on registration

When it first proposed registration, the SEC didn't try to take on the tough job of defining "hedge fund." (Chapter 1 looks at the many ways that people use the term.) Instead, it created a new term for it, "private fund," and used that to extend the coverage of the Investment Advisers Act of 1940 to include what we typically think of as a hedge fund. As a policy matter, the agency required that certain funds register in order to ensure that investors in these funds receive a minimum level of disclosure about management practices. The SEC also wanted to ensure some level of oversight and enforcement power at the Commission's disposal.

The SEC wasn't concerned with investment strategies — only fund operations. Specifically, the Commission looked at the following criteria for a registered hedge fund:

- Are the principals qualified to run the fund's money?
- Can investors find out if they're qualified?
- Have the fund managers explained the risks of the fund's strategy?
- Are accounting systems in place to value the fund's assets and handle the cash flow?
- Can investors withdraw their money on a timely basis?

Recognizing that hedge funds operate in an entrepreneurial industry and that the process is expensive, the Commission voted in 2004 to require registration only of funds with $25 million in assets or more. Smaller funds, which are more apt to attract less-sophisticated investors and have more trouble meeting operational requirements, didn't have to register. Most of the problem funds (which you can read about in Chapter 18) fall into the smaller category because they're less likely to be of interest to larger, more experienced investors.

In other words, the big investors who were protected because of their own market power gained no new safeguards, and smaller investors who lacked negotiating power with hedge fund managers continued to be without safeguards.

The main reason that the court threw out the hedge-fund registration requirement is that it felt the SEC didn't have the authority to require registration without an act of Congress. A secondary reason is that the requirement didn't seem to address abusive funds that harmed smaller investors.

Without the protection of registration, investors must look out for themselves when entering the hedge fund world for the most part. The following sections aim to arm you with info that can help out during the process.

First thing we do, we hire the lawyers

As a prospective hedge fund investor, you may find it helpful to know what a hedge fund manager goes through when setting up a fund. Knowing the right way to do business will help you better identify folks who go about it the wrong way.

For starters, a hedge fund manager needs a strong legal team, and her lawyers should be specialists in SEC compliance matters to help ensure that all paperwork is filled out correctly and turned in on time. A lawyer with a focus on SEC compliance specializes in securities cases and has handled registration for other investment advisers. A strong legal team also gives you, the prospective investor, some assurance that the fund is professionally managed. And no, it isn't cheap to the fund, which is one of many reasons why hedge funds charge relatively high fees (see Chapters 2 and 4).

The securities industry is considered to be self-regulating, but that doesn't mean that hedge funds regulate themselves. Instead, it means that the SEC has delegated much of the compliance work to the exchanges and related organizations: the New York Stock Exchange, the National Association of Securities Dealers, and the Commodities Futures Trading Commission, among others. A good securities lawyer should know these organizations inside and out and will make sure that anybody required to receive paperwork will get it.

In addition, the SEC requires a registered hedge fund to do the following:

- ✔ Maintain certain records, such as trade histories and banking records
- ✔ Establish in-house compliance monitoring procedures
- ✔ Have a compliance officer on staff

A compliance officer will probably be a lawyer who has securities experience. No matter what degree the compliance officer holds, he or she needs to have extensive experience with SEC regulations, exchange policies, and good trading and documentation practices. You should ask about the hedge fund's legal counsel and registration policies when you conduct an interview with the fund manager (see Chapter 18).

Reviewing the registration process

The Securities and Exchange Commission requires funds to go through several steps if they decide to register (to attract more investors, for example) — a process that the fund can handle electronically. The Commission is one of several sponsors of the online Investment Adviser Registration Depository, www.iard.com, which walks the hedge-fund operator through the whole process. At the conclusion of the process, many of the documents become public information, so you can use them to help evaluate fund managers.

The Investment Adviser Registration Depository Web site is deceptively simple. Don't be fooled — registration isn't a do-it-yourself project. An error or omission may have tremendous repercussions down the line. A hedge fund manager should shell out the money for qualified legal advice, and a hedge fund investor should run in fright from a firm that doesn't have access to good counsel (see the previous section for more on legal matters).

The National Association of Securities Dealers (NASD) oversees the registration process as a whole. The following list outlines some of the many forms that a fund has to complete under the watchful eye of this organization:

- ✔ **Entitlement Forms:** Before the National Association of Securities Dealers lets a firm begin the filing process, it requires the firm to show that it's a bona fide investment business with proper eligibility and to list the persons who will have access to the system. In other words, not just anyone can start an investment business. If you're evaluating an unregistered hedge fund, you may want to use the entitlement form to help generate some due-diligence questions. If it helps the NASD determine if a fund is bona fide, it can help you.

- ✔ **Form ADV Part 1:** Form ADV registers an investment advisory firm. (ADV is short for "advisory".) Part 1 includes information on the advisor's experience, business history, and last 10 years of disciplinary history. It also requires the advisor to identify his business within the fund. The advisor must file this form electronically, so you can look up an advisor's information at www.adviserinfo.sec.gov. And if a fund isn't registered, you can use a blank copy of the form to help design your due diligence.

✔ **Form ADV Part 2:** Part 2 of the ADV lays out the fund's services, fees, and investment strategies. Money-management firms don't have to file Part 2 with the SEC, but they must keep the forms current and make them available upon request to the Commission and to current and prospective clients. Part 2 gives the kind of information a hedge fund investor should expect, whether or not the fund is registered. A hedge fund manager can give you this information without putting it on file.

✔ **Form ADV-W:** Notice of Withdrawal as an Investment Advisor. When a firm leaves the investment business for whatever reason, it files this form with the SEC. You may see many forms going on file now that the courts have ruled that registration isn't necessary. The filing of the form doesn't mean that hedge fund is a bad one; just that it's no longer doing the legal work involved in staying registered.

✔ **Form ADV-H:** This is the hardship exemption, allowing firms to postpone the electronic filing of their Form ADVs. The SEC usually grants the exemption for technical difficulties with access to the electronic filing system. The filing of this form isn't something you should expect to see from a well-run hedge fund, so you should avoid a fund that asks for the exemption.

✔ **U4:** Do you remember the permanent record that your elementary school counselor told you would follow you for the rest of your life? The U4 is the closest thing to it for employees at registered broker/dealers and investment advisory firms, which may include registered hedge funds, funds of funds, and brokers who sell hedge funds. Fund operators must fill out detailed information on where they've lived and where they've worked for the past 10 years. They also need to submit fingerprints, and any disciplinary information is included. Data from the U4 is available for two years after a person leaves a registered firm; you can look up fund operators at the NASD's BrokerCheck at `pdpi.nasdr.com/PDPI`.

Yes, the NASD checks those fingerprints. A new employee at a money-management firm where I worked noted on her job application that she had never been convicted of a felony. But when she filed her U4 and the NASD checked her fingerprints, it found that she was convicted for felony shoplifting. Ooops! The firm promptly fired her for lying on her job application. Others have passed the fingerprint screen but embellished their educational or work experience. Lying on a U4 isn't a crime, but it is subject to civil disciplinary action — fines, a ban on working in the industry, and so on. Most employers see it as a firing offense. A prospective investor who uncovers a falsehood during due diligence should consider placing his or her money elsewhere.

✔ **U5:** A notification that an employee at a registered firm has left the firm. The U5 includes the reasons for the departure. Firms use the U5 to update a person's U4.

Meeting investor needs with regulation

What does the regulation process have to do with you, the hedge fund investor? Should hedge funds even be regulated? Many would make a case that hedge funds shouldn't be subject to regulation because their advantage lies in their ability to invest freely without disclosing their activities. But in exchange for relief from regulatory requirements, it seems likely that the government will make funds made available to fewer investors. Would you rather have more regulation or a stricter accredited-investor requirement (see Chapter 2)? It all depends on where you stand. The following list outlines some benefits of regulation:

- ✔ Regulation may give the SEC more tools for detecting fraud and more teeth after a detection. In particular, tougher rules may allow the agency to find fraud at an early stage, before investors have lost all their money.

- ✔ Regulation may improve the markets by finally giving everyone reliable information about the numbers and types of funds in operation. To date, such data has been the province of consulting firms (see Chapter 17), which charge for their services and may be biased in how they collect and report information. The lack of information has allowed some hedge funds to misrepresent themselves and make it harder for market researchers to model different risk scenarios.

- ✔ Finally, regulation would help smaller hedge funds establish good compliance practices. Many large funds already have compliance practices in place, whether or not they actually register. Other funds haven't paid much attention to the practices, placing the entire burden on the investor during due diligence.

Realizing that "registered" doesn't mean "approved"

No need to fret because the registration requirement has been repealed — at least for a while. Registration wasn't and will never be a seal of approval. The Securities and Exchange Commission ensures only that a fund has met the disclosure requirements of the law; it doesn't let you know if a fund is properly operated or a good investment. Do your own due diligence if you want to stamp a seal of approval (see Chapter 18 for more information).

The SEC considers a fund's registration to be effective when it's made. However, Commission staff members will review the registration for completeness, and they may ask the hedge fund for changes or to submit additional information.

Pulling laws out of the blue sky

The term "blue sky laws" has been used for about 100 years, but the exact source of it is unknown. It appears to come from criticisms of fraudsters who conned investors into schemes with no basis other than the sky above. These laws predate Federal securities laws.

By 1996, it became clear that the blue sky laws were more effective at creating additional work for lawyers than for providing information and protection to investors. The National Securities Markets Improvement Act of 1996 repealed blue sky laws that duplicate Federal laws, leaving most states toothless.

In some cases, if a firm files incorrect or incomplete information on its Form ADV (see the previous section), the knowledge of the mistake doesn't come out until after the fund collapses or people make allegations of fraud. For example, many advisors have lied on their U4s but get discovered only when a prospective investor calls up their Ivy-covered alma maters to verify their graduation dates. The SEC doesn't approve of a firm's filings; it only verifies that the filings are complete, which is why you need to investigate a fund even if it registers with the SEC.

Addressing registration at the state level

Just because the Feds don't require registration right now doesn't mean that certain state legislations won't step into the void. Many hedge funds are headquartered in the state of Connecticut, and that state is considering stricter regulations as of press time because it believes that the current SEC regulations are inadequate. And you can bet that if a spectacular hedge-fund collapse happens in any state, elected officials looking for political gain will promote a new round of regulations.

If a hedge fund does register with the SEC, it doesn't need to register with any state. But if it isn't registered, the fund may have to register in states where it operates or where it has investors. How do you know? The quickest way to an answer is a phone call to your appropriate state regulator. You can find a directory on the North American Securities Administrators Association Web site — www.nasaa.org.

Going Costal: Avoiding the Registration Debate through Offshore Funds

One way to get around U.S. investing laws is to operate outside of the United States. No kidding! Most nations have their own securities laws that apply, but one class of hedge funds seems to be almost lawless: *offshore funds.* Offshore funds are operated out of offshore banking centers — a handful of locations that allow investment businesses to operate with limited regulation and taxation. The International Monetary Fund defines offshore banking centers as

✔ Locations with relatively large numbers of financial institutions working primarily with nonresidents.

✔ National financial systems with external assets and liabilities that are out of proportion to the domestic financial needs.

✔ Places where low or zero taxation, light financial regulation, banking secrecy, and anonymous transactions are readily available.

Among the many offshore banking centers found around the world appear in Bermuda, the British Virgin Islands, the Cayman Islands, Marianas, Mauritius, and Singapore. (Of course, a fund manager may be making investment decisions from an office in his house in Greenwich, Connecticut. Hey, it's a global economy, and bandwidth is cheap.) But even places like New York, Tokyo, and London offer services that qualify under the International Monetary Fund's definition — as long as you aren't a citizen of the country.

An offshore hedge fund may be able to shelter money from taxes and operate free of regulation better than a fund located in a more traditional financial market. The lack of regulation can greatly increase the potential for increased return and reduced investment risk, but only if you qualify and if you know the other risks that you're taking. In general, a U.S. citizen or resident alien may not invest in offshore funds. These funds are for citizens outside of the United States, residents outside of the United States, and individuals who are in the United States for less than 180 days a year. In addition, U.S.-based tax-exempt institutions (such as pensions or foundations; see Chapter 8) and offshore corporations may invest in offshore funds.

U.S. investors participate in offshore funds, of course. If you want to join one, you could set up a corporation in Mauritius and fund it with money that would then be invested in a hedge fund based in the Cayman Islands. You could also set up a charitable-remainder trust to create a tax-free vehicle, or you could buy into the fund through an offshore life-insurance policy.

The structures that taxable investors in the United States need to use to invest in offshore funds are complicated. If you're interested in going the offshore route, you need a lot more advice than you can get from this book.

Because offshore funds have little regulation, you have little recourse if you run into problems. Your best protection is a good contract and extraordinary due diligence (see Chapter 18).

Investing in a Fund without Registration

Until Congress passes legislation authorizing the SEC to regulate hedge funds, you're investing without a net. That doesn't mean that all hedge fund managers are shysters or that you have no protections after you enter a fund. After all, registration had plenty of limits; it didn't apply to funds with less than $25 million in assets or fewer than 15 investors, and it didn't allow investors to withdraw money for two years.

So, what do you do to protect yourself and to ensure that you receive all protections coming your way? You read the contract the hedge fund manager proposes to you, and you do your due diligence; I cover these topics in more detail in the following sections (and in Chapter 18).

Contracting the manager's terms

When you buy shares in a hedge fund, you sign a contract agreeing to the terms that the hedge fund manager has set. You have to certify that you're an accredited or qualified investor (see Chapters 1 and 2 for these definitions). Some of these terms of the contract may be negotiable; negotiations give you a chance to see if you can change the reporting, withdrawal, or other components of the fund's operations to your liking.

After you sign the contract, it becomes governed by contract law. The contract should give the court jurisdiction in the event of a dispute; the contract will almost definitely identify a state court, and the hedge fund manager will prefer to set the state where she lives to reduce her travel costs. (The investor, of course, will prefer that the jurisdiction be closer to his or her house.)

The securities industry has long relied on binding arbitration to settle disputes, so don't be surprised if the hedge-fund contract requires that you handle any problems that way. In most cases, the contract states that the

American Arbitration Association (www.adr.org) sets the rules and policies for the arbitration. Most securities lawyers are familiar with the arbitration process, but a lawyer who doesn't specialize in the investment business may not be. Should you need to take a case to arbitration, do yourself a favor and find a lawyer who has experience (see the section "First thing we do, we hire the lawyers" earlier in this chapter); many believe that players in the securities business prefer arbitration because it's so often favorable to the industry, not the investor.

Covering yourself with due diligence

Is your hedge fund manager who she says she is? What about the company that issued the bonds she wants to invest in? It's on you to find out — especially if you don't have the backing of registration with the SEC to rely on for protections.

Registration and contract law are no match for the investor who heads off problems by checking out the players. *Due diligence* is the process of verifying the information that you have. (Sometimes people refer to it as "due dilly," but I think that's silly. I'm a snob that way.) Chapter 18 gives you the information you need to get started, but here's a quick list you can use with a little information specific to this chapter:

- Yes, do a Google search, but don't stop there. Search for information about the manager and the fund on Lexis-Nexis or another news database.

- Look up the fund manager's U4 (see the section "Reviewing the registration process" earlier in this chapter) or get a copy of his résumé, and then pick up the phone and verify the employment and educational information you find on it.

- Ask other investors about their experiences with the fund.

- Call the hedge fund's prime broker, accountant, and lawyer. Be sure to go through the switchboard at those firms, on the outside chance that the hedge fund manager gave you the cell-phone number of an accomplice who will lie to you.

- Get complete information on the hedge fund's investment style, cash-distribution policies, investor-communication policies, fees, and commissions. Do you understand them? If not, and even if so, you may want an experienced lawyer or consultant to review them (see Chapter 17 to find out more about consultants).

Do you know your regulations?

This chapter covers a lot of regulatory information, which can be difficult to remember. Here's a little quiz to help you review:

1. U4 is the

   a. Fourth album by the Irish band U2.

   b. Connecticut law that regulates hedge funds in that state.

   c. Form hedge funds use to register with the Securities and Exchange Commission.

   d. Employment and disciplinary record of someone who works in the securities industry.

2. Blue sky laws are:

   a. Indoor air-quality regulations that prohibit smoking at trading desks.

   b. Federal securities laws.

   c. State securities laws.

   d. Obsolete.

3. Which of the following isn't an exemption from SEC registration?

   a. Having fewer than 15 U.S. investors

   b. Allowing international investors into a hedge fund

   c. Forbidding withdrawals for two years

   d. Having less than $25 million in assets

4. When the Securities and Exchange Commission approves a registration,

   a. It says only that the filing is complete and accurate.

   b. It issues a seal of approval that funds may use in their marketing materials.

   c. The hedge fund has no further compliance responsibilities.

   d. Investors are insured against investment losses.

5. Investors need to do due diligence

   a. Only on unregistered funds.

   b. Only on offshore funds.

   c. Only if they have the time.

   d. Before committing their money to any investment.

6. Investors in offshore funds

   a. Need a valid passport.

   b. Must live outside of the United States for at least 60 days each year.

   c. Must not be subject to U.S. taxes.

   d. Must be citizens of either Bermuda or the Cayman Islands.

Answers: 1) d 2) c 3) b 4) a 5) d 6) c

Chapter 4

How to Buy into a Hedge Fund

*A*n open-end mutual fund, which you probably know about if you're considering a hedge fund, continuously offers stock to the public. You find a fund that interests you through an advertisement, on the Internet, in the papers, or through a financial advisor; you read the prospectus that the fund issues; you fill out a form; you write your check; and viola! You're a mutual-fund shareholder. A hedge fund is nothing like that. When you enter into a hedge fund, you join a private-investment partnership.

If you want to enter the hedge-fund world, you have to be prepared to jump through some hoops. Few hedge funds have Web sites, let alone toll-free numbers you can call to contact helpful, licensed sales representatives. You can't call a hedge fund to place an order like you can with a mutual fund. In fact, you can't get into many funds, even if you're an accredited investor (one with $200,000 in annual income [$300,000 with a spouse] or a net worth of $1 million; see Chapter 2). Hedge fund managers may not want to take more money than they can handle, given the strategies that they follow (for more information on dealing with managers, see Chapters 1 and 2). And, as hedge funds are unregistered, they may not be able to increase their asset base or their investor headcount without running afoul of Securities and Exchange Commission (SEC) requirements (I discuss these requirements in great detail in Chapter 3).

Still, hedge funds need investors as much as investors need hedge funds. They have no job if they have no money to run! In this chapter, I tell you what you need to know to enter this private world.

You don't need a broker to buy into a hedge fund, and you don't need a broker to buy into a mutual fund, but a broker sometimes helps the process. For more on finding consultants, see Chapter 17, and read on!

Using Consultants and Brokers

If you can't call up a hedge fund manager, how do you know that he's out there? The key is networking. Hedge fund managers often work with consultants who track hedge-fund performance and help market the funds. The hedge funds place their trades through *prime brokers* — brokerage firms that handle most of their trades and back-office work. Many of these brokerage firms have sales reps who work with high-net-worth individuals, pension funds, and endowment funds. Some prime brokers encourage communication by holding conferences each year to bring their hedge fund clients and prospective investors together. (You can find more about consultants in Chapter 17.)

A hedge fund manager won't take your investment unless he's certain that you're an accredited investor — you have a yearly income of $200,000 ($300,000 with a spouse) or $1,000,000 in assets. Otherwise, he's breaking the law. You may not be asked to prove it, but you will be asked to sign a statement attesting to your accredited status.

Your mission is to find appropriate hedge funds that are open to taking your investment. If you're interested in buying into a hedge fund, you should start by talking to your financial advisor. If you work at a pension or endowment, you probably deal with consultants who can point you in the right direction. If you're an accredited individual investor, your broker, lawyer, or accountant may be able to put you in touch with brokers or consultants who can find hedge funds for you.

However, hedge-fund investing is very much a private club. If you don't know anyone in the hedge-fund world but want to invest, your best bet is to work with a broker at a very large, brand-name brokerage firm. Such firms are likely to serve as prime brokers to hedge funds, and they may put on conferences for prospective hedge fund investors.

Some large brokers are more likely than others to have connections to hedge funds. When using a broker to find a hedge fund, you should inquire about the relationship between the hedge fund and the broker. Specifically, what financial arrangements are in place?

Keep in mind that brokerage-firm employees have to follow strict rules when marketing hedge funds. The National Association of Securities Dealers, which regulates brokerage firms, says that its member firms must adhere to the following:

- ✔ Provide balanced disclosure of the different funds under consideration
- ✔ Perform a reasonable determination of the investor's suitability
- ✔ Provide supervision for anyone in the firm selling hedge funds
- ✔ Train staffers in the risks, features, and suitability of hedge funds

If your broker isn't providing you with these services, go elsewhere.

Marketing to and for Hedge Fund Managers

Most hedge funds are too small to have dedicated marketing staffers. Instead, funds rely on personal connections, relationships their prime brokers have, and consultants to find the money they put in their funds. In some special cases, the manager's reputation within the industry may be enough to bring in money.

If Joe Dokes the trader goes out on his own after making money for his old investment employer, people who witnessed his abilities will want to invest with him. Joe will probably talk to any accredited investors among his friends and family to see if they're interested in investing. At that point, he'll talk to his prime broker, which may know of interested investors. The brokerage may arrange for a road show, during which Joe meets with potential investors all over the country (or even the world). Joe will probably also meet with the consultants who advise hedge fund investors. (Chapter 17 has more information about the roles consultants play.)

These points are where you come in. You need to determine what types of hedge funds will help you meet your investment objectives (I cover styles in Part III) and then start asking contacts in the business about funds in those categories that are open to new investors. The process is basically old-fashioned networking. If someone known to a fund introduces you, even through a few degrees of separation — and if the introducer can vouch for your accredited status (see Chapter 2) — you'll find that doors open quickly.

You may not want to invest in a fund's start-up phase, opting instead to track the initial performance of the fund. Later on, if the fund manager starts another fund, expands the current fund, or needs someone to buy out a current investor's stake, he'll know whom to turn to.

Because funds can't market to non-accredited investors (see Chapter 2), they're reluctant to do anything that may be construed as an advertisement. Most funds have no Web sites, and some don't even put their phone numbers in the phonebook.

When you obtain a meeting with the manager (a broker or your consultant may set up the meeting), you get a chance to review legal forms that discuss the fund, which may include an offering circular, private placement memorandum, or Securities and Exchange Commission Form ADV that describes who the manager is and what the fund strategy involves. (Chapter 3 gives you a description of these documents.) At that point, you'll most likely have a chance to meet with the manager to find out more about the investment style and whether the fund is a good fit for you.

No matter who recommends the hedge fund, how prosperous the manager looks, or how logical the investment strategy seems, don't invest until you check out the fund manager (Chapter 18 provides more information on what to look for). This process is called *due diligence,* and it's a key step in buying into a hedge fund.

Hedge funds often want to control the amount of money under management, so if the fund has more interested investors than it can handle, the fund manager can choose among them. A prospective investor with less experience or greater liquidity needs may lose out to a person who has invested in hedge funds before and who doesn't foresee a need to make withdrawals.

Most managers also prefer more experienced investors because their level of patience may be higher, making them less likely to withdraw money if the funds hit some rough patches.

Investor, Come on Down: Pricing Funds

When you buy into a hedge fund or cash out your shares, you need to know what the shares are worth. When a fund forms, setting the price is simple: The total value of the fund is the total value of the cash put into it. If the fund disbands, setting the prices is also simple: The hedge fund manager sells all the securities, pays all the bills, and distributes the remainder proportionately.

You own a percentage of the partnership that translates into your holding. This is a better way to describe a hedge-fund holding than "holding shares."

If a stake in the fund is added or withdrawn, by the investor or the fund manager, at any time between when the fund forms and when it's liquidated, calculating the value of each investor's share is much tougher. Even if the investor isn't selling, she may have other reasons for needing the value of the hedge-fund investment. If the investor is a pension plan, for example, the plan must report the value of the assets in its hedge-fund investments to the plan's sponsor, its trustees, and its beneficiaries on a regular basis.

And, of course, you need to know what the shares are worth to calculate performance (see Chapter 14 for more information on performance calculation). In this section, I cover net asset value calculation, including dealing with illiquid securities. With the use of these tools, you'll have a sense of how the fund comes up with the value of your investment.

Prices are all over the place. Some funds report values to consultants annually or quarterly, but many don't. Minimum investments are all over the place, too. Some funds will take $25,000 investments, and others insist on $10 million.

Calculating net asset value

Hedge funds are priced on their net asset value. Also called book value, *net asset value* is the total of all the fund's assets minus all the fund's liabilities.

Sounds simple, right? Well, here's one catch: finding the value for all the fund's securities, calculated at the end of each trading day. If a fund invests entirely in one market and one type of investment, the pricing is straightforward — the New York Stock Exchange (NYSE) closes at 4:00 p.m. ET, so if all your investments trade there, you simply price at the close. But in a global market, who decides when the trading day ends? What if you also have futures (financial contracts that trade on a different exchange)?

Here are some global considerations that you must deal with:

- ✔ The Chicago Board of Trade's Dow Jones futures contracts trade on the floor of that exchange until 4:15 p.m. ET.

- ✔ The London Stock Exchange closes at 10:30 a.m. ET, but if a big-news event involving a listed company occurs, trading takes place over-the-counter (between buyers and sellers, using electronic networks rather than the floor of the exchange) until the LSE opens again at 4:30 a.m. ET the next morning.

✔ The Tokyo Stock Exchange takes an hour-and-a-half break from trading at lunchtime, but no one in New York knows because they're asleep.

Many hedge funds rely heavily on over-the-counter trading to take advantage of short-term discrepancies in prices. A large fund that does business in many markets around the world may have staffers working around the clock. If assets are in constant motion, when does the clock stop so you can calculate net asset value?

So, as simple as the concept of net asset value may seem, be sure to ask the fund manager when and how the fund calculates the value. It should be spelled out in the contracts that you sign when you enter the fund. Table 4-1 shows you how the hour of the pricing affects the fund's value that day. For simplicity, this table covers the total U.S. dollar value of each security. For the London stock, it tracks how the price changes in after-hours trading.

Table 4-1	Net Asset Value Calculated at Different Times				
	Security A	*Security B*	*Security C*	*Futures D*	*Security E*
Time of Day (Eastern)	*London Stock Exchange*	*London After-Hours*	*New York Stock Exchange*	*Chicago Board of Trade*	*Tokyo Stock Exchange*	*Net Asset Value*
1:00 a.m. (Tokyo Closes)	$1,000		$1,050	$(800)	$900	$2,150
2:00 a.m.	$1,000		$1,050	$(800)		$1,250
3:00 a.m.	$1,000		$1,050	$(800)		$1,250
4:00 a.m.	$1,000		$1,050	$(800)		$1,250
5:00 a.m.	$980		$1,050	$(800)		$1,230
6:00 a.m.	$1,002		$1,050	$(800)		$1,252
7:00 a.m.	$992		$1,050	$(800)		$1,242
8:00 a.m.	$982		$1,050	$(801)		$1,231
9:00 a.m.	$983		$1,050	$(802)		$1,231
10:00 a.m.	$984		$1,051	$(802)		$1,234

Time of Day (Eastern)	Security A London Stock Exchange	Security A London After-Hours	Security B New York Stock Exchange	Security C Chicago Board of Trade	Futures D Tokyo Stock Exchange	Security E Net Asset Value
11:00 a.m. (London Closes at 10:30 a.m.)	$986		$1,056	$(801)		$1,241
12:00 p.m.		$987	$1,057	$(802)		$1,242
1:00 p.m.		$1,135	$1,063	$(803)		$1,395
2:00 p.m.		$1,146	$1,052	$(803)		$1,396
3:00 p.m.		$1,158	$1,053	$(802)		$1,408
4:00 p.m. (NYSE Closes)		$1,146	$1,054	$(802)		$1,398
5:00 p.m. (CBOT Closes at 4:15 p.m.)		$1,135		$(802)		$332
6:00 p.m.		$1,123			$900	$2,023
7:00 p.m.		$1,112			$901	$2,013
8:00 p.m.		$1,112			$902	$2,014
9:00 p.m.		$1,112			$902	$2,014
10:00 p.m.		$1,112			$902	$2,014
11:00 p.m.		$1,112			$902	$2,014
12:00 a.m.		$1,112			$902	$2,014

If you calculate the net asset value when the New York Stock exchange closes, it would be $2,298. Calculate it at 5:00 p.m. — the end of the business day in New York — and the price is $2,286. Wait until midnight and the price is $2,266. If you add the values at the closing time for each market, the price is the sum of the price at each market's close (ignoring the after-market trading):

$986 + $1,054 − $802 + $900 = $2,138

No calculation method is inherently better; the key is that the method is disclosed and applied consistently.

Valuing illiquid securities

Because hedge funds can limit how often clients withdraw money (see Chapter 7), and because they tend to take a broad view of possible investments, they often put money in *illiquid securities* — investments that don't trade very often and are difficult to sell on short notice.

Academic theory says that the market price is the correct price for an asset, but this statement assumes that markets are perfectly efficient. One requirement for an efficient market is perfect liquidity, in which buying or selling has no effect on the price. The price in the market is the correct price. (See Chapter 6 for more on this topic.)

In reality, supply and demand drive markets, so short-term buying and selling can have an enormous impact on prices. If an asset trades all the time, the value is widely known. It's easy to know what a share of Microsoft stock is worth because millions of shares are bought and sold every day, for example. If an asset doesn't trade, you have no observable, unbiased market indicator of what the true price should be. Think about a house. My house isn't exactly like my neighbor's house. They were built at the same time, but my neighbor added a bathroom, and I installed custom bookcases. When the time comes to sell, there may not be a ready buyer for either of our houses. If I have to sell quickly, I may take the first offer that comes my way, even if it's low. If my neighbor puts her house on the market at the same time but doesn't need to move right away, she can hold out for a higher price. Houses are just one example of an illiquid, tough-to-price asset.

Hedge funds have many techniques to use to assign values to illiquid securities:

- ✔ **Net present value:** The discounted value of all the expected cash flows.
- ✔ **Black-Scholes:** A complicated mathematical model used to find the value of an option.
- ✔ **Relative valuation:** Basing the security's price on a similar security that trades frequently.

I discuss different valuation methods in Chapter 5.

If a hedge fund you're interested in invests in illiquid securities, find out what its policy for valuation is. And know that you take on some risk if the fund buys a lot of these assets — the price assigned to the fund may not hold when the illiquid securities have to be sold (quite a catchy rhyme, don't you think?).

Managing side pockets

A *side pocket* in a hedge fund is a group of securities held by only some of the fund's investors. And unlike side pockets in jeans, they don't make your hips look larger.

Hedge funds set up side pockets — also called *designated investments* or *special investments* — for two main reasons:

- ✔ **To hold illiquid securities (see the previous section) away from money that investors can redeem.** For example, the fund may allow investors to pull money out of the main part of the fund once per quarter, but it may decide that investors can redeem funds in the side pocket only once every two years. Likewise, new fund investors can't enter into the side pocket so that the valuation of those investments doesn't become an issue for them. If you invest in a fund that's just starting out, part of your investment may be held in a side pocket

- ✔ **To allow certain fund investors access to securities that other investors may not have.** The fund may provide performance enticements or other special benefits that attract specific investors. A fund may also set up a side pocket to meet the needs of a large institutional investor that can put a great deal of money into the fund. For example, some people who work in the securities business may not be able to invest in Initial Public Offerings of stock, so they may invest in a side pocket that does not buy these securities. An endowment with a long time horizon may be interested in illiquid securities, so they fund may have a side pocket just for them to hold these securities.

Side pockets are priced separately from the rest of the fund. Because they're often set up just to hold illiquid investments, their price may be more uncertain.

Purchasing Your Stake in the Fund

After a hedge fund investor and a hedge fund manager decide to work together after setting up interviews through brokers or other connections and determining the price of your investment (see the previous sections of this chapter), the next stage in the process starts: the purchase. The investors (lucky you!) and the manager have tons of forms to fill out, and, of course, you have to transfer some money before you can turn a large profit. This section covers those logistics.

Fulfilling paperwork requirements

Besides the initial partnership-agreement forms, you have other forms to fill out and provide and other obligations to meet. The U.S. Treasury Department's Financial Crimes Informant Network (www.fincen.gov), which investigates money laundering, requires financial institutions to have enforcement procedures in place to verify that new investments aren't made from ill-gotten funds.

The hedge fund's staff must verify that they know who the investors in the fund are and where their money came from, so you have to provide the following when you open a hedge-fund account:

- ✔ Name
- ✔ Date of birth
- ✔ Street address
- ✔ Place of business
- ✔ Social Security number or taxpayer identification number
- ✔ Copies of financial statements from banks, brokerages, and other accounts showing that you're accredited and that you have enough money to meet the initial investment

If you want to open an individual account, you should also be prepared to provide your driver's license and passport. If you want to open an institutional account, you have to provide certified articles of incorporation, a government-issued business license, or a trust instrument.

Working with brokers

After you sign all the forms and do all the hand-shaking (not the fraternity kind, probably), you can deposit your cash. The money you put up goes to the fund's prime broker, which holds it in escrow until the fund is ready to add new money. To minimize the cash-flow effects on investment returns, the fund may add money only once a month, once a quarter, or once a year (see Chapter 2 for more information on how hedge funds manage cash flows).

If you already have an account for your other investments at the same firm as the fund's prime brokerage, you'll have an easy transfer. If your money comes from a bank or another brokerage firm, you may be required to obtain signature guarantees before you can transfer the funds. The brokerage or bank will probably send the money electronically, although you may be required to send a certified or cashier's check, which you can obtain through your bank. (In the United States, most brokerage and bank functions are separated. In other parts of the world, the same institution may handle both services.)

After you send your money to the brokerage, you can begin monitoring your fund's ride in the markets. Whether it behaves like a raft through class-five whitewater rapids or a ship on a sail through quiet seas, you won't get a visit from Julie the Adventure Director. Instead, the taxman may come along. (For more on tax considerations for hedge fund investors, see Chapter 8.)

Reporting to the taxman

On top of the identity paperwork you fill out at the beginning of the purchasing process (see the section "Fulfilling paperwork requirements"), you have forms to fill out for tax reporting down the road. IRS Form W9, for example, keeps your taxpayer information on record.

Each year, you'll receive a K-1 form from the fund, which reports your share of the hedge fund's profits. (The hedge fund itself files form 1065 with the IRS.) As a partner, you need to report your share of the fund's earnings to the IRS, even if you haven't received any cash. This is a different reporting structure from most other forms of investment income, which are usually reported on 1099 forms and handled through schedule B and schedule D of IRS Form 1040.

The fund itself doesn't pay the taxes — you do.

Signing Your Name on the Bottom Line

When you buy into a hedge fund, you buy shares in an investment partnership. This purchase carries some specific contractual obligations that both parties — you, the investor who purchases as the limited partner, and the hedge fund's general partners — have to meet. The following sections give you some background, but I suggest also calling a lawyer before you commit $5 million of your hard-earned money by signing a contract. A lawyer may be able to negotiate changes on different provisions, like withdrawal procedures or disclosure levels, to get them working in your favor.

Drawing up the contract

When you enter into a hedge fund, the fund manager presents you with a contract drawn up by the fund's law firm (make sure any fund you choose has a law firm and a brokerage firm). The contract will be more or less standard, but it will be written to favor the general partners' interests.

The fund manager may refer to the contract as a *partnership agreement,* a *subscription agreement,* or a *private-placement memorandum;* however, its legal status as a contract is similar, no matter the document's title. Some contracts can be so sided to the managers that they'll be open to doing anything they want with the money, investment-wise. I strongly advise you to have a lawyer with you when going over the contract.

Addressing typical contract provisions

The hedge fund contract sets forth many pieces of information you need to know:

- ✔ The fund's general partners
- ✔ The fund's status with regulators (turn to Chapter 3 for more information on regulation)
- ✔ The fees that the fund charges and how it calculates them
- ✔ The fund's limits on withdrawals

The contract may also discuss the fund's investment strategies, the assets that the fund will and won't invest in, and reporting requirements, but it doesn't have to.

A partnership agreement also sets forth how the fund will handle any conflicts. Most likely, limited partners give up the right to sue; you have to take disputes to arbitration, which is the norm in the investment business. The agreement you sign should discuss who will oversee the arbitration and where it will take place, should a hearing become necessary.

By signing the document, you agree to the terms and certify that you're an accredited investor (an investor with a net worth of $1 million and an annual income of $200,000 [$300,000 with a spouse]; see Chapter 2 for more).

Finding room for negotiation

When you get the contract — either in person, electronically, or in the mail — your first impulse will be to mark every clause you don't like and then go to the fund's general partners and ask for changes. In most cases, you'll get rebuffed. Hedge funds are popular investments, and many people want to hop on the bandwagon. Good fund managers can — and do — set their own terms.

But keep this in mind: If the fund you're interested in is small; if the manager is relatively new; and if you have plenty of money to commit, you may have some leverage. You may be able to ask for sales-fee reductions, fewer withdrawal restrictions, or other changes that meet your needs. In hedge funds, as in life, it never hurts to ask.

Part II
Determining Whether Hedge Funds Are Right for You

The 5th Wave   By Rich Tennant

"Choosing the right investment strategy is like choosing the right hat. You find the one that fits you best and then you stick with it."

In this part . . .

Although hedge fund managers have more flexibility than many other money managers when it comes to generating high returns relative to the amount of risk taken, a hedge fund isn't an appropriate investment for every type of investor. In Part II, you get information on how to choose a hedge fund — or any other type of investment — by doing some asset research, determining your risk and return preferences, surveying your tax situation, and considering other special needs that you may have. With the information here, you can make smarter decisions about how to manage your money.

Chapter 5

Hedging through Research and Asset Selection

A hedge fund manager's job is to survey the world's markets to find investments that meet the fund's risk and return parameters. But how does the manager actually do it?

The fund manager has to have a system in place for determining what to invest in and for how long. He looks for opportunities to make money in an asset that's going to change in price, and he looks to reduce the risk of the portfolio. Without discipline, he can't make good decisions, which makes your job of evaluating performance impossible. Anyone who invests money has several available techniques for increasing returns and reducing risk. Some hedge fund managers simply do better research, and others rely on technical analysis, short-selling, and leverage to generate the returns that their clients expect. (I discuss technical analysis later in this chapter, and I cover short-selling and leverage in Chapter 11.)

This chapter gives you a basic overview of the different financial assets available and tells you how fund managers may value them. I hope to help you understand what kinds of assets a hedge fund might invest in. I can't give you an easy answer as to how or whether these assets should be used in a hedge fund, but armed with this information, you can make better investment decisions for yourself and ask better questions of a hedge fund manager, who wants to make the decisions for you.

First Things First: Examining Your Asset Options

You can't invest wisely unless you know what you're investing in. If you don't understand what a hedge fund manager is talking about when he's discussing prospective asset classes or strategies, you're more likely to make mistakes with your hard-earned money. On the other end of the spectrum, if you completely understand the characteristics of different asset classes, you may see investing alternatives that fit your needs and don't involve hedge funds at all. (You don't have to be a millionaire to take advantage of some of these opportunities.) Now, for a middle ground. By understanding the asset classes the hedge funds may focus on, you can make sound investing decisions with hedge funds.

Most investors should hold a diversified mix of securities in order to get their optimal risk and return payoff. The exact proportion depends on your needs. (Chapters 7, 8, and 9 cover the details you need to consider when structuring your portfolio.) Likewise, hedge fund managers have different targets for risk and return, and they turn to different assets in order to meet their targets. They spend time doing their research, and you should do the same (see the section "Kicking the Tires: Fundamental Research" later in this chapter).

A hedge fund or a group of hedge funds may use the assets you see here in many different ways. Hedge fund managers often use traditional assets in non-traditional ways, for example, so no hard and fast rules are there to rely on. But if you have some basic understanding, you'll be in a better position to ask good questions. The chapters of Part III cover some of the investment strategies and styles that hedge funds use. Consider this chapter to be a companion.

In practice, "asset" and "security" are synonyms, and derivatives are considered to be a type of asset. But to be precise, these three aren't the same. An *asset* is a physical item — examples include a company, a house, gold bullion, or a loan. A *security* is a contract that gives someone the right of ownership of an asset — a share of stock, a bond, or a promissory note, for example. A *derivative* is a contract that draws its value from the price of a security.

Sticking to basics: Traditional asset classes

Although many hedge funds pursue esoteric strategies and exotic assets, all funds have some investment positions in ordinary investment classes. Traditional assets can be parts of profitable trades, so don't assume that a hedge fund manager who steers clear of swaps traded on the Zimbabwe Stock Exchange is a bad fund manager.

Just because a hedge fund invests in securities that you've heard of doesn't mean it isn't taking on risk. Some hedge funds buy very ordinary and safe securities, such as U.S. government bonds, but they goose up the returns — and the risk — by using borrowed money to finance almost the entire position.

The following sections give you a roundup of the usual suspects used to manage risk and return in hedge funds. You may be surprised that they don't look much different from what you would see in any investment portfolio.

Taking stock in stocks

A *stock* (also called an *equity*) is a security that represents a fractional interest in the ownership of a company. Buy one share of Microsoft, and you become an owner of the company, just as Bill Gates is, for example. He owns a much larger share of the total business, obviously, but you both have a stake. Stockholders elect a board of directors to represent their interests in how the company manages itself. Each share represents a vote, so good luck getting Bill Gates kicked off the Microsoft board! Hedge fund managers often buy and sell stocks in order to meet their investment objectives.

A share of stock has limited liability, which means that you can lose your entire investment, but no more than that. If the company files for bankruptcy, creditors can't come after shareholders for the money that the company owes them.

Some companies pay their shareholders a *dividend,* which is a small cash payment made out of firm profits. In fiscal year 2005, for example, Microsoft paid each shareholder a dividend of $0.36 per share, paid out at a rate of $0.09 each quarter. The ratio of the dividend to the stock price is called the *yield.*

Any bonds today?

A *bond* is a loan that hedge fund managers often invest in to meet their investment objectives. Hedge fund managers invest in many different types of bonds at different times; it all depends on the fund's investment objectives, what techniques the fund uses, and the prices in the market at any given time.

A company or a government issues a bond in order to raise money to cover expenses or investments that can't be funded out of current income or savings. In other words, companies and governments borrow money for the same reasons that individuals do. The bond issuing process goes as follows:

1. **The bond buyer gives the bond issuer money.**

2. **The bond issuer promises to pay interest on a regular basis.**

3. **The bond issuer then repays the money borrowed — the *principal* — on a predetermined date, known as the *maturity*.**

Bonds generally have a maturity of more than 10 years. In the realm of government bonds, short-term bonds are referred to as *notes,* and bonds that mature within a year of issuance are referred to as *bills.* Among business issues, short-term bonds are often called *commercial paper.* The interest payments on a bond are called *coupons.*

Over the years, enterprising financiers realized that while some investors needed regular payments, others wanted to receive single sums at a future date, so they separated the coupons from the principal. The issuer sells the principal payment, known as a *zero-coupon bond,* to one investor, and sells the coupons, called *strips,* to another investor. A borrower makes the payments just like with a regular bond. (Regular bonds, by the way, are sometimes called "plain vanilla.")

A borrower who wants to make a series of payments with no lump-sum principal repayment seeks an *amortizing bond* to return principal and interest on a regular basis. If you think about a typical mortgage, the borrower makes a regular payment of both principal and interest. This way, the amount owed gets smaller over time so that the borrower doesn't have to come up with a large principal repayment at maturity.

Coupon clippers

If you look on a bulletin board in a coffee shop or other community space, you'll probably see a "car for sale" or "apartment for rent" sign with little information slips cut into the bottom. If you're interested, you can rip off a slip and contact the advertiser later. Bonds used to employ the same strategy. The bond buyer would receive one large certificate good for the principal, with many smaller certificates, called coupons, attached. When a payment was due, the owner would cut off the matching coupon and deposit it in the bank. Some old novels refer to rich people as "coupon clippers," meaning that their sole labor in life is to cut out their bond coupons and cash them in.

Nowadays, you can handle bond payments electronically, so you now reserve the coupon-clipper label for bargain hunters looking for an extra $0.50 off a jar of peanut butter.

Other borrowers may prefer to make single payments at maturity, so they seek out *discount bonds*. The purchase price is the principal reduced by the amount of interest that otherwise needs to be paid. In other words, if a discount bond paid 10 percent interest and was due in a year, it would sell for $909 today. The buyer would receive no interest payments; instead, he would get a check for $1,000 in a year.

If a company goes bankrupt, the bondholders get paid before the shareholders. In some bankruptcies, the bondholders take over the business, leaving the current shareholders with nothing.

Surveying cash and equivalents

Cash is king, as they say. Hedge fund managers have money readily available to purchase securities for the portfolio or to meet customer redemptions. For the most part, the interest rate on cash is very low, so hedge funds try to keep as little cash on hand as possible. However, they do look for some cash and cash-equivalent investments that can pay off handsomely.

One way that hedge fund managers make money from their cash holdings is by making short-term loans. Collectively known as *money market securities* or *cash equivalents,* these loans are expected to mature within 30 days or even overnight.

For example, a multinational corporation may need to borrow money for one day to meet payroll. It issues what's called a *repurchase agreement:* It borrows the money for one night by selling the hedge fund a bond and then pays the money back by repurchasing it for a slightly higher price the next day. The risk for the hedge fund is very low; the interest rate is low, too, but it's higher than if the money just sat around.

Other forms of money-market securities include the following:

- ✔ Long-term bonds that are about to mature (say, a bond issued 15 years ago that matures next week)
- ✔ Uninsured bank CDs
- ✔ Government securities that will mature within 90 days

The first key decision a manager makes is what currency to keep the cash in. Currency fluctuates rapidly, which makes even recent stories sound like ancient history. (Cue the storytelling music!) For example, once upon a time, a few years back, the dollar was very strong relative to the euro. In 2002, I sent everyone in my family sweaters and rugby shirts from Ireland and Scotland as their Christmas presents. I purchased them online and sent them to the United States. Even figuring in the shipping costs, the prices were better than I could've received in the United States. But about a year later, when we took a family vacation to Ireland, the dollar dropped dramatically. In just 15 months, the euro's value increased 25 percent. Someone who purchased euros in late 2002 and waited until early 2004 to bring them out of the pocketbook would've seen a huge profit (see Figure 5-1).

Euros Increase in Value Relative to Dollars

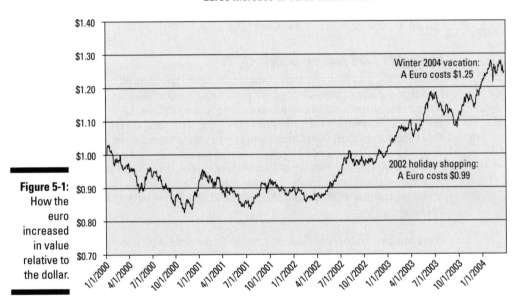

Figure 5-1: How the euro increased in value relative to the dollar.

Going for some flavor: Alternative assets

You may think that geeks armed with MBAs and HP12C calculators dominate the world of finance, but the field is filled with creative people who break the mold. Investment bankers are slicing and dicing streams of cash flow into all kinds of new and nontraditional assets that meet specific needs for people who need money and people who have money to invest. Hedge fund managers, sniffing out opportunities to meet their investment objectives, often turn to the alternative assets we outline in the following subsections.

In popular usage, an *alternative investment* is anything other than stocks, bonds, or cash (see the previous subsections in this chapter). Hedge funds themselves are often considered to be an alternative investment class, but they shouldn't be. A hedge fund is an investment vehicle. Because of their light regulations and limits on withdrawals, hedge funds have more freedom to invest in alternative asset classes. They may be structured with a risk profile that's completely different from a traditional asset, but they're not in and of themselves alternative assets.

Real estate

Real estate isn't always considered an investment. In most cases, it's a store of value, which is an excellent hedge against inflation. In other words, over the long run, you expect the price to increase by inflation and not much more. This expectation is particularly appropriate for raw land and, believe it or not, single-family houses.

Yes, I know, you must think I'm on something, because your grandmother bought her house for $20,000 in 1955 and sold it for $200,000 in 2005. But on a compound basis, she earned 4.7 percent per year. She lived rent-free, but she had to take care of ongoing maintenance and repairs. Not to mention that $20,000, adjusted for inflation, was the equivalent of $142,000 in 2005 dollars, making her real, after-inflation return less than 1 percent per year. That return is about what you'd expect from a store of value, not from an investment.

But real estate can be an investment, too. An office or apartment building generates a steady flow of rental income in addition to the stored value of the land. Agricultural real estate, including timberland, generates a steady flow of income from the sale of the commodities produced. Real estate that contains minerals generates profits when the minerals are extracted and sold.

Raw land may increase in value if demand for it changes. Take the following as examples of this demand-motivated value increase:

- ✔ A developer may convert an abandoned manufacturing building to residential loft condominiums, if a market's taste shifts that way.

- ✔ If people want to move to the far reaches of an urban area, farmland may become more valuable when converted to a residential subdivision.

- ✔ Young families may refuse to consider certain city neighborhoods and then change their minds when the public schools improve.

- ✔ A sleepy farm community may take on a completely different character when engineering graduates from a nearby university start semiconductor companies in their garages.

Hedge funds rarely purchase raw land for investment purposes, but they may provide lending to real-estate investors, help finance construction projects, or take shares in mineral projects (see the following section for more information). It's entirely possible that a hedge fund you invest in will put your money into real estate. Now that you know a little more about that asset, you're in a better position to understand and evaluate the hedge fund manager's strategy and results (see Chapter 14 for more on performance evaluation).

Commodities

Commodities are basic, interchangeable goods sold in bulk and used to make other goods. Examples include oil, gold, wheat, and lumber. A hedge fund probably won't buy commodities outright, but it may take a stake in them in one of a few different manners:

- ✔ By purchasing real estate that generates income from commodities produced, like timberland or agricultural holdings (see the previous section)

- ✔ Through futures contracts, which change in price with the underlying commodities (see the upcoming section "Betting your future on futures")

- ✔ By managing its stock investments based on the exposure of the company issuing the stock to different commodity trends

Commodities are popular as a hedge against inflation and uncertainty. In general, commodity prices tend to increase at the same rate as prices in the overall economy, so they maintain their real (inflation-adjusted) value. They may also be susceptible to short-term changes in supply and demand. A cold winter increases demand for oil, for example, a dry summer reduces production of wheat, and a civil war may disrupt access to platinum mines. If you invest in a hedge fund that works with commodities, the info here should help you understand why the value of your investment will fluctuate.

Venture capital

Great entrepreneurs often have fabulous ideas held captive by thin wallets. To fund their business ideas, they look for investors willing to take great risks in hopes of high returns. Heady investors provided the start-up capital for business like Google, Yahoo!, and America Online — think of how much money they made for getting in on the ground floor! But for every success story, you have the sad tales of companies that went under before they even got started.

Many hedge funds are in the business of taking on high risk in exchange for potential high returns, so venture capital fits neatly. Some hedge funds become partners in venture capital firms (private partnerships that often operate like hedge funds), and others seek out promising new businesses to invest in directly. (See Chapter 12 for more on venture capital.)

Derivatives

Derivatives are financial contracts that draw their value from the value of an underlying asset, security, or index. For example, an S&P 500 futures contract gives the buyer a cash payment based on the price of the S&P 500 index (adjusted for interest rates) on the day that the contract expires. The contract's value, therefore, depends on where the index is trading — not the index itself, but the value derived from the price of the index.

Hedge funds often use derivatives to manage risk. By selling an S&P 500 future, for example, a fund can effectively sell off its exposure to the stock market. This action helps the fund maintain its market-neutral position. Other hedge funds use derivatives to increase return or reduce other forms of risk, such as interest rate or currency risk. A handful of funds invest only in derivatives. (You can discover more about risk and return in Chapter 6.)

Some hedge funds use futures contracts to *speculate* — to make bets that the price of the underlying assets will go up or down in price. Futures contracts are highly liquid — they're easy to trade — which makes them attractive for a hedge fund that wants to take a very short-term position in an asset class.

Opting for an option play

An *option* is a contract that gives the holder the right, but not the obligation, to buy or sell the underlying asset at an agreed-upon price at an agreed-upon date in the future. An option that gives you the right to buy is a *call,* and an option that gives you the right to sell is a *put.* A call is most valuable if the stock price is going up, whereas a put has more value if the stock price is going down. Here's a quick sentence to help you remember the difference: You call up your friend to put down your enemy.

For example, a call named MSFT 2006 Mar 22.50 gives you the right to buy Microsoft at $22.50 per share at the expiration date of mid-March, 2006. (*Note:* Traders refer to Microsoft as "Mr. Softy" because MSFT is Microsoft's trading symbol and because traders have a sense of humor.) If Microsoft is trading above $22.50, you can exercise your option and make a quick profit. If Microsoft is selling below $22.50, you can buy the stock cheaper in the open market, so the option would be worthless.

Hedge funds sometimes use options to manage risk or to profit from price changes.

You can find great information on options, including online tutorials, at the Chicago Board Options Exchange Web site, www.cboe.com.

Warrants and convertible bonds

A *warrant* is similar to an option (see the previous section), but a company issues it instead of it being sold on an organized exchange. It gives the holder the right to buy more stock in the company at an agreed-upon price in the future. Company-issued employee stock options are more like warrants than exchange-traded stock options. Related to the warrant is the *convertible bond,* which is debt issued by the company. The company pays interest on the bond, and the bondholder has the right to exchange it for stock. Which option the holder should exercise depends on interest rates and the stock price.

Hedge funds sometimes use warrants and convertible bonds to manage risk or to profit from price changes.

Betting your future on futures

A *futures contract* attaches the obligation to buy a set quantity of the underlying asset at set price and at a set future date. Futures started in the agricultural industry because they allowed farmers and food processors to lock in their prices early in the growing season, reducing the amount of uncertainty in their businesses. Futures have now been applied to many different assets, ranging from pork bellies (which really do trade; manufacturers use them to make bacon) to currency values. A simple example is a lock-in home-mortgage rate; the borrower knows the rate that the mortgage company will apply before it closes the sale and finalizes the loan.

Most futures contracts are closed out with cash before the settlement date. Financial contracts — futures on currencies, interest rates, or market index values — can be closed out only with cash. Commodity contracts may be settled with the physical items, but almost all get settled with cash.

Futures contracts are useful for hedge fund managers who want to lock in prices. They also give managers exposure to commodity prices without having to handle the actual assets. After all, the average financial wizard doesn't want to care for live cattle, operate grain silos, or keep freezers full of pork bellies! (Most futures that investors trade are interest rates, used by people who need to manage interest-rate risk and people who hope to profit from it. Pork bellies are much less common, but they're a lot more fun to talk about!)

Forwards (not backwards!)

With a *forward contract,* an investor buys a currency, commodity, or other asset now at the market price, but the delivery doesn't take place until an agreed-upon future time. This strategy allows an investor to lock in the current price. In many cases, a hedge fund manager uses forward contracts to cover a futures contract — the manager locks in the current price in hopes that the future value is different, creating a profit on the difference. The difference is known as the *spread.*

Forward contracts are generally customized and arranged as private transactions. Futures, by contrast, actively trade on organized exchanges such as the Chicago Mercantile Exchange (www.cme.com) and the London International Financial Futures Exchange.

Visiting the center of the financial universe

If you ever get to visit an exchange, you should, because the energy is fantastic. Many exchanges have education and visitors' centers, and some have galleries where the curious can catch the trading action. Should you ever be offered a visit to the floor of an exchange, jump on it! Very rarely, an exchange trader or employee will be allowed to show a guest around. You may have to meet a dress code and go through tight security, but the experience is worth it. I've been on the floor of the New York Stock Exchange and the Chicago Board Options Exchange; I've watched from the galleries at the Chicago Board of Trade, the Tokyo Stock Exchange, and the London Stock Exchange; and I've loved every minute of it!

Swaps

A *swap* is an exchange of one cash flow for another. For example, say a company has issued bonds that pay interest in U.S. dollars. However, it decides to incur expenses in Japanese yen to offset profits that it makes in Japan. So, the company finds another company making payments in yen that would rather be making payments in dollars, and they swap their payments. As a result, each company can better manage its internal currency risk.

In many cases, one or both parties in the transaction are banks or financial services firms — like hedge funds. The fund looks to profit on the difference between the different currencies, different interest-rate structures, or different payment times.

Swaps are customized contracts arranged through banks or brokerage firms; they aren't traded on an organized exchange.

Custom products and private deals

We often think of securities trading as people in funny jackets running around and waving their hands like crazy on the floor of an exchange. And this still happens; however, most trading takes place over the counter. Traders for hedge funds, banks, brokerage firms, and mutual funds get on the phone or send electronic messages to each other to buy and sell securities.

Many kinds of securities trade seldom, if at all. These securities are often privately negotiated deals between a person who needs money and a person(s) (or a firm) who has it. A lottery winner, for example, may want to exchange his annual payments from the state for a single lump sum. He finds an investor who's looking for a regular income, and the two will cut a deal.

Hedge funds often participate in private transactions and offbeat investments so they can meet their desired risk and return characteristics better than they can with readily traded securities. Contract law governs private transactions; only rarely does the Securities and Exchange Commission have any say in them. In this section, I discuss a few such private transactions, like mezzanine financing and payment-in-kind bonds, but you may come across many others.

Mezzanine financing

Mezzanine financing is a combination of debt and equity used to support a company until it can go to the public markets. The debt and equity may be used as late-stage venture capital, when the new business isn't quite ready to sell its stock to the public, or it can go toward financing an acquisition. The lenders of the financing don't get paid until the company settles all other debts, making the financing almost like equity in that mezzanine lenders can lose everything if the company goes bankrupt.

Payment-in-kind bonds

Distressed companies, or companies in financial trouble, often issue *payment-in-kind bonds.* Instead of paying interest on its debt, the company gives the investors that own its bonds, known as *bondholders,* other bonds or securities, which creates many interesting trading opportunities. For example, a hedge fund manager may notice that the price of a payment-in-kind bond doesn't fully reflect the value of the bonds that the company will pay out in place of interest. Hedge funds like these opportunities.

Tranches

Bonds are often issued in several classes, known as *tranches.* ("Tranche" is the French word for slice; in essence, a security is sliced up into smaller securities when it's issued in tranches.) Each tranche may have a different interest rate and payment term. For example, one tranche may pay interest only after the first three years. Another may be a zero-coupon bond, which helps a company meet unique cash-flow needs. Tranches are often designed with the buyer's needs in mind as well. A hedge fund or other bond buyer may be looking for a structure that fits in with its overall portfolio construction, and a unique tranche may be a good fit.

Bonds issued in tranches aren't plain vanilla bonds (see the section "Any bonds today?"), and the design of some tranches is often negotiated with the buyers, which is why I include them in this section.

Viaticals

A *viatical* is a life-insurance policy purchased from the insured as an investment. Many terminally ill people need money now. They have life-insurance policies with big benefits, but their policies aren't helping the sick today. So, these sick people find investors who are willing to give them money now in exchange for the death benefits later. Viaticals are enormously risky investments, because sick people get better and researchers develop new cures all the time. In the 1980s, many viatical buyers focused on AIDS patients, but new treatments transformed AIDS into more of a long-term chronic illness, not a certain death sentence. Some contracts investors expected to pay off in 2 years haven't paid off almost 20 years later.

Because the time to maturity is unknown, viaticals are difficult to price. However, some hedge funds are willing to take on that risk, because some funds have aggressive risk-and-return objectives (see Chapter 6). Viaticals aren't common investments, but if you see them in the future, you'll have a better sense of what to ask.

Kicking the Tires: Fundamental Research

After you can identify different assets classes and how hedge funds use them, you need to figure out what they're worth. If you invest in a hedge fund, the fund's manager will do the valuation work. If you're making investment decisions yourself, you have to bear the burden. My point is that someone has to have a system for figuring out the price to buy a security and the price to sell a security.

Fundamental research is the process of answering questions to come up with a value for securities. Whether an investment is plain vanilla or exotic, the investor has to know what the investment is worth now, what its outlook is, and what risks affect its value. To discover this information, the investor needs a system of analysis. Investors use several different approaches to valuation. Most settle on two or three that fit the assets they invest in, their personalities, and the investment objectives of their funds.

No form of fundamental analysis is the "right way." People can, and do, debate which research techniques are best. However, the technique an investor uses isn't the most important factor; what's important is that the investor applies the technique in a consistent, explainable, and logical manner. The choice of an analysis method seems to be a function of personality and style as much as anything.

Fundamental research looks at the assets and cash flows of a business to determine how much its securities are worth. A fund must ask the following fundamental questions:

✔ How fast is the company growing its sales?

✔ Does it have any great new products?

✔ Does it have patents that the balance sheet doesn't reflect?

✔ Will a change in energy prices affect the company?

Beware the fund manager who does a little bit of everything. Too much jargon, too many analytical techniques, and too much vague information often mean that the fund manager's past performance is more due to luck than skill. Without having a good system in place for doing research, the fund manager won't fully understand why one investment works and why another doesn't. The manager may have a sense of panic when market conditions change, and his or her fund investors won't get good accountability or explanations. When you hear, "We don't want to be hemmed in by one style" or "The fund uses a top-down, bottom-up, micro and macro plus or minus market conditions approach," run away!

Top-down analysis

Top-down fundamental analysis examines the overall state of the economy. The researcher uses the findings to identify specific assets that he or she expects to benefit or suffer from the changes in the overall state of the economy, like price increases, employment levels, and interest rates. A top-down analyst, for example, may look at consumer-debt levels, project future changes, and then look for companies affected by the changes. Will an increase in consumer debt help or hurt car and appliance manufacturers? High-end retailers? Bargain retailers? Financial-service firms that emphasize lending or savings? If the researcher has a framework in place for analyzing the trends of the overall changes in the economy, he or she can select companies expected to change in price and structure the portfolio accordingly.

Top-down investing is sometimes called *theme investing,* because a fund manager looks for a handful of broad trends and invests based on those trends. The fund may look to benefit from an aging population, higher energy prices, or increased defense spending, for example. In some cases, a firm may have a portfolio strategist who works to determine the themes. The firm's other analysts, who may use different analytical approaches, have to narrow their search to securities that fit the themes.

One major theme of top-down fundamental research is the use of economic analysis. Hedge funds often use economic analysis as part of their investment strategies, no matter their overall research styles. And if the funds invest in several of the world's markets, economic analysis is especially important.

Hedge fund managers perform economic analysis in order to determine the best ways to profit from changes in economic trends, like inflation, unemployment, interest rates, or growth in a nation's gross domestic product. Most hedge fund managers at least think about the underlying economy when making investment decisions, and some hedge funds, known as macro funds, base their entire strategy around economic changes (you can read more about macro funds in Chapter 13).

The following sections explore the different levels of economic analysis within top-down research.

A microeconomic approach

Microeconomics relates to the structure of small units in the economy, like individual companies or households. Microeconomic analysis looks at conditions, like how much competition or regulation exists in a market, how easy it is for new companies to enter a market, and how taxes cause a specific company to behave. Microeconomic analysis is practically synonymous with fundamental research, because the hedge fund manager wants to know how changes in prices, competition, and product trends affect the prospects for a given company.

A macroeconomic approach

Macroeconomics looks at the overall national or even global economy. Macroeconomic analysis is concerned with exchange rates, interest rates, price levels, growth, and employment. Hedge funds that invest heavily in government bonds, financial derivatives, and currencies generally pay attention to macroeconomic analysis. Managers of these funds use data published by government agencies, central banks, and non-governmental organizations such as the United Nations and the World Bank to develop forecasts for changes in price levels.

Secular versus cyclical trends

Trends fall into two categories: secular and cyclical. A *cyclical trend* is related to economic cycles. For example, when employment improves, more people are working, and these new employees need clothes to wear to work, so they buy more threads, increasing revenue for apparel companies. A *secular trend* represents a fundamental shift in the market, regardless of the cyclical trends.

For example, in the 1970s, a growing number of women took jobs. These women needed clothes, creating an entirely new market: business clothes for women. Retailers like Talbots grew and changed to meet the new market demand.

Another secular trend in the clothing industry is the move toward casual dress in the office. In the 1990s, the economy boomed and white-collar employment grew, but folks were wearing khakis and golf shirts rather than suits and ties. Sales were strong at retailers that sold casual apparel, but sales dropped off at traditional suit makers like Brooks Brothers. Even if professionals bought their golf shirts at suit stores, they spent less money than they would've on crisp white shirts and expensive silk ties.

The challenge for an investor is separating the cyclical economic trend, which is temporary, from the secular economic one, which is not.

Demographics

Demographics, or the makeup of the population, are drivers for many businesses and economies. Companies need to worry about the demographics of their employee and customer bases, and nations need to worry about the people within their borders. Young populations tend to have cheap, unskilled workers, and older demographics usually have highly skilled, experienced, and expensive work forces. Young people tend to borrow money to spend; older people spend their savings; and people in the middle tend to set aside more than they spend.

Demographic research is economic research. Understanding the nature of the demographics within a population can help hedge fund managers make better decisions and separate cyclical from secular trends (see the previous section).

Bottom-up analysis

A *bottom-up* investor looks for individual companies that he expects to do especially well or especially poorly in the future. The investor starts his fundamental research by examining the company itself — its financial statements, its history, its product line, the quality of its management, and so on. He then makes a judgment about the company's value on its own merits. The researcher incorporates broad market trends only as they directly affect the business, which sets bottom-up analysis apart from top-down analysis (see the previous section). The bottom-up investor believes that he can find good and bad investments in any industry at any time.

A subset of bottom-up research is known as the *story stock* — an offbeat company with complex products or unusual circumstances that require elaborate explanations. Sometimes story stocks prove to be good investments — meaning that they go up in price as those who tell the stories expect them to — especially if the companies are harbingers of change in their industries;

other times, these companies make good shorts (see Chapter 11 for more information on short-selling).

I'm a bottom-up fundamentalist with an accounting bias, myself (see the following section for more on accounting). I like tying an investment's value to the issuer's performance, assets, and prospects. I don't fully understand technical analysis, and I make no apologies for that (see the section "Reading the charts: Technical analysis" later in this chapter). (I know, I know, I should pick up *Technical Analysis For Dummies,* just to see what the fuss is about!) If you like following patterns and looking for trends more than you like crunching numbers and reading regulatory filings, technical analysis may be for you.

Focusing on finances: Accounting research

Some bottom-up investors (see the previous section) look only at a company's reported financial statements, ignoring other aspects of its business. These investors look for evidence of fraud, unsustainable growth, or hidden assets. This examination is known as *accounting research.* Often accountants themselves, the accounting analysts who examine the companies understand the many nuances and judgment calls that go into preparing financial statements. In most cases, the goal of accounting research is to identify potential short ideas (see Chapter 11 for more information on short-selling).

Gnawing on the numbers: Quantitative research

Quantitative research looks strictly at numbers. These numbers may represent accounting figures (for example, accounts receivable relative to sales), or they may be sensitivity factors (for example, how much a company's profit changes when oil prices increase by 1 percent). Quantitative analysts, often called *quants,* tend to put the information they find into complex mathematical models, and the solutions that result correspond to the securities that investors should put into the portfolio. Firms that rely heavily on quantitative analysis are often called "black-box shops," because the quants put numbers into a computer, which then spits out the portfolio selection, and only a handful of people understand how it works.

Quantitative analysis is often derived from a refinement of the Modern (Markowitz) Portfolio Theory, which I discuss in great detail in Chapter 6. The Modern (Markowitz) Portfolio Theory says that a security's performance is related to its overall sensitivity to the performance of the market. A refinement of the theory is the Arbitrage Pricing Theory (APT), which looks at a security's sensitivity to a range of macroeconomic factors (for example, commodity prices, exchange rates, interest rates, and unemployment) rather than just the market. Equations based on the Arbitrage Pricing Theory are long regressions used to measure how well a given security fits with the forecast for the factors.

Reading the charts: Technical analysis

Technical analysis involves looking at charts of the price and volume of trading in a security. The charts show the historic supply and demand for the security, which may indicate where future prices are heading. The information shows a measure of sentiment. Analysts look to any number of questions: Is the number of buy orders increasing? Are the orders increasing while the price goes up or while the price goes down? Is the stock's price rising steadily, or does it go up in bursts around news announcements? Technical analysts use the answers to these types of questions to make investment decisions. The following list goes into more detail about technical issues:

✔ **Price:** The first statistic that technical analysts look at. The price-review process goes as follows:

   1. Analysts often start with a bar chart that marks the opening, high, low, and closing prices for each day of trading. The visual charts help the analysts see if prices are generally trending up or generally trending down.

   2. Next, they find out if trading is causing the trend line to change (a *reversal*) or if it follows the trend (a *continuation*). The answers give a sense of how the future performance will follow.

   3. Finally, analysts look at resistance levels. Does the price keep going up, or does it normally stick or start to go down at a certain level? Does the price keep going down, or does it seem to bottom out before going back up at a certain level?

✔ **Volume:** Shows how many securities are traded each day. When compared to prices, volume tells the analyst how many investors care about the security enough to move the price. Big price changes on small volume may indicate that investors are manipulating the price.

For further fundamental research, technical analysts calculate money flow, which is the average price for the day ([high + low + close] ÷ 3) multiplied by the volume for the day. If the price ends up for the day, the money flow is given a positive number; if the price ends down, the money flow is given a negative number. At that point, analysts calculate a ratio with the number of days of negative money flow in the numerator and the number of days of positive money flow in the denominator. Analysts consider money flow in the range of 30 percent to 70 percent normal. Above that, the security may be about to decline in price; below that, the security may be about to increase in price.

✔ **Patterns:** In addition to the basic measures of price and volume, technical analysts look for patterns that may indicate where a security's price will move. They often look for patterns by drawing lines to show how the trends are moving.

Although they have clever names like "head and shoulders," "teacup and handle," "flag and pennant" — not to mention wedges, triangles, rectangles, and channels — the patterns can be difficult to recognize. Some hold for short time periods, and others hold for longer eras. In fact, some technical analysts look for patterns called *Elliott waves* and *Fibonacci waves,* which may explain prices over decades and even centuries.

✔ **Momentum:** An accelerating security price change is said to show *momentum.* Positive momentum is good, and negative momentum is bad (ground breaking, I know). Many growth-stock investors look for a combination of technical momentum and earnings momentum (accelerating earnings growth) to identify stocks that they expect to show above-average price appreciation.

Few funds rely on technical analysis exclusively, but many investors use it regularly as a check on their fundamental research. Technical analysis is complicated, which means that the dabbler can run into trouble.

How a Hedge Fund Puts Research Findings to Work

So, what happens when a hedge fund's research identifies some great opportunities in different assets? Well, the fund takes a position. It can go long — buy in hopes that the asset goes up — or go short — sell in hopes that the asset goes down. The fund can also trade securities, monitor positions that may pay off in the future, or look for other ways to turn the information into a return for the hedge-fund investor. I discuss these options and more research findings in the pages that follow.

The long story: Buying appreciating assets

When a hedge fund manager or other investor buys a security, he or she is said to be *long*. An investor has only one reason to go long: He or she thinks that the asset will go up in price. Some hedge fund managers look for longs that will work over an extended period of time — possibly years — and others prefer to make their profits over very small stretches of time — possibly seconds.

Buying low, selling high

The secret of making money is buying low and selling high. Easy, huh? But what marks low and high? Answering this question is where research comes in. The fund buys the security (with cash on hand or with leverage; see Chapter 11) and holds it until it reaches a higher price or sells it if it becomes clear that the investment isn't working out. The research should set the price targets for establishing and selling the position.

When the asset reaches its price target, the fund may sell it or go back to its research methodology to see if the fund should set a new target. The difference between the purchase price and the sale price — adjusted for borrowing, interest, and commissions — is the profit (or loss) for the position.

Trading for the short term

Many hedge funds are aggressive traders, meaning that they often take positions for only a very short time. They look to capture small increases in price, but they do it every day, over and over again, so that the amounts compound into a very large return. The hedge fund structures of light regulation, limited investor liquidity, and maximum return for a given level of risk very much favor trading.

Holding for the long term

Some hedge funds take a long-term outlook with their securities. They look to buy and hold, to establish a position and then wait weeks, months, or even years to be proven right.

The buy-and-hold style is less common in hedge funds than in other investment vehicles, such as mutual funds or individual accounts, because the hedge-fund structure is less of an advantage to the investor with a long-term outlook than to the active trader. Still, many hedge funds do buy and hold — especially if they're playing with private and illiquid investments (see the section "Custom products and private deals" earlier in this chapter).

The short story: Selling depreciating assets

Hedge funds can make money by selling securities, and not necessarily securities that they own. A *short-seller* borrows a security from someone else (usually from a brokerage firm's inventory) and then sells it. After a while — ideally, after the security goes down in price — the short-seller buys back the security in the market and repays the loan with the asset that he originally borrowed. The lender doesn't have to repay the original dollar value, just the security in question. The profit (or loss) is the difference between where the short-seller sold the security and where he bought it back, less commissions and interest charged by the lender (see Chapter 11 for more on short-selling).

In the derivatives markets, someone who's short has an obligation to sell in the future, but it doesn't matter if he or she holds or has borrowed the underlying security now (for more on derivatives, see the section "First Things First: Examining Your Asset Options").

Protecting long positions

Hedge funds are in the business of reducing risk, and short-selling is one risk-reducing method. By selling off part of the risk, the fund can make money while hedging the long position. For example, if a fund's quantitative research finds that a given investment is heavily exposed to the price of oil, the fund can get rid of that risk by shorting oil futures. The fund offsets any gain or loss in the investment's price caused by sensitivity to oil with the gain or loss of the futures position.

Investment shorts (unlike the shorts you can't get rid of)

An *investment short* is a short-sell taken in a legitimate business that the fund doesn't expect to do well. A fund may make the decision to go with an investment short as part of a matching long position in a competitor that it expects to do well, as part of a risk-management maneuver, or purely for investment success.

Fraud shorts (nope, not Capri pants)

A *fraud short* is an investment that the fund expects to go down in value because of suspicions that the company is guilty of misrepresenting its products, its financial results, or its management (see the section "Focusing on finances: Accounting research"). These investments are rare, but funds make a few of them every year. A fraud short is risky stuff — the management of a company that a fund heavily shorts will probably fight back, sometimes with ugly tactics, and short sellers who are anxious to get the news flow moving in their favor have been known to resort to lies and threats.

Naked shorts (excuse the oxymoron)

A fund exacts a *naked short* when it sells a security that it hasn't borrowed in hopes that it will go down fast enough that the fund can buy back the security and settle with the buyer. Naked shorting is against exchange regulations in most markets, but it still happens. The advantage for the fund is that it can sell short without paying interest to the lender, and it can sell short even if no lender will loan the fund the security. The downside is that if the fund can't repurchase the security in time to settle its sale, the exchanges will find out and probably shut down the fund.

Because of the illicit nature of the technique, you shouldn't invest in any fund that admits to naked shorting.

Chapter 6

Calculating Investment Risk and Return

*T*he goal of a hedge fund is to decrease investment risk and increase investment return. People who study finance in an academic sense tend to think about risk and return differently than other folk, so it helps to understand the dominant thinking. I'm not saying that all hedge funds follow the academic principles, but they may use the language.

Many hedge fund managers are smart people, and they often look the part — a bit nerdy. They may not be the slick folks who throw great parties and drive fancy cars. Instead, they often have finance PhDs and love nothing more than calculating market strategies to exploit investment opportunities that other investors haven't discovered. I'm sure they like fancy cars, too, though. Running a hedge fund is more interesting to a manager than teaching undergrads, and it increases the likelihood that the car in her garage will be a Porsche rather than an econobox.

Understanding research that dives into the market's mechanics can help you make better decisions for where to place your hard-earned savings. And if you decide not to put your money into hedge funds, some knowledge of the theories behind risk, return, and diversification can make sure you avoid fads that don't help you meet your investment goals. Even if some of the theories in this chapter seem far-fetched to you, they'll help you understand what drives other investors who buy and sell securities.

This chapter gives you a quick summary of investment theory. I present it from an academic perspective, but don't let that scare you off. I have very good reasons for doing this! You'll run into this material when you talk to hedge fund managers and other investment professionals, so you may as well know what they're talking about, or at least where to look. After you read this chapter, you'll be prepared when investment discussions turn to alpha, beta, or standard deviation. Some of the material is technical, but hedge-fund management and investment is a technical business.

Market Efficiency and You, the Hedge Fund Investor

When people try to describe the securities market, they start with one key assumption: The market is *efficient*. Efficiency means that a security's price reflects all information, good and bad, about the security. It doesn't mean that the price predicts the future. All kinds of surprises can and do happen. However, if someone knows something, the knowledge shows up in the price. This definition leads to one of the many popular economics jokes:

> **Q.** How many investors does it take to change a light bulb?

> **A.** None — the market price already reflects the change.

If the market isn't efficient, the price of an asset will be very different from its actual value.

Hedge fund managers and their analysts spend their days looking for ways to make money in efficient markets. Their research also contributes to efficiency because they find information that investors can use to figure out where they want to buy and sell particular stocks or bonds. In the next few sections, I'll show why this process should matter to you.

Why efficiency matters

Why should you care about market efficiency? Well, a hedge fund manager's attitude toward efficiency determines how she goes about making money (making you money, in other words). If she believes in perfect efficiency, for example, she's likely to pursue a strategy that involves risk management through leverage instead of emphasizing securities selection (see Chapter 11 for more information on leverage). If she believes in total inefficiency, she's likely to spend much of her time doing research on specific securities and then committing a good portion of the fund's money to securities that she thinks will outperform the market. You should find a manager whose beliefs in efficiency and resulting strategies match up with your investment objectives.

When you evaluate performance claims (see Chapter 14 for more on evaluating performance), keep in mind that markets tend to be efficient over the long run. In investing, as in life, if it sounds too good to be true, it probably is. If a hedge fund manager tells you that her strategy will make huge profits by exploiting massive inefficiencies, you want to find out what she considers to be an inefficiency, why she thinks that the inefficiencies exist, and what will happen if another investor acts on the discovery. (See Chapter 18 for more on doing your due diligence.)

Perusing profitable inefficiencies

Sometimes, the research of a fund manager or an analyst uncovers inefficiencies where a fund can make a profit. Such inefficiencies aren't easy to find, but they do exist. Investors are most likely to find *profitable inefficiencies* in markets that aren't well researched, like some emerging markets (countries with newly developing economies and stock markets). They also exist where investor psychology seems out of step with the underlying value of the assets (witness the dot-com bubble). Some researchers have pinpointed common inefficiencies; for example, stocks with a low price-to-book value (that is, a low stock price relative to the balance sheet net-worth) tend to outperform the stock market as a whole.

Efficiency and the random walk

When hedge fund managers talk about securities prices, they sometimes use the term *random walk*. What they mean is that without new information, a security's price moves randomly. Some days the price is up a little, and some days it moves down a little, but you can't predict the price. Only new information changes the magnitude and direction of a price change, and those changes also come in a random and unpredictable fashion; after the market (that is, everyone trading all the stocks and bonds on the exchanges) assimilates the news, the price goes back to changing randomly.

Eugene Fama of the University of Chicago developed the random-walk theory in the mid-1960s; Burton Malkiel, a professor at Princeton, later wrote a popular book based on Fama's work titled *A Random Walk Down Wall Street* (W.W. Norton & Company).

Fund managers who believe in the random walk believe in the strongest possible market efficiency. They often invest only in index funds — mutual funds that invest in the stock market in the same proportion as a major market index, such as the S&P 500 (an index prepared by the Standard & Poor's corporation that includes the stock of 500 large U.S. companies and that's designed to measure the overall performance of the stock market). They also claim that throwing darts at the quotes page of the Wall Street Journal is as likely to generate a top-performing stock portfolio as any intensive research.

Keep in mind that if the markets are mostly efficient and if stock prices are mostly random, it's very difficult for hedge fund managers and other investors to outperform the market. It's possible, and it happens, but it isn't easy.

One reason that academic theory about market behavior may seem so unrealistic is that almost all the research assumes that markets are efficient. In the real world, markets have pockets of inefficiency — sometimes they last ten minutes, and sometimes they last for years (think of the infamous dot-com bubble). But keep in mind that scholars are working on models of what could happen in ideal conditions. Without models, researchers and analysts can't perform the tests that improve our understanding of why things work the way they do. If you can keep this in mind, market theories will make a lot more sense.

Using the Modern (Markowitz) Portfolio Theory (MPT)

Harry Markowitz, as a graduate student at the University of Chicago in 1946, wrote his doctoral dissertation on how investors balance risk and return. His dissertation was the first step in what's now known as the *Modern Portfolio Theory* (MPT). Markowitz believed that investors are rewarded for taking risk. Investors who buy many different securities will find that the risk of each offsets the risk of the others, leaving the investor with only the risk in the market. In other words, the only risk that pays off is market risk. Investors who want more risk than the market should borrow securities (use leverage; see Chapter 11) to increase their exposure to market risk. Likewise, investors who want less risk than the market should mix up their market investments with low-risk assets like treasury bonds.

No Nobel Prize in Economics?

Here's some trivia about the Nobel Prize in Economics: Alfred Nobel's 1895 will, which created the other Nobel Prizes, didn't mention it, and the Nobel Foundation, which awards the physics, chemistry, medicine, literature, and peace prizes, doesn't give it. The economics prize is affiliated, however. The Prize in Economic Sciences in Memory of Alfred Nobel was created in 1968 by the Bank of Sweden, which awards the prize.

The MPT is the way that almost all professional investors think about the world. It's a basis for structuring portfolios, evaluating trades, and explaining performance. Even when investors have disagreements with the theory, they use its language to describe what they're doing. If you plan to invest in hedge funds, you need to have an understanding of how fund managers think about investing.

As time went on, the theory seemed to outgrow the label "modern," and Markowitz's work seemed deserving of even more honors than his 1990 Nobel Prize for the revolutionary approach to finance. Nowadays, many people honor the good professor by having the "M" in MPT stand for "Markowitz." If you do more financial reading or talk to people in the financial field, you'll hear "Markowitz Portfolio Theory," "Modern Portfolio Theory," and "MPT" used interchangeably. To help you keep it straight, I combine them in this book: the Modern (Markowitz) Portfolio Theory (MPT).

So what's risky?

Markowitz defined *risk* as a function of standard deviation — a statistic that shows how much your return may vary from the return that you expect to get. Say, for example, that a fund manager expects a security to have an average return of 10 percent over two years. If it returns 10 percent the first year and 10 percent the second year, the manager sees no deviation between any one return and the average return. But if the security returns 20 percent one period and 0 percent the next, it still returns an average of 10 percent, but it has big deviations from the 10-percent mean. The more a security swings around the expected return, the riskier it is.

Table 6-1 shows the math that goes into a standard-deviation calculation. (Nope, you don't need to know this for a final; I just include it to show you where the magic numbers come from.) It takes the closing prices for Johnson & Johnson and Yahoo! in December of 2005, calculates the percent changes each day, and then finds that each of the daily percent changes varies from the average of all the month's daily percent changes. The table shows a measure of how much each return can vary from the mean.

Table 6-1	Calculating Standard Deviation					
Date	*J&J Closing Price*	*Change from Previous Day*	*Standard Deviation*	*Yahoo! Closing Price*	*Change from Previous Day*	*Standard Deviation*
30-Dec-05	$59.76	−0.25%	0.0059	$39.18	−0.96%	0.0132
29-Dec-05	$59.91	−0.28%		$39.56	−1.71%	
28-Dec-05	$60.08	0.20%		$40.25	0.78%	
27-Dec-05	$59.96	−1.33%		$39.94	−1.70%	
23-Dec-05	$60.77	−0.33%		$40.63	−0.49%	
22-Dec-05	$60.97	0.71%		$40.83	0.89%	
21-Dec-05	$60.54	0.17%		$40.47	−0.52%	
20-Dec-05	$60.44	−0.67%		$40.68	−0.90%	
19-Dec-05	$60.85	0.55%		$41.05	−3.00%	
16-Dec-05	$60.52	1.17%		$42.32	1.37%	
15-Dec-05	$59.82	0.08%		$41.75	1.09%	
14-Dec-05	$59.77	−0.23%		$41.30	0.24%	
13-Dec-05	$59.91	0.17%		$41.20	2.79%	
12-Dec-05	$59.81	0.08%		$40.08	−0.57%	
9-Dec-05	$59.76	0.03%		$40.31	−0.10%	
8-Dec-05	$59.74	0.07%		$40.35	0.60%	
7-Dec-05	$59.70	−0.72%		$40.11	−0.20%	
6-Dec-05	$60.13	−0.96%		$40.19	−0.69%	
5-Dec-05	$60.71	−0.26%		$40.47	−1.80%	
2-Dec-05	$60.87	−0.77%		$41.21	0.34%	
1-Dec-05	$61.34			$41.07		
Average	$60.26	−0.13%		$40.62	−0.23%	

Mathematically speaking, *standard deviation* is the sum of the squares of the difference between each return and the average return over an entire time period. If you want a gander at the equation, here it is:

$$s = \sqrt{\frac{1}{N-1}\sum_{i=1}^{N}(x_i - x)^{-2}}$$

The result is a single number: the standard deviation for each stock for the month. And in that period, Yahoo! had a higher standard deviation.

One problem comes with the standard deviation calculation: It considers getting a greater return than expected to be as risky as getting a lesser return. In the real world, most people disagree — they pay more attention to the likelihood and magnitude of potential losses than to the range of potential gains. Behavioral finance addresses this problem; I get to that topic in the section "Investing on the Cutting Edge: Behavioral Finance."

Reviewing risk types in the MPT

The MPT does more than just define risk as the standard deviation of returns. It goes further to classify standard deviation as coming from company-specific factors or market-related factors. If the entire stock market crashes, for example, all stocks will go down in price, at least for a day or two — even if many of the companies are doing fine. Simply by being part of the market, companies take on some risk — a position Markowitz called *systematic risk* (and which some people refer to as *market risk*).

Each security also has its own unique risk. A stock's performance may depend on management's skill within a company, new product introductions it makes, or its relationships with government regulators. These unique factors affect the security but not the market as a whole. Markowitz found that if investors hold diversified portfolios, as hedge funds and individual investors often do, all the unique risks of all the different securities cancel out, leaving only systematic risk. That's why the unique risk of securities is often called *diversifiable risk* (along with *unsystematic risk* or *specific risk*).

So, why do you care? Well, in theory, you don't get paid for diversifiable risk, because you can easily eliminate it. In practice, however, hedge fund managers and other investors often take on diversifiable risk, either because they see little pockets of market inefficiency or because the assets are so unusual that investors really can't offset them with other securities (see the section "Market Efficiency and You, the Hedge Fund Investor" for more).

Distributing risk

Investors usually assume that the standard deviation (the measure of risk in the MPT) is arranged evenly around the mean return — forming a nice bell shape. What the distribution signifies is that returns that come in higher than average are just as likely as returns that come in lower than average. If higher and lower returns are equally likely to happen, a portfolio manager has an easier time managing risk. A normal risk distribution curve looks like the one in Figure 6-1.

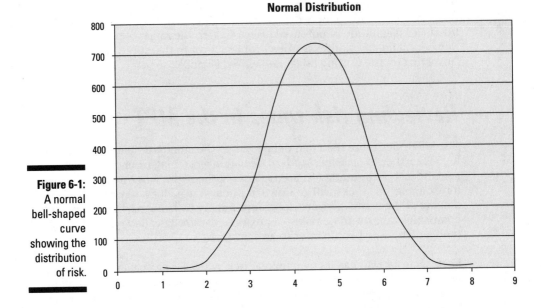

Normal Distribution

Figure 6-1: A normal bell-shaped curve showing the distribution of risk.

Risk isn't always distributed so neatly, however, and an uneven distribution can cause issues for hedge funds. If risk in a hedge fund is *almost* distributed normally, a hedge fund manager will *almost* be able to manage the risk involved. Occasionally, a high-flying hedge fund is brought down by a sequence of unpleasant events (interest-rate increases, currency collapses, stock market crashes, and the like) that people in the industry knew were possible, but the possibility turned out to be more likely than anyone expected.

Such events can destroy an investor very quickly, even if the market returns to normal in short order. Long-Term Capital Management, a hedge fund run by a group including two Nobel-Prize winning economists, was ruined in 1998 when a handful of rare events occurred at the same time (see Chapter 1 for more discussion on this fund).

Even though you may not want to see any more statistics, I throw some more at you here (sorry!). Two types of risk distribution come up when people talk about hedge funds: long-tail risks and fat-tail risks. If you know the difference, you can have smarter conversations with hedge fund managers — conversations that lead to smarter decisions about your money.

Hunting long-tail risk

When looking at the normal curve in Figure 6-1, you see that both of the ends are the same size. This indicates a balance between the likelihood of good things happening and the likelihood of bad things happening. Now, suppose a hedge fund manager spots an event that's possible but highly unlikely. In this situation, the curve would feature one end that's way out beyond the end of the normal curve — known as a *long-tail distribution.* You can see an example in Figure 6-2. In short, long-tail risk says that just because an event hasn't happened yet doesn't mean it won't happen.

Long-tail Distribution

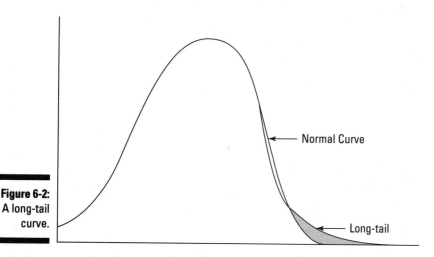

Figure 6-2:
A long-tail
curve.

One example of long-tail distribution is wealth in the United States. Only 10 percent of Americans had a net worth of more than $831,600 in 2004, according to the Federal Reserve Bank. That 10 percent includes the thrifty worker who paid off his mortgage and maximized his 401(k) contribution, and it includes Bill Gates' billions. The huge amount between a person who has exactly $831,600 and the founder of Microsoft is an example of a long-tail distribution.

In terms of hedge-fund risk, the long-tail includes risks that are remote but possible — like the collapse of the U.S. government or an earthquake that destroys Tokyo. One concern within the industry is that some hedge funds earn abnormally high returns by taking on large numbers of long-tail risks. No matter how unlikely some events are, anything can happen, and the results of an unexpected event can be catastrophic. One of the many contributing factors that led to the collapse of the fund Long-Term Capital Management was Russia's refusal to pay back its debts (see Chapter 1 for more detail on the fund). Until that point, financial scholars always assumed that a government would figure out a way to pay back what it borrowed — by printing money if it had to. So, financial analysts put the risk of default way out in the long tail, if they considered it at all.

Focusing on fat-tail risk

If certain extreme events are more likely to occur than other events, the look of a distribution gets a little chunky at the ends of the bell. Such a distribution is called a *fat-tail distribution*. If an investment has fat tails, the price of the security probably swings a lot more than otherwise expected, so you're more likely to get really high — or really low — returns than otherwise expected.

You can see the difference between a normal curve and a fat-tailed distribution in Figure 6-3. The difference isn't huge, but you can spot it, and you'll want to know as much as you can about it if your return sits on one of those tail ends.

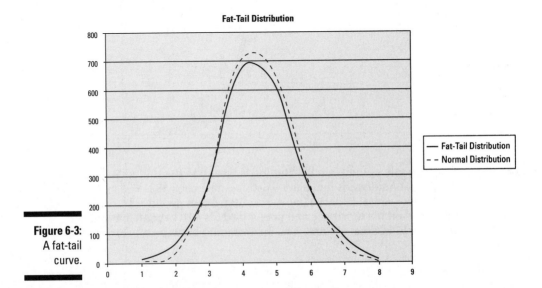

Figure 6-3: A fat-tail curve.

What I'm trying to say is that if your hedge fund has a fat-tail return, you may make more money than you expect or you may lose more money than you expect. If the fund's risk-management system assumes a normal distribution of returns when it actually has a fat-tailed distribution, you and the fund could run into trouble.

Determining the market rate of return

The Modern (Markowitz) Portfolio Theory looks at how an investment performs relative to the market. (The market, in financial theory, is anything and everything that one can invest in.) The tricky part of the theory is figuring out how the market performs. Most people start by coming up with a definition for the market. In most cases, investors use a market index like the S&P 500, because the index is designed to sample the market. Often, investors have the option to buy index funds or exchange-traded funds, which are investments designed to perform exactly like the market index. Thanks to these funds, investors have an easy way to get market performance — which also means that they expect more return or less risk when they choose a hedge fund instead.

The *market rate of return* reflects the risk of investing in the market rather than in a risk-free asset. The risk-free asset is usually a short-term U.S. government security, like a treasury bill. The market return you look at is the *market risk premium,* which is the difference between the market return and the return on the risk-free asset. (If you flip to the section on the Capital Assets Pricing Model, you'll see that it looks at that difference when calculating the expected return on an asset.)

Naturally, academic researchers debate the size of the risk premium. The matter is complicated by which time period they use to calculate it. The following list gives some different schools of thought:

- ✔ The New York Stock Exchange has been in existence since 1792, and some price data is still floating around out there from its inception. It isn't necessarily accurate or fully comparable to more recent data, but the motivated researcher can find and use it.

- ✔ Others prefer to look at the risk premium after the 1929 stock-market crash. That date marks a low point in the market; you can find accurate data from that date; and the U.S. government passed new regulations after the crash to ensure market integrity. Some regulations are still in place, and you can read all about them in Chapter 3.

- ✔ Still others prefer to use data after the end of World War II, when the United States became a dominant world power and the economy entered its modern era.

Does it matter which time frame investors use for the risk premium? Yes, because the size of the average market return over and above the risk-free rate of return affects people's expectations for the market. A hedge fund manager who assumes that a 7-percent risk premium is normal has a different investment approach than a manager who assumes that a 9-percent premium is normal. Some hedge fund managers invest without regard to market expectations, but others use the market to peg their investment strategies. It's hard to say which technique is better, but the choice affects a manager's market expectations and strategies.

Beta: Ranking market return

In the 1960s, William Sharpe, a professor at Stanford University and a Nobel laureate; John Lintner, a professor at Harvard Business School; and Jack Treynor, an employee at Merrill Lynch did some work on Markowitz's model and came up with an application for it: the *Capital Assets Pricing Model,* or CAPM. The CAPM is a refinement of the MPT; the model says that investment return is a function of the general rate of return on the market combined with how sensitive a given asset is to the market's performance. The number used to measure that implied risk is called *beta.* Hedge fund managers use beta to rank the systematic risk of an asset. The following sections present the math involved with beta and its real-world applications.

Doing the beta math

I know that math probably makes your eyes glaze over, but you have good reasons to recognize the equations involved with beta and understand what they mean. Some hedge fund managers really do use this stuff — or at least their own versions of it. (In Chapter 11, for example, you can find plenty of discussion on beta-neutral hedge funds.)

If you know what beta is, you'll have an easier time understanding what your fund manager is doing with your money. And even fund managers who sneer at the CAPM because the real world is a lot messier than the theory makes it out to be — you can find plenty of people who hold this opinion out there — often use beta as a way of discussing market risk and comparing investment returns.

Without further ado, here's the beta equation:

$$E(r) = B(r_m - r_f) + r_f$$

where E is the expected return on a security, *B* is beta, r_m is the market rate of return, and r_f is the risk-free rate of return. In sentence form, it says that "the expected return on a security is equal to beta times the difference between the market rate of return and the risk-free rate, plus the risk-free rate."

The formula for beta is complicated. It compares the standard deviation of a security to the standard deviation of the market itself. In most cases, the performance of an index, like the S&P 500 in the United States or the Nikkei in Japan, measures the "market." But people argue all the time about how to define the market to come up with beta. To make matters even more complicated, a given security's beta changes over time.

Hedge fund managers who use beta have a few choices for finding their magical numbers. They may run their own internal computer programs, using their own definitions of the market, or they may subscribe to research services that calculate figures for them. If you're curious about the beta of any particular stock, you can find numbers through such online stock quotation services as Yahoo! Finance (`finance.yahoo.com`) and MSN MoneyCentral (`moneycentral.msn.com`).

You can bet, though, that a hedge fund manager uses a different source than Yahoo! Finance; if you're talking to a fund manager who relies heavily on beta, ask how his fund workers calculate beta and how frequently it's revised.

If you think back to your algebra days, you may notice that the Capital Assets Pricing Model looks a lot like the equation for a line — y = mx + b, where m is the slope of a line, x is a value on the X-axis, and b is the intercept on the Y-axis. Similarly, the Capital Assets Pricing Model describes a rate of return that changes according to the slope, beta; times the amount equal to the market rate of return minus the risk-free rate of return; with the risk-free rate being the place where the line crosses the Y-axis.

Math's great, but what does beta mean?

What? You don't care about the math involved with beta? You say you aren't working on your MBA, so you just want to know how the number affects you and your investments? Okay, okay, I'll tell you.

It's like this: The market has a beta of 1. A financial researcher expects a stock with a beta of more than 1 to move in the same direction as the market, but at a greater level. So, if the market goes up, a stock with a beta of 1.5 goes up by a greater percentage. Likewise, a stock with a beta of less than 1 moves in the same direction but at a lesser percentage. And a stock with a negative beta moves in the opposite direction of the market.

So, if you think that the market is going up, you (or your hedge fund managers) should buy plenty of high-beta securities to get a greater return. If you want to reduce your exposure to the market, you should buy securities with betas less than 1. And if you think the market is going down, you should look for securities with negative beta because they'll go up when the market goes down. One easy way to create negative beta is to short a stock with a high positive beta (see Chapter 11 for more on shorting), which is exactly what many fund managers do when they expect the market to go down.

Now you know how hedge fund managers can use beta to manage the risk and return parameters of their portfolios. Whew!

Alpha: Return beyond standard deviation

Ready for some more Greek? Allow me to introduce alpha. Hedge fund managers love to use the word *alpha* — the measurement of investment performance over and above market risk taken. Alpha is a factor financial researchers add to the CAPM. Here's the equation for alpha under the CAPM:

$$E(r) = B(r_m - r_f) + A + r_f$$

That letter A, or alpha, stands for some kind of additional return that the market doesn't explain (see the previous sections to find out what the rest of the variables represent). To most academic types, alpha doesn't exist. They claim alpha is 0, because in an efficient market, the unexplainable differences would disappear. Some research has shown that alpha may exist in some situations, however. For example, stocks with low prices relative to their book values (assets minus liabilities) have been shown to perform better than expected on a measure of beta alone.

Alpha appears before beta in the Greek alphabet, so why did I list Beta before Alpha in this chapter? Beta is listed before alpha because beta came first in the evolution of the CAPM, and because alpha has less support in theory. But hedge fund managers love to talk about alpha, and that's one of the reasons why I also discuss it in Chapter 1.

To most hedge fund managers, alpha isn't an esoteric subject for PhD candidates to debate during late-night bull sessions. Alpha is real to them, so much so that it's their reason for being in the hedge-fund business. Alpha represents a fund manager's proprietary investment strategy, her great skill, and her justification for the fund's high fees (see Chapter 2). Basically, alpha represents the value a hedge fund manager adds to the fund. A typical presentation to prospective investors by a typical hedge fund manager includes the magic words, "We generate alpha by . . .," at which point the managers launches into a description of a research or arbitrage strategy (you can read more about the strategies that fund managers use in their quest for alpha in the chapters of Part III).

Just keep two things in mind. First, if positive alpha exists, and it seems to, so does negative alpha, which means that a hedge fund manager could do such a bad job that she actually removes value from the portfolio. Second, fund managers who find positive alpha consistently are also likely to demand high fees for their stellar skills. Comprehensive due diligence (see Chapter 18) can help you sort out the better managers from the clunkers.

Many hedge fund managers who discuss alpha don't necessarily use — or even believe in — the Capital Assets Pricing Model. They simply use the word to describe what they plan to do for investors who invest money with them.

The Arbitrage Pricing Theory (APT): Expanding the MPT

The Capital Assets Pricing Model (CAPM) states that investment returns depend on the risk-free rates of return and the market risk premiums (see the section "Determining the market rate of return" for more). The CAPM sums up this definition in an equation for a line, and generates numbers like "beta" and "alpha" that fund managers and investors can use as shorthand for other investment concepts.

But as neat as it is, the CAPM has some flaws. One particular flaw is logical: Doesn't it seem like investment returns might depend on things other than the risk-free rate of return and the risk premium for the market? Maybe the reason that securities have different betas, and the reason that betas change over time, is that something other than the market dictates their movement. And maybe alpha can be broken out and identified. These thoughts were running through the head of Stephen Ross, a finance professor, when he developed the *Arbitrage Pricing Theory,* or APT. The math looks like this:

$$E(r) = f_1(rp_1) + f_2(rp_2) + f_3(rp_3) + r_f$$

where f_1, f_2, and f_3 are different economic factors (like unemployment, commodity prices, and commercial interest rates), and rp_1, rp_2, and rp_3 are the returns related to those factors. In English, the theory reads as follows: "The expected return on an asset is equal to how sensitive the asset is to different factors in the economy, multiplied by the risk premium that each of these factors has relative to the risk-free rate, plus the risk-free rate of return." Depending on the version of the theory used, an investor can look at only one or two factors, or he can look at dozens. If you think about it, the CAPM is just a version of the APT that cares about only one fact: sensitivity to market risk.

Many hedge fund managers use a version of the Arbitrage Pricing Theory to guide their asset selections. You may find a manager who has developed a model internally that fits his own research and his own approach to the market. APT models are almost always proprietary, so investors in the fund don't get to see what the model looks like. Funds that rely heavily on the APT and similar models are sometimes called *black-box shops,* because they feed data into computer programs and wait for lists of securities to pop out, but investors never quite see what goes on with the program in the middle.

Even if a hedge fund you're interested in is a black-box shop, it doesn't prevent you from getting some information about how the fund constructs its model and what factors go into it. You should get an explanation before you invest in the fund, during your due diligence (see Chapter 18) or before.

Discovering How Interest Rates Affect the Investment Climate

In the Capital Assets Pricing Model (CAPM; see the section "Beta: Ranking market return"), the market rate of return depends in part on the risk-free rate of return — the return that people want for giving up the use of their money, even if they're certain to get it back. For example, you can give your mother a dollar tonight, and you know she's good for it, but if you go through a tollbooth on the way home tomorrow, you may be really bummed that you gave up that money.

An *interest rate* is the price of money. It reflects three things:

- ✔ Giving up the use of the money (also called *opportunity cost*)
- ✔ The risk of not getting money back
- ✔ Inflation (the decline in purchasing power because of a general increase in prices throughout the economy)

In this section, I explain the factors that go into interest rates and how interest rates relate to hedge funds (and you). I also show you the power interest rates have when they compound.

Seeing what goes into an interest rate

You hear financial types describe interest rates in two ways: real interest rates and nominal interest rates. *Real interest rates* reflect risk. *Nominal interest rates* reflect risk and inflation. Nominal rates are the rates you see posted in the papers. You can't get a quote on a real interest rate; you have to back inflation out of a nominal interest rate. And yes, some people care about the proportion of real interest rate included in the nominal rate, especially when inflation levels are high. The following sections dive into the three factors reflected in an interest rate.

Compensation for the use of the money

In the United States, the rate of return on short-term U.S. government securities — treasury bills — is usually thought of as the risk-free rate (see the section "Determining the market rate of return"). The rate reflects the market opportunity cost for giving up the use of the money, and because the bills generally mature within 90 days, inflation isn't an issue. And if the U.S. government doesn't pay back its debts, all investors will have bigger problems than determining the exact rate of interest in the economy (see Chapter 1 for more on what can happen in this situation).

Risk of repayment

The risk of repayment varies with the overall economy — are people making money and doing well, or are they struggling? — as well as with the attributes of the specific borrower. Individuals have credit histories that show how much debt they should be able to handle, and businesses and governments have histories, too. The greater the likelihood of repayment, the lower the interest rate. This is a simple example of the risk-and-return tradeoff.

Inflation

Inflation is a change in price levels in the economy. If prices go up, people expect their investment returns to go up, too. If the returns don't match the change in price levels, the investors give up money on a real basis when they invest.

In general, when inflation is high, so are interest rates. A little inflation is good because it gives people reason to invest. Too much inflation, though, causes people to spend money as fast as it comes in.

Inflation is the single biggest risk that most investors face. Investments that people think of as safe often don't return enough to beat inflation. Sure, you can simply lock up your cash in a safe, but you lose purchasing power every day that your cash sits there. In the long run, as long as you spend less money than you earn and get a return that meets or beats inflation, you'll be okay, no matter if you put your money in a flashy hedge fund or in a more traditional investment, like a mutual fund.

Deflation

Deflation is the opposite of inflation — it's the general decline in price levels in the economy. Deflation may seem like a good thing, but it isn't. Instead of consumers reveling in bargains around every corner, they become afraid to invest, and the economy comes close to shutting down. In fact, if interest rates are negative, consumers can increase their purchasing power by holding onto their money. Many historians believe that deflation caused the Great Depression in the 1930s.

Deflation is rare, but it happens. And if it does happen, you want to invest your money in a different country where it isn't taking place.

Relating interest rates and hedge funds

Interest rates have many effects on risk and return within a hedge fund, and in turn on hedge fund managers and their strategies. In the following list, I cover some of the effects of interest rates:

- ✔ **Hedge funds as borrowers.** Many hedge funds pursue strategies that rely on leverage, which means that they borrow money for investment purposes. (You can read more about leverage in Chapter 11.) Naturally, when a hedge fund borrows money, it has to pay interest, so if interest rates are high, the fund will have higher expenses. Higher expenses lead to a reduced investment return.

- ✔ **Hedge funds as lenders.** Hedge funds lend money out when they buy bonds. Many hedge funds actively buy and sell bonds day in and day out as part of their investment strategies. Interest rates affect the value of derivatives, currencies, and stocks, too. The level of the rate affects the return on investments, so hedge fund analysts pay plenty of attention to risk and inflation in the overall economy.

- ✔ **Hedge funds as risk managers.** Most hedge funds are designed to reduce investment risk. Because opportunity cost, business risk, and inflation (the three factors that affect interest rates) are all risks that can affect a hedge fund investor's returns, many hedge funds pay attention to interest rates to improve their risk management. To manage interest-rate risk, they often use derivative securities such as futures and swaps, which I describe in Chapter 5.

- ✔ **Hedge funds as speculators.** Some hedge fund managers try to predict the direction of interest rates, using their predictions to speculate on stocks, currencies, bonds, and derivatives. Predicting the future is always risky, but some funds have computer models that may accurately show how different securities will react to different combinations of economic events. Interest-rate speculation is a high-risk endeavor that may pay off with high returns, which is what some hedge fund investors want.

Witnessing the power of compound interest

Albert Einstein may have concentrated on the theory of relativity, but he was just as fascinated with compound interest. Compound interest is a simpler concept than physics, yet so many investors ignore the power of compounding to their detriment. *Compound interest* is interest on interest, and it can make a dramatic difference in the value of your investments. As financiers often say, those who don't understand compound interest are doomed to pay it. Hedge fund managers know all about the power of compound interest, and that's one reason they prefer to keep their investors' money locked up for relatively long periods of time.

Table 6-2 gives you a simple example of compound interest. Say you invest $1,000 at 8-percent interest for 10 years. If you take the $80 earned each year and spend it, your investment won't grow. You'll collect and spend a total of $800 over the time period, which you can see in the left side of the table.

Table 6-2	Simple Interest versus Compound Interest			
	Simple Interest: Cashing Out Each Year		*Compound Interest: Earning Interest on Interest*	
	Principal	Interest	Principal	Interest
Year 1	$1,000	$80.00	$1,000	$80.00
Year 2	$1,000	$80.00	$1,080	$86.40
Year 3	$1,000	$80.00	$1,166	$93.31
Year 4	$1,000	$80.00	$1,260	$100.78
Year 5	$1,000	$80.00	$1,360	$108.84
Year 6	$1,000	$80.00	$1,469	$117.55
Year 7	$1,000	$80.00	$1,587	$126.95
Year 8	$1,000	$80.00	$1,714	$137.11
Year 9	$1,000	$80.00	$1,851	$148.07
Year 10	$1,000	$80.00	$1,999	$159.92
Total Earned		$800.00		$1,158.92
Difference in Dollars				$358.92
Difference in Percentages				44.9%

Now, say that you keep the interest in your account and let it build up. Each year, your money grows by the amount of interest earned the years before. At the end of the 10 years, you'll collect a total of $1,158.92 — almost 45 percent more money.

Another great thing about compound interest is that small differences can add up over time. Table 6-3 shows the value of an investment compounded at 8-percent interest and the value of an investment at 8.1 percent. After 10 years, the difference between the earnings of the two is small — only $20.00 — but it has widened to almost 1.7 percent compared to 0.1 percent at the start. Carry this difference out over 20 years, and you see an even greater difference.

Table 6-3	Noticing How Small Differences in Interest Rates Matter			
	Interest Rate of 8%		Interest Rate of 8.1%	
	Principal	Interest	Principal	Interest
Year 1	$1,000	$80.00	$1,000	$81.00
Year 2	$1,080	$86.40	$1,081	$87.56
Year 3	$1,166	$93.31	$1,169	$94.65
Year 4	$1,260	$100.78	$1,263	$102.32
Year 5	$1,360	$108.84	$1,366	$110.61
Year 6	$1,469	$117.55	$1,476	$119.57
Year 7	$1,587	$126.95	$1,596	$129.25
Year 8	$1,714	$137.11	$1,725	$139.72
Year 9	$1,851	$148.07	$1,865	$151.04
Year 10	$1,999	$159.92	$2,016	$163.27
Total Earned		$1,158.92		$1,179.00
Difference in Dollars				$20.07
Difference in Percentages				1.7%
Year 11	$2,159	$172.71	$2,179	$176.50
Year 12	$2,332	$186.53	$2,355	$190.80

	Interest Rate of 8%		Interest Rate of 8.1%	
	Principal	**Interest**	**Principal**	**Interest**
Year 13	$2,518	$201.45	$2,546	$206.25
Year 14	$2,720	$217.57	$2,753	$222.96
Year 15	$2,937	$234.98	$2,975	$241.02
Year 16	$3,172	$253.77	$3,217	$260.54
Year 17	$3,426	$274.08	$3,477	$281.64
Year 18	$3,700	$296.00	$3,759	$304.45
Year 19	$3,996	$319.68	$4,063	$329.11
Year 20	$4,316	$345.26	$4,392	$355.77
Total Earned		$2,502.03		$2,569.04
Difference in Dollars				$67.00
Difference in Percentages				2.7%

For a hedge fund dealing with millions or billions of dollars, the differences in compounded interest add up to greater and greater amounts. Table 6-4 shows you the same information as Table 6-3, but it features an initial investment of $1,000,000 rather than $1,000. The initial difference in interest rates of 0.1 percent means a difference in income of $20,000. That's real money!

Table 6-4	Seeing How Small Differences Matter More when the Dollars Are Big			
	Interest Rate of 8%		Interest Rate of 8.1%	
	Principal	**Interest**	**Principal**	**Interest**
Year 1	$1,000,000	$80,000.00	$1,000,000	$81,000.00
Year 2	$1,080,000	$86,400.00	$1,081,000	$87,561.00
Year 3	$1,166,400	$93,312.00	$1,168,561	$94,653.44
Year 4	$1,259,712	$100,776.96	$1,263,214	$102,320.37
Year 5	$1,360,489	$108,839.12	$1,365,535	$110,608.32

(continued)

Table 6-4 (continued)

	Interest Rate of 8%		Interest Rate of 8.1%	
	Principal	**Interest**	**Principal**	**Interest**
Year 6	$1,469,328	$117,546.25	$1,476,143	$119,567.59
Year 7	$1,586,874	$126,949.95	$1,595,711	$129,252.57
Year 8	$1,713,824	$137,105.94	$1,724,963	$139,722.03
Year 9	$1,850,930	$148,074.42	$1,864,685	$151,039.51
Year 10	$1,999,005	$159,920.37	$2,015,725	$163,273.71
Total Earned		$1,158,925.00		$1,178,998.54
Difference in Dollars				$20,073.54
Difference in Percentages				1.7%

Table 6-4 illustrates why hedge fund managers spend so much time and energy looking for very small advantages in the market. They know that given enough time and enough money, they can make little differences add up.

Investing on the Cutting Edge: Behavioral Finance

The Capital Assets Pricing Model (CAPM; see the section "Beta: Ranking market return") and the Arbitrage Pricing Theory model (see the section "The Arbitrage Pricing Theory [APT]: Expanding the MPT") start with two basic assumptions: They both assume that markets are efficient and that market participants are rational.

Like human beings are ever rational? You see the problem.

Many financial researchers are working on ways to account for the fact that people can do crazy things when dealing with money. That goes for fancy-schmantzy hedge fund managers with Nobel prizes and for high-school grad-uates trying to pick out investment options for their company-sponsored retirement plans. The field in which these researchers work is called *behavioral finance* — a field that's trying to explain the common deviations from rationality and efficiency so that people can better understand how financial markets move.

And some of these researchers are picking up their own Nobel Prizes, too.

Examining the principles of behavioral finance

Traditional, stale finance insists that markets react immediately to information and that, as a whole, the participants in the market are rational. It allows for *some* irrational behavior but remains steadfast that it all cancels out. People of this thinking believe that the overly optimistic trader and the overly pessimistic trader counteract each other, and the logical people win out.

Traditional finance also says that the more information that comes into the market, the more efficient the market will be. But as data continues to get cheaper, the market hasn't become more rational and efficient. If anything, the dramatic increase in instant news and free stock-price services has caused investors to overreact and get carried away with trends.

Anyone with Internet access can get free information that professionals once had to pay dearly for and even wait two or three days to receive. (Believe it or not, there was a time when investors waited to receive earnings announcements in the mail before making buy-and-sell decisions.)

Behavioral finance has a different thought process. It says that investors make decisions by using quick rules, not rational analysis; it says that the presentation of a decision can influence investors; and it says that markets are inefficient. These are the principals of behavioral finance — a field that's still in its newer stage — and I outline them in the following sections.

Using quick and easy rules: Heuristics

A *heuristic* is a guideline for making a decision — a step-by-step approach that says, "When you see this, do that." This approach is a great way to make decisions quickly, but it can keep people from being more efficient or from noticing details that make the current situation different from the situation last week, on which the heuristic worked just fine.

For example, many stock traders believe that you buy on the rumor and sell on the news. When they hear whispers about a corporate takeover, they start buying the company's stock and then they sell it when an announcement hits the airwaves. Sometimes, that strategy works like a charm. Other times, it causes a trader to acquire stock for no good reason and to sell it before a bidding war breaks out.

Professional investors spend their days bombarded with price changes and news feeds. The information comes so fast that they may not have the luxury of thinking carefully about whether the rules of the game have changed. The sheer volume and speed at which information flows into the market makes rational analysis impossible. The use of heuristics may lead to an analysis that's almost, but not quite, rational.

Harnessing the power of presentation: Framing

In this chapter, I've presented a few equations dealing with financial theory. Equations are great because they strip a problem of emotion; they even strip it of words. Strings of letters, numbers, and symbols simplify a situation so that you can make a rational decision. But the real world is all about story problems, and many people respond to language better than to equations buried within.

The *framing* of a question is the way that someone presents it. If I offer you a 90-percent chance to make a dollar with a 10-percent chance of losing a dime, you'll probably take my offer. If I offer you a 90-percent chance of making $10 million and a 10-percent chance of losing a million, you may focus on that big loss and turn the offer down. However, the risk and return is the same for both.

Investors see losses as terrible occurrences, which causes them to avoid taking risks — even risks where the likelihood of a gain is greater than the likelihood of a loss. Fear also causes investors to hang on to losing investments instead of admitting defeat, in the hopes that maybe, possibly, the price will go up.

Professionals are better at pulling a problem away from its frame than most individual investors, but they aren't perfect. When December rolls around, a hedge fund looking at a big year-end performance fee is likely to become conservative in order to protect that bonus. A hedge fund that sits under the bonus threshold may get incredibly aggressive in the hopes that an investment will stick. Neither situation may suit the best interests of the fund investors.

Battling inefficiency: Pricing anomalies

When the market is clearly inefficient, academics say that pricing anomalies exist. Most of these anomalies disappear as soon as investors discover them.

Years ago, researchers found that stocks tended to perform better in January than in any other month of the year. They called it the "January effect," and it seemed to defy market efficiency. However, soon as investors found out about the January effect, they started buying stocks in December so that they could take advantage of it. This rush led to such a demand in December that it became the best-performing month of the year. At that point, investors started buying stocks in November to take advantage of the December effect that preceded the January effect. Eventually, the whole anomaly disappeared, and nobody really talks about it much anymore.

Other anomalies seem to hold because of messy investor psychology, which gives behavioral-finance experts some good areas for research.

The following sections show you some other sources of market inefficiency that create pricing anomalies. Researchers in behavioral finance are exploring these sources, and at some point, investors will have practical information that they can apply. For now, you should keep these things in mind when evaluating a hedge fund manager and discussing investment performance.

Groupthink

You know how in junior high everyone does things just because everyone else does them? And how the worst thing in the world is to be different? People in the investment world follow the same mentality, I'm afraid to say. On occasion, everyone seems to think alike — often called *groupthink* or the *herd mentality*.

In the late 1990s, for example, every investor was so sure that Internet stocks would enjoy enormous success for years to come that people who dared to point out that maybe, just maybe, the valuations were crazy faced becoming a social outcast, getting fired, or just being pitied.

The problem is that people can be right, but the truth can take a long time to come to the light, and plenty of money can be lost in the meantime. John Maynard Keynes, a famous economist who died before the Swedes started giving Nobel Prizes in Economics, once said, "The market can remain irrational longer than you can remain solvent." Several hedge fund managers were proven right about dot-com valuations in 2000, but many of those people lost their clients before the truth came out.

Wage and price stickiness

In an efficient market, prices go up and down equally, and they respond to information. In the real world, however, prices often don't go down as much as expected. Instead, they stick to some floor level. If a company needs to cut its payroll, it has the option of cutting the salary of every worker equally. More likely, however, the company will fire some workers so that others on the job will make as much as before or even more. If a candy company enjoys a drop in its ingredient prices, it will probably keep the difference as profit. If it decides to give customers some of the savings, it will most likely increase the size of its candy bars instead of cutting the price it charges for them.

George Soros and the theory of reflexivity

Not everyone working in behavioral finance is a university professor. George Soros, a legendary hedge fund manager, developed one of the more interesting theories of how the market behaves (you can read more about Soros in Chapter 1). And because of his status, people pay attention to what he has to say.

Soros' *theory of reflexivity* says that there's a limit to how efficient security prices are because the prices of securities influence future economic and market behavior. Instead of merely reflecting information, prices start to affect it, which leads to periods where the market is out of balance. Because security

prices cause these situations, they no longer respond efficiently.

For example, if a stock price is going up, investors sometimes take that observation as proof that a company is attractive, so they buy more of the stock and bid up the price. When small companies in the same industry see that prices are rising, they're more likely to issue their stock to the public in an Initial Public Offering, or IPO. When venture-capital investors see the profits being made on IPOs, they're more likely to fund new start-up companies that may go public. *Note:* In this example, the driver is the rising price of stock, not the information about how the underlying business is performing.

As long as some economic factors are less than perfectly efficient, the prices of related securities will be less than perfectly efficient.

Bias toward the present

In academic theory, interest rates reflect the time value of money. The longer you lend out your money, the more compensation you should expect for giving up the use of the money and for any losses in purchasing power due to expected inflation. In practice, however, investors seem much more interested in making money today. They don't pay much attention to the effect on potential return for holding money into the future or whether they're getting compensation for waiting.

Applying behavioral finance to hedge funds

As comfortable as they are with numbers and equations, most hedge fund managers believe that markets are driven by more than pure logic. Many fund managers pay attention to behavior to find investment opportunities (such as George Soros; see the sidebar "George Soros and the theory of reflexivity").

Some fund managers incorporate information about how investors are behaving into their expectations, and they make buy-and-sell decisions based on their observations. Other fund managers look at how people are behaving and go with the opposite strategy, on the theory that crowds are often wrong.

Other fund managers stick to their investment strategies — even during periods when the strategies aren't working — under the assumption that rationality will return at some point. One reason that hedge funds limit withdrawals is so fund managers have time for their investment ideas to play out. If fund investors panic and demand the return of their investments, the fund managers have to play into near-term market irrationality, even if that isn't the best strategy for the hedge fund in the long run.

Chapter 7

You Want Your Money When? Balancing Time and Liquidity

In This Chapter

▶ Bringing your cash needs to light

▶ Keeping track of the time on your investment horizon

▶ Examining your principal needs

▶ Managing liquidity after you enter a fund

*H*edge fund managers have the ability to make big profits on short-term trades. It isn't unusual for a fund manager to hold a security overnight, or even for only a few minutes, in the pursuit of profit. Fund managers, however, aren't keen on sharing their investment perks. They don't let investors in their funds trade in and out with the same frequency. A mutual-fund investor, on the other hand, can cash out at any time.

The money you invest in a hedge fund may be locked up for years (see Chapter 2 for more on the structure of hedge funds). Therefore, you need to consider your cash-flow needs and your time horizon before making an investment, and you need to find out how your needs match with those of the fund manager. The needs of both parties may determine how much money you should allocate to a hedge fund. You also need to know what to do if the hedge fund returns money to you outside of a withdrawal. In this chapter, I give you advice on how to handle liquidity challenges in your portfolio, including when to make withdrawals, what to do when you receive a distribution of fund assets, and what to do in case of fund disbandment. Time to put my money where my mouth is!

Considering Your Cash Needs

Whether you're an individual investor trying to figure out what to do with your annual bonus or a pension fund employee trying to allocate this year's contribution, you need a plan for your money, and you need to pick investments that match your plan. The decision is a three-step process that involves answering questions and examining your cash needs:

1. Do you need the money to meet any obligations in the next year? If so, you probably don't want to put it into a hedge fund. Instead, check out a short-term investment, like treasury bills or a money-market fund.

2. If you don't need the money right away, do you have enough cash to meet the minimum deposit for the types of investments you're interested in? It isn't unusual for a hedge fund to require an initial investment of $250,000 or even several million dollars (see Chapter 2 for more on initial payments).

3. If you're interested in hedge funds, but don't have enough money on hand, you may need to start saving! Even though you may not need the money for years, you may need to invest it for the short term. Saving for a fund can be like saving for the down payment on a house: The house itself is a long-term investment, but you need to produce the money to buy it in short order.

Like Dollars through the Hourglass: Determining Your Time Horizon

The answers to two questions go a long way toward determining how to invest your money and what to invest it in:

- When do you need your money?
- What do you need your money for?

How much money you need to generate from an investment is closely related to your *time horizon*. If you need money next week, you'll invest it differently than if you need the money in 40 years. Your monetary needs can change over time, too. For example, a relatively new business may have a pension plan but no retirees. Until its employees start retiring, the company can manage its pension assets for maximum total return, without regard for income. When employees start retiring, though, the company will have to reallocate some funds to generate income to meet each month's pension payments.

No matter the answers you give to the two major questions, they'll influence the risk you can take, the return you need to shoot for (see Chapter 6), the asset classes that are open to you (see Chapter 9), and how much time you can allocate toward the investment.

Generally speaking, investable money falls into three categories:

- ✔ **Temporary (or short-term) funds** that you'll need in a year
- ✔ **Matched assets** that you invest to meet a specific liability, like a college education
- ✔ **Permanent funds** that you invest for such a long term that, for all practical purposes, you'll never spend them

After you determine what you have planned for your money and when you'll need it, you can make better decisions about where to invest it. After all, a hedge fund that forbids withdrawals for two years is a terrible investment for you if you need your money in one year, no matter how good the fund's track record looks. The following sections cover the three investment categories in more detail.

The rate of return on an investment reflects not only the risk, but also the investor's time horizon, because you give up the ability to spend your money. Investors expect compensation when they give up access to their cash. In economic terms, giving up your right to spend money now is called the *opportunity cost* of an investment.

Taking stock of temporary funds

Temporary funds stay invested for a very short time. You may need the money put in a temporary fund at any time, so you don't want to tie it up. For example, you may set up an emergency fund with six months worth of expenses. A business may keep cash on hand to take advantage of bargains on inventory. You may also set up a fund used to repay a loan due this year.

Investors usually keep temporary funds in treasury bills, money-market securities, and bank accounts. The return on these investments is low, but so is the risk that comes with the investments. You can get your money out easily — in some cases simply upon demand — with the assurance that the value will hold. For these reasons, hedge funds aren't suitable for temporary funds.

Hedge funds charge high fees. Standard charges include a management fee of 2 percent of assets and a bonus payment of 20 percent of the fund's profits (see Chapters 2 and 4). Because fund managers need time to earn these fees, they want money that investors can set aside for long periods.

Fathoming matched assets and liability

When an investor needs the funds he or she invests to meet a specific liability at some point in the future, the investor is said to have *matched assets.* The mother of a newborn knows that in 18 years, she will probably have a college tuition to fund. A human-resources manager at a major multi-national corporation knows how much money the corporation is likely to pay out in pensions every year for the next 50 years. Investors can meet these liabilities by investing assets now in order to earn a return sufficient enough to meet the liabilities. The greater the expected return, the less money that a person will have to invest.

The higher the rate of return on an investment, the lower its present value — a good thing if you're saving money, but bad if you're borrowing it. Also note: The higher the expected rate of return, the higher the expected amount of risk.

Table 7-1 shows the amount of money you'd have to invest today to generate $1,000,000 in 10 years, figured at different rates of return. *Note:* This table shows the value of the $1,000,000 as of press time. Notice that as the expected rate of return increases, the amount of money you have to set aside today decreases.

Table 7-1	Money and Expected-Return Percentage Needed to Generate $1 Million in 10 Years				
Investment Return	3%	5%	7%	9%	11%
Amount to be Invested Today	$744,094	$613,913	$508,349	$422,411	$352,184

Some investors establish investment plans to meet a single obligation at an approximate future point, like a college education. Other investors have a range of obligations to meet. A pension fund, for example, has to pay out money each month to retirees in the plan, and it has to invest money to pay the youngest firm employee her benefits from the day she retires until the day she dies, possibly 70 years from now. The folks in charge at the pension fund will sit down with some actuaries and work out a schedule of the money due at different dates. At that point, they invest money to generate the necessary return to meet the targets. The fund treats the money needed to meet this year's payments to retirees as temporary funds, kept in short-term investments (see the previous section). The fund may then invest money that it doesn't need for many years or a few decades in risky or illiquid investments, including hedge funds.

Whether a hedge fund is an appropriate match for an upcoming financial need depends in large part on the risk profile of the hedge fund. An absolute-return fund, which is designed to have low risk and a steady, low, return (see Chapter 1), is usually a good match with an intermediate-term obligation, for money that you don't need until after you meet any lockup periods on the fund. Directional funds, which pursue high-risk strategies in exchange for higher expected returns, are a better match for financial needs that reach far into the future.

Peeking into permanent funds

Some investors put away money with a plan that would drive shopaholics crazy: To never spend it. Instead, the investors plan to spend only the income generated from the investments' interest and dividends. They can then reinvest the capital gains so that the initial amounts invested get larger, which causes the amount of income that the investments can generate to grow.

And who are the lucky folks who can put away money forever if they choose? Some very wealthy families hold money in trust for generations. More often, university endowments and charitable foundations choose this investment route. These organizations generally spend a small amount of their assets each year — often only 5 percent — to support their activities. They invest any return over and above the 5 percent to expand the total investment pool, from which money is rarely spent. The amount of an investment pool in a permanent fund can be huge: The Bill and Melinda Gates Foundation has $28.8 billion under management as of press time (not including the fortune that Warren Buffett plans to donate to this foundation), and the State of Alaska Permanent Fund, which manages and distributes a share of oil profits to state citizens, is worth $30.0 billion. Both funds allocate some money to hedge funds.

What's 5 percent of $28.8 billion? Yep, $1.4 billion, which means the Gates Foundation can do plenty of good in the world while growing its principal.

Money managers sometimes talk about the 11th Commandment: "Thou Shalt Not Invade Thy Principal." *Principal* is the amount of money you invest. If you spend it, you can't generate any income, the investment can't grow larger, and you can't pass money on to the next generation.

Permanent funds are often great investment candidates for hedge funds. Most hedge funds are designed to generate steady capital gains, and they limit withdrawals, so your fund's money should build up over time.

Few managers structure hedge funds to generate income, so if producing income is one of your key investment objectives, you should allocate your funds to other types of investments, like bonds or dividend-paying stocks.

Poring Over Your Principal Needs

Investors have three primary investment objectives to consider. These are the types of return that they hope to get from their investments:

- **Income:** Generates regular payments
- **Capital appreciation:** Attempts to grow the principal without regard for income generated
- **Total return:** Combines income and capital appreciation

Managers generally structure hedge funds for capital appreciation, although a few are managed for total return. Hedge fund investors often look to increase their principal through capital appreciation. If you count yourself among this honorable fraternity, you need to answer two questions:

- When do you need the money?
- How much leeway do you have in the amount you need?

If you absolutely need a fixed amount of money at a specific date in the future — for example, if you have folks expecting pension checks — you probably need to go with a low-risk investment. That may include a hedge fund, but it may not. The more flexibility you have, however, the more a hedge fund may be suitable as part of your portfolio. What determines your flexibility? You should consider three important factors:

- **Is the hedge fund investment relative to the size of your overall portfolio?** If you want to put almost all your investable assets into a hedge fund, you better be investing money you don't really need. In fact, if you have to invest most of your assets, that may be a sign that the investment really isn't suitable for you.

It's paradoxical, I know, but the larger your overall portfolio, the more flexibility you have and the more suitable hedge funds are for you. Yes, yes, the rich get richer, as the saying goes, but hedge funds just aren't suitable for smaller investors. That caveat is one reason why managers open funds only to accredited investors (see Chapter 2). Don't fret, though. I provide some advice on how to use hedge-fund techniques in smaller portfolios in Chapter 16.

✔ **What are the consequences if you're a little bit off in your calculation?** If your return is less than you expect, will you have to work an extra year or two or scale down to only one retirement house rather than two? Or will a small return cause you to default on a contractual obligation? If you don't have the flexibility to handle a return that's less than you expect, hedge funds aren't suitable for you.

✔ **How much time do you have between now and when you need the money?** The longer the time, the more risk you can take because you'll be able to make mid-course corrections in case your investment isn't working out as you had planned. If you allocate the hedge fund investment in support of an obligation due 30 years from now, you have more flexibility than if you need the money in 2 years.

What flexibility shows is that a hedge-fund investment is most appropriate for the permanent portion of your portfolio (see the section "Peeking into permanent funds"). You don't need the money now or in the near future to support your life or any necessary obligations. You want to maximize your return, of course, but you can afford to take some chances in terms of the risk and the illiquidity.

A university endowment that needs to turn over only 3 percent of its assets for spending and that adds money each year from donations, for example, has far more flexibility than many other types of investors, which is one reason universities have been big hedge-fund investors. Harvard University's endowment, which has been in operation for centuries and was valued at $25.9 billion at the end of fiscal year 2005, receives new donations every year. At Harvard, the endowment management personnel have to consider how to generate the income promised to the university budget, oversee the investment of the permanent principal, and put the new money coming in to work.

What can you do if you can't make a withdrawal from a hedge fund, but the fund is performing so miserably that you're in danger of losing all your money? Unfortunately, not much. Although rare, it can happen. As a general rule, you shouldn't invest money that you can't afford to lose in any illiquid investment, hedge fund or otherwise. If you get in over your head, you may have to stand by helplessly while your portfolio value goes to zero.

Handling Liquidity After You Make Your Initial Investment

Most prime brokers are household-name brokerage firms and banks, like Morgan Stanley and Bear Stearns. Choosing and entering a fund is a big, tough process, but your work doesn't stop after you hand over your investment and ride out the minimum lockup period. Your hedge fund will (hopefully) generate money for your investment, giving you additional investment opportunities. The fund may allow you to withdraw funds so you can meet other objectives (but it comes with a price). The fund may also start sending you checks to reduce its burden, or it may decide to disband altogether. The following sections give you factors that can affect your investment objectives after you enter into a hedge fund.

Taking advantage of additional investments

After you meet the strict requirements to get into a hedge fund, find the right fund for your investment objectives, and go through initiation (just kidding), you can begin to enjoy the perks of the fund: additional investment opportunities. Your hedge fund manager may look to raise more money in order to pursue interesting investment strategies that he sees in the market. His likely initial inquiries will be with his current investors. A hedge fund is a partnership, after all, and if all partners are happy, you'll want to work together some more. On the flip side, if you come into money that you want to add to the fund, let your fund manager know. He may not need the money now, but he may want it in the near future.

Your fund manager plans to reinvest the returns from the hedge fund. Every time the fund manager receives an interest payment or sells an investment at a profit, you make money that goes into the fund. Your underlying investment increases as long as the fund has a positive return.

From the fund manager's perspective, cash in the fund is a problem unless he can invest it to meet the risk-and-return profile that investors expect (see Chapter 6). Sometimes, the manager simply can't find enough investments out there that meet the fund's investment criteria. It's also possible that the fund doesn't want to take on more money, although the manager will allow you to buy shares from another investor — another good way to make additional investments after you enter a fund.

Investors make money when they buy low and sell high, as the cliché goes. The best time to put more money into the fund is when its performance is bad, because the assets that it invests in will be cheaper. Of course, this time happens to be when you're most likely to want to get out of the fund to cut your losses. Knowing when to cut and when to buy more isn't easy, but the savvy investors who can do it will have better returns than investors who chase return by buying high and selling low. Success in this regard is a combination of luck, skill, and experience. If I knew a sure-fire way to get it right, I certainly wouldn't tell you, because I'd be on a beach in Maui.

Knowing when (and how) you can withdraw funds

At some point, you may need to pull out money from your hedge fund. Maybe you need to match an expense, or you need to move your money to another investment that seems more suitable for your objectives. No matter your reasons, any good investment plan requires ongoing reevaluation of your investment objectives (using material in this chapter) and how well your investments are meeting them.

A hedge fund's offering documents should set out how often you can make withdrawals and how you should request a withdrawal. A hedge fund isn't like a mutual fund, where shares are continually issued and redeemed. You can't get online and transfer money with a few keystrokes whenever you like. Hedge funds are closed investments with only a few investors (see Chapters 1 and 2 for more info on how hedge funds are structured).

You won't find a standard withdrawal policy in the hedge-fund industry. A hedge fund manager may even negotiate different policies for different investors in the fund. Rumor has it that one really big, really secretive fund locks up investors for five years. Others may allow withdrawals once a month with advance notice. You need to know your needs before you invest in a hedge fund so that you know what policies will match your portfolio requirements.

Instead of the rapid redemption services that mutual funds, brokerage firms, or bank accounts offer, you'll probably have to send written notice to a hedge fund manager in advance of your withdrawal. The manager may lay out very specific terms for how you should send the request (for example, certified postal mail) if you want to get your money. The turnaround time between when the manager receives the request and when he approves the withdrawal may be a month; the hedge fund's partnership agreement probably specifies the time period (see Chapter 2 for more information).

The fund manager has some options when it comes to raising your with-drawal funds. She can

- ✔ Meet your request with cash on hand.
- ✔ Sell off some assets to raise the cash.
- ✔ Sell your shares to another investor.

You'll receive the proceeds from the bank or prime broker that handles the fund's investments.

A hedge fund manager may not want to sell investments just to meet your withdrawal request because it may screw up a carefully crafted investment position or require her to sell an asset at a near-term loss. Also, some fund investments are illiquid, meaning that they're difficult to sell on demand. As a result, a fund manager may view your withdrawal as something that will hurt the fund's remaining investors. To offset the hurt, some hedge funds impose withdrawal fees, especially if investors want to pull out more than a small amount (say, 5 percent of their total investments in the fund).

Your fund manager may also hold back some of your money until the fund's accountants have a chance to calculate the performance of the fund up to the date of your withdrawal. It isn't easy to calculate the value of some invest-ments like venture capital (see Chapter 12), so the fund manager wants to wait until she knows the value before settling up with you.

Receiving distributions

Although few hedge funds are designed as income investments (see the sec-tion "Poring Over Your Principal Needs"), they sometimes send checks to their investors. The checks may be distributions of income and capital gains, or they may be returns of capital. The difference may appear academic on the surface, but it affects your portfolio — especially when it comes time to pay your taxes (see Chapter 8). Which distribution is which, and why do the funds start sending you checks like grandma on your birthday? Read on to find out!

Income

Income is money generated from interest, dividends, rental payments, and similar sources. Hedge funds usually reinvest income into their funds, but sometimes they pay it out to their investors. You may receive a check to help you meet your tax obligations, or your fund may send it to manage the size of its investable assets.

Whether or not you receive income checks, you have to pay taxes on the income and capital gains realized by your fund during the year (see Chapter 8). Your fund manager may give you guidance on your estimated liability as the year progresses.

You can do whatever you want with the money that you receive (after taxes). You can use it to meet spending obligations, or you can reinvest it elsewhere; it all depends on your portfolio objectives.

Returns of capital

Capital gains are profits made when an investment goes up in price. These gains are *paper gains* when the fund still holds the asset that goes up in price, and *realized gains* when the fund sells the asset, locking in the profit in the process. Realized gains are taxable, but paper gains are not. In most cases, hedge funds want to reinvest their capital gains into new investments.

Your hedge fund may send you a check for your capital gains, reducing the amount of principal in the fund. If the fund manager doesn't see great investment opportunities in the market that would meet the fund's desired risk and return profile, he may want to whittle the fund's size down to something more likely to generate big profits given the current market climate. Sure, the fund manager is giving up the asset-management fee by returning the capital gains, but he's also increasing the potential size of the profit bonus.

You may think that income and capital gains are the same thing, but they aren't. The government taxes them at different rates, and people handle them differently for accounting purposes. In most cases, capital gains are taxed at lower rates than income, which is enough of a reason to keep them separated.

A return calculation has two parts: the dollar amount of the profit, and the dollar amount of the underlying principal. A $100,000 gain represents a 10-percent return on $1,000,000 in principal, for example, but it's only a 1-percent return on $10,000,000 in principal. The larger the fund gets, the harder it is to generate enough dollar return to represent big percentage return. Therefore, a hedge fund manager may have an incentive to reduce the amount of principal in his or her fund in order to increase the percentage return reported.

Managers of top-performing funds have been known to kick investors out. It sometimes happens when relationship issues arise between the manager and the investor. After all, a hedge fund is a partnership, and sometimes partners don't get along. The offering documents that you sign when you enter the fund explain if and when the fund manager can do this. The policy may screw up your portfolio, and all the paper gains will suddenly fall into the realized (taxable) category.

Moving on after disbandment

One final factor can affect your investment objectives after you enter into a hedge fund: the life of the fund. For many reasons — mostly related to poor performance — a fund manager may decide to disband the fund and return the money to investors.

Hedge Fund Research, a hedge-fund-performance analysis firm (www. hedgefundresearch.com), reports that 11.4 percent of the hedge funds in its 9,000-fund database shut their doors in 2005, the highest rate recorded. For funds of funds, which are investment pools that place money in several different hedge funds (see Chapter 15), the liquidation rate was 9.4 percent. The rate of abandonment also increased from 2004, when 4.7 percent of hedge funds closed.

When your fund disbands because of poor performance, you're happy to get your money back. But poor performance isn't the only culprit. A fund may have a new manager who realizes that it can be hard to raise enough money and earn enough of a return to make the venture worthwhile.

However, there are two main problems with fund abandonment:

- ✔ **Poor performance may be a temporary blip.** A given investment strategy may be having an off year, which actually presents a good opportunity to buy assets cheap in order to take advantage of better performance in the near future. If the fund closes, though, its investors lose the opportunity to buy low in order to sell high. This is one reason that funds like having as long a lockup period as possible.

- ✔ **It may not be easy for a fund investor to find a new investment that meets his or her risk-and-return needs.** The likelihood of you finding another suitable investment is called *reinvestment risk*. Based on Hedge Fund Research's 2005 numbers, your chances may be running at about 10 percent or so.

If disbandment looks like a possibility for your fund, you really can't do anything except start looking for new places to put your money. Disbandment is one of the risks you take when you invest in hedge funds.

Chapter 8

Taxes, Responsibilities, and Other Investment Considerations

*I*nvestors face all sorts of constraints when setting investment objectives and choosing hedge funds and other investment vehicles to meet them. In Chapter 7, I cover time and liquidity considerations. In this chapter, I cover some constraints that aren't set by the hedge fund manager, but by regulators and others outside of the fund, including taxes, fiduciary responsibilities, and social restrictions, to name a few. If you want to put your money into a hedge fund, you need to know what your requirements are or you'll run into big problems. For example, many hedge funds follow strategies that generate both high returns and high tax liabilities. These funds may be appropriate only for pensions, foundations, and other investment groups that aren't subject to the taxman.

You aren't in the fight alone, however; your hedge fund manager has to deal with these constraints as well. No matter how the fund is regulated, its manager has certain responsibilities to meet. Understanding the constraints faced by certain types of fund investors can help the fund manager create and market new hedge funds that meet investors' needs.

Taxing You, the Hedge Fund Investor (Hey, It's Better than Death!)

Hedge fund investment returns come in two forms: capital gains and income. A *capital gain* is the increase in value an asset experiences over time. *Income* includes interest, dividends, or rent — in other words, any ongoing payments made to the investor. You may not care about the classification of your return, as long as you make money, but you need to care that the U.S. tax code treats these returns differently. (I discuss capital gains and income in more detail later in this section, and you can check out Chapter 7 for even more detail.)

No matter your form of return, the hedge fund you're in must have an investment strategy to produce the return, and different investment techniques have different tax effects. Some hedge-fund strategies make great money, but not after the fund pays taxes. If you have to pay taxes, you need to make sure your hedge fund is managed with that responsibility in mind. This section covers how tax considerations can (and should) affect your choice of a hedge fund, or whether you can buy into a hedge fund in the first place. (Chapter 4 discusses the paperwork involved in buying into a hedge fund, much of which is related to taxes.)

You may have to pay taxes on your share of your hedge fund's income and capital gains each year, whether you take any money out of the fund or not. After all, you *are* considered to be a partner in the business; alas, responsibility comes with a cool title (see Chapter 1). Talk to your tax advisor for more information.

You aren't done after the Feds get their cut; your state probably wants a share of your profit, too, and the city or country where you live may also take a piece of your investment profits. There are too many state considerations to cover in this book; just make sure you look into it, for your own sake.

Making sense of capital-gains taxes

A *capital gain* is the increase in value of an asset over time. If you buy a share of stock at $10, hold it while the company introduces great new products and generates tons of profits, and then sell it after the stock reaches $52, you have a capital gain of $42. You don't pay taxes until you sell the asset. Your basis is the price you paid to acquire the asset, and your gain is the price you sell it at less the basis.

Capital gains are classified as short term or long term, based on how long you hold your investment. *Long-term capital gains* come from assets that you hold for more than one year, and *short-term capital gains* come from assets that you hold for one year or less. You can net capital gains against capital losses. If you lose money when you sell one investment, you can deduct that loss (up to $3,000) against a gain incurred when you sell another. If you have more than $3,000 in losses, you can carry the extra into next year and deduct it then. You can also net any short-term capital losses against long-term capital gains, which may reduce your liability.

The advantage of capital gains is that the government taxes them at a lower rate than income (see the following section). If you have to pay taxes, 28 percent — the maximum rate on capital gains as of press time — is less than 35 percent — the current maximum rate on income. In addition, long-term capital gains — on assets held for more than one year — are taxed at lower rates than short-term capital gains.

Most hedge funds generate at least some returns from capital gains. Investors in a hedge fund are expected to pay taxes on those gains each year out of other sources of funds, because the fund manager probably won't distribute money to investors so they can pay the taxes. (You can read more about hedge fund distributions and withdrawals in Chapter 7.) If a hedge fund gets almost all its returns from short-term capital gains, the tax burden will be higher than with a fund that gets almost all its returns from long-term capital gains.

Tax laws change every year. Be sure to check the IRS's latest guidance on investment tax issues, because this book may be out of date when you do your taxes in the future. Don't think that I'm going into an audit with you! The IRS Web site, www.irs.gov, is a great source of information.

Taxing ordinary income

Many investment gains are classified as ordinary income. *Income* is money that an asset generates on a regular basis — for example, interest on a bond, dividends on common stock, or rent from a commercial real estate stake. You report this income on your taxes, and you pay the same rate on it that you pay on earned income from your job. The good news? You can deduct any investment interest you pay, such as interest paid in leveraging or short-selling strategies. (See Chapter 11 for more information on leveraging and short-selling.)

The government taxes dividends, or payouts of company profits, at a lower rate than other investment income because the company that issues the dividend has already paid taxes on its profits before it issues the dividend out of what's left over. Many companies pay their shareholders small amounts of money out of their profits each year. In 2005, for example, Johnson & Johnson shareholders received $1.32 in dividends for each share owned. The maximum tax rate on dividend income as of this writing is 15 percent.

A hedge fund that generates much of its return from interest income carries a higher tax burden than one that generates return from dividend income or from long-term capital gains (see the previous section).

On occasion, a hotshot trader makes an investment that generates tons of money, only to find come April 15 that the earnings are classified as income and the expenses are classified as capital losses. With no expenses to deduct, the investor finds that the taxes more than offset the realized profit. This situation is rare, but it happens. Allow me to illustrate. The following table shows the pre-tax profit on this investor's initial investment:

Initial investment	$1,500
Ending value	$2,000
Pre-tax profit	$500

The $500 represents the ending value of the investment less the initial investment. The next table shows how the taxes affect the investment's profit, less income taxes due, when the costs are capital and the profits are income:

Profit for tax purposes	$2,000 (1,500 cost disallowed)
Income taxes due at 33% rate	$660
Realized profit	–$160

How do you avoid this situation? If an investment is subject to income taxes, your best bet is to work with a hedge fund manager who has enough experience to understand the tax implications of different trading strategies. Because taxes can eat into an investment return, hedge fund investors who pay taxes should ask potential hedge fund managers about the tax implications of their funds' investment strategies.

Exercising your right to be exempt

With all these crazy tax implications, it's a wonder anyone invests in hedge funds. Think about it — you could have to pay huge amounts in taxes each year on money that the fund locks up for two years. Who would do that? A tax-exempt investor would. But doesn't everyone pay taxes? No. Two primary types of investors don't pay taxes:

- ✔ Qualified retirement and pension plans
- ✔ Bona-fide charitable foundations and endowments

Not surprisingly, these groups are among the biggest investors in hedge funds. It doesn't hurt that they often have a lot of money, a long-term investment horizon, and that they don't have to worry about income and capital-gain tradeoffs because of their exempt status. The following sections dig a bit deeper into the workings of these organizations.

Tax-exempt investors have to meet stringent IRS requirements and possibly other standards to retain their status. If you're responsible for choosing any investment options for a qualified tax-exempt investment fund, talk to a lawyer to make sure you don't make a mistake that could have your foundation or endowment writing a big check come April 15. I doubt your organization will be as charitable with your position, in that case!

Identifying qualified plans

A *qualified plan* is a pension plan that meets certain IRS provisions. Among other things, the plan has to benefit all employees, not just a few highly paid workers.

There are two types of qualified plans:

- ✔ **Defined benefit plans:** The employer agrees to pay the employee a set monthly amount upon retirement, based on the years that the employee worked and the income that he or she earned. The defined benefit plan is a traditional pension fund, and it's becoming rare. You most often see this plan offered by large, unionized employers, who often invest in hedge funds for their plans.

- ✔ **Defined contribution plans:** The employee sets aside some money from each paycheck and determines where he or she wants to invest it. The employer may match some of the employee's contribution. A familiar example is a 401(k) plan.

   Defined contribution plans don't invest in hedge funds, because no employee's annual contribution would be large enough to meet a hedge fund's initial investment requirements.

If a plan meets the qualification rules, an employer can deduct contributions made to the plan from its taxes, and the employee pays no tax until the money is withdrawn. Investment returns on the plan assets aren't taxed.

Getting the gist of foundations and endowments

Nonprofit institutions, such as foundations or endowments, are often supported by large pools of money that generate annual investment income used to support the organizations' work. In some cases, the amounts of money involved are huge. The Bill and Melinda Gates Foundation, for example, has $28.8 billion in assets as of press time, and Harvard University, where Bill Gates was enrolled before he dropped out to start his own company, sits on $25.9 billion. Most foundations are quite a bit smaller, however.

A *foundation* is set by a wealthy individual or a company. Charitable organizations that need money for activities send grant applications to foundations, explaining how they plan to use the money to support the foundations' goals. Examples include the Ford Foundation and the John D. and Catherine T. MacArthur Foundation, both of which provide support for a wide range of endeavors.

An *endowment* is a pool of money that the charitable organization controls itself. Endowments can be quite small — my church has an endowment of about $300,000, for example — or they can be on the scale of Yale's $15.2 billion or Harvard's $25.9 billion.

Donations made to foundations and endowments are usually deductible from income taxes. The investment income earned by the organizations is also tax-free as long as they meet certain requirements. Foundations, for example, must distribute 5 percent of their assets each year. Some very large foundations eschew hedge funds because they don't want to risk a large return. Sounds crazy, huh? They want to give money to charities for responsible use, but they don't want the charities to have so much money that they give it away to wasteful projects.

Free money here! Just read!

Okay, so this advice doesn't pertain to hedge funds, but I'd be remiss if I didn't share this simple financial trick. If your employer operates a 401(k) or other defined contribution fund, and the employer matches your contribution, be sure you set aside at least as much money each year as the company will match. If your employer matches the first $1,000 that you contribute, your $1,000 contribution automatically doubles. That's free money! You can't beat that with any investment, in a hedge fund or elsewhere.

Can you invest your IRA in hedge funds?

"Aha!" you say. You have the answer to the tax problem for an individual investor: Just invest in hedge funds through an IRA (an Individual Retirement Account, which gives income tax advantages to the account holder)! That way, all the taxes are deferred until withdrawal, and the tax problem goes away.

If only it were that simple. The first flaw in this plan is that an individual investor is unlikely to have enough money in a retirement account to put in a hedge fund. After all, many funds require that investors put in $1 million or more (see Chapter 2). Even hedge funds that take smaller amounts of money usually ask investors to put in a minimum of $50,000. Still, an individual with a substantial rollover from a 401(k) or executive deferred compensation plan — a type of employee benefit that puts bonus money into a retirement plan — may be able to meet a hedge fund's high minimum investment.

The next snag is that in order to put the IRA into a hedge fund, it has to be set up as a self-directed IRA (an IRA account that the owner manages instead of assigning the management to a mutual fund or other organization). Most banks and brokerage firms can handle the paperwork for this structure because IRAs are set up as trust accounts; however, very few hedge funds, if any, want to operate a trust business.

So, the biggest question is, will a hedge fund want your retirement account? A fund runs into some obstacles when it comes to handling retirement accounts. A hedge fund manager who handles retirement funds has to file with the U.S. Department of Labor, which oversees retirement accounts. A fund manager can't invest IRA accounts in some asset classes, such as metals and gems. Finally, a fund must price retirement accounts monthly, which may be difficult for a hedge fund holding many illiquid securities (securities that don't trade often and thus may not have an easily determined value).

Larger endowments, on the other hand, often turn to hedge funds because they can afford to lock up large sums of money for two years; they don't have to worry about taxes; and they appreciate the increased return relative to the risk taken. If you're making investment decisions for a foundation or an endowment — especially one with more than $5 million in assets — you should at least consider hedge funds. That's what this book is all about!

Figuring Out Your Fiduciary Responsibility

If you're responsible for managing money for another person or an organization, you take on a *fiduciary responsibility*. You're responsible for acting in the best interests of the person (or organization) who owns the money. The exact description of how a fiduciary should act varies with the type of account involved. A pension fund manager has to meet different fiduciary duties than a trust account manager, for example.

People involved in the selection and administration of funds also have fiduciary responsibilities. If your job involves mailing out statements to employees who participate in a pension plan, fiduciary responsibilities and laws affect you. If you make the decision to put a pension or an endowment into a hedge fund, these responsibilities and laws definitely affect you. Your fiduciary responsibilities form a key constraint on your decision of whether to invest in hedge funds in the first place, let alone which one. And if you do invest in hedge funds, your fiduciary responsibilities affect how you monitor your investment.

As a fiduciary, you must employ the following characteristics:

- ✔ **Care:** By applying skills, knowledge, and insight.
- ✔ **Discretion:** By protecting the client's confidentiality.
- ✔ **Impartiality:** By treating all clients and beneficiaries the same.
- ✔ **Loyalty:** To serve the beneficiary.
- ✔ **Prudence:** By behaving appropriately to preserve investment capital.

I discuss some of the big concepts — and big governing laws — in this section. If you have any questions about what laws cover your responsibilities or how to follow these laws, you may need to consult a lawyer and an investment consultant (see Chapter 17) — the courts take fiduciary responsibilities seriously, and so should you.

Coming to terms with common law

Allow me to start the discussion of fiduciary responsibility by giving you some information on how fiduciary responsibilities have evolved over time. Legal standards that are based on court decisions rather than on laws passed by elected representatives are called *common laws.* Fiduciary responsibility developed in the common law before legislators started writing laws about the investment business. And, in general, the courts look down upon money managers and advisors who take advantage of their clients.

The foundation of fiduciary responsibility in U.S. law is the so-called *prudent person rule,* which Judge Samuel Putnam first laid out in an 1830 court ruling: "All that can be required of a trustee to invest, is, that he shall conduct himself faithfully and exercise a sound discretion. He is to observe how men of prudence, discretion, and intelligence manage their own affairs, not in regard to speculation, but in regard to the permanent disposition of their funds, considering the probable income, as well as the probable safety of the capital to be invested."

The problem with the prudent person rule is that the court didn't set out the qualifications and behavior in checklist form. Instead, Judge Putnam assumed that you would know a prudent person when you meet one, but your idea of prudence may be very different from mine. Furthermore, he established a standard that preservation of the initial investment (also called *capital* or *principal*) is more important than investment return, which isn't always the case.

What's the difference between a prudent person and a prudent expert? Here's something to chew on. My sister-in-law is a smart woman who teaches first grade. She has the responsibility of teaching 24 kids to read and do math in a safe, supportive environment. You don't get much more prudent than that. If you hand her $20,000,000 in pension-plan assets and tell her that she must manage that money, she may turn it over to a bank and put it in certificates of deposit (CDs) because she doesn't know what else to do; she isn't a financial expert. Bank CDs are safe investments, so she has met the prudent person standard. The situation is different if you decide to give the $20,000,000 in pension assets to a fancy portfolio manager with 15 years of experience, several degrees from brand-name colleges, and plenty of initials after his name. If he puts it in bank CDs because he doesn't know what else to do with the money, he violates the prudent expert standard. (***Note:*** Bank CDs may be a good investment for a pension plan, given market conditions and the plan's needs, but the decision to go this route should be an active one, not a default choice.)

Tackling trust law

A *trust* is a complex legal relationship in which one person or legal entity gives money to another person to manage for the benefit of a third party. People can set up trusts for plenty of reasons, but many individuals use them for estate planning. By having a trust inherit assets rather than a person, you can avoid some estate taxes. You can avoid other problems, too: A trust may stipulate that a minor can have only a small part of her inheritance until she reaches a certain age, thus preventing her from running amok with too much money and too little control.

Persons managing larger trusts may sometimes invest in hedge funds, so trust laws apply to their investments. Each state is unique, but most trust laws have a few things in common:

✔ The trustee, who has responsibility for the trust, must act as a prudent person, not necessarily as a prudent expert (see the previous section).

✔ The trustee's primary responsibility is preservation of the initial investment.

✔ The person who sets up the trust may create restrictions that would be difficult for the trustee or the beneficiary to change.

People who run pension and retirement accounts, charitable foundations, and university endowments often set them up as trust accounts; however, these investments are governed by different laws based on trust laws, but designed to meet the specific needs of those funds. You can read more about these laws throughout this section.

Uniform Management of Institutional Funds Act (UMIFA)

Over the years, each state has passed its own fiduciary standards, which led to a hodgepodge of contradictory rules within the United States. Finally, between 1972 and 1984, most states adopted the Uniform Management of Institutional Funds Act (UMIFA), a standard law that regulates the management of charity and endowment funds. UMIFA is enforced on the state level, but the standardization makes it easy for money managers and the people who hire them to follow the rules. A charity or endowment that wants to invest in hedge funds must heed the guidance of the UMIFA.

UMIFA says that investors handling the affairs of charity and endowment funds must follow standards of business care and prudence. UMIFA fiduciaries don't have to be investment experts, only prudent persons. The assumption is that the fiduciary acted properly, so if an accuser presents allegations of impropriety, the burden of proof falls on the accuser.

UMIFA stipulates that an investor should invest funds at reasonable risk for reasonable return. UMIFA leaves the key word, "reasonable," undefined. What the investor needs to know is that she can lose some of the initial investment and still be acting prudently if she has evidence of a long-run strategy that meets the charity or endowment's needs (see Chapters 7 and 8 for more on investment objectives; you can discover more about investment strategy in the chapters of Part III).

Employee Retirement Income Security Act (ERISA) of 1972

The Employee Retirement Income Security Act of 1972 is one of the most powerful pieces of federal legislation in the investment world. Because "Employee Retirement Income Security Act of 1972" is a mouthful, people almost always refer to the law by its nickname, ERISA (rhymes with "Alyssa"). Legislators wrote ERISA to regulate pensions, but it applies to many other types of employee benefits. ERISA says that a fiduciary is anyone who exercises control over any portion of the pension plan. The law holds fiduciaries to a prudent expert standard, meaning that each person in a fiduciary role must have the education, experience, and training to meet his or her assigned responsibilities (see the section "Coming to terms with common law" for more on prudent experts). The U.S. Department of Labor handles ERISA enforcement.

Under ERISA, a pension plan's fiduciaries must act in the best interests of the plan's beneficiaries. Confusion can sometimes arise within a company, as it's usually the company that sponsors the pension plan for its employees that makes decisions about how to invest the money. Those decisions can't benefit the company; they have to benefit the employees who will receive the pension when they retire.

If an accuser brings forth allegations of fiduciary irresponsibility, the burden of proof falls on the fiduciary, not on the accuser. This is a higher standard than in other fiduciary laws (such as UMIFA).

Plans that fall under ERISA, which is almost all pension plans and many other employee benefit plans, must have written investment plans calling for diversified portfolios. An ERISA plan can take investment risks that may result in short-term losses as long as the plan meets its long-run investment policy and the fund considers its portfolio as a whole rather than any particular plan. That second requirement is tough for some hedge funds to meet, because they may not report performance frequently enough to meet fiduciary responsibilities. The pension plan's fiduciaries must evaluate and report on the pension's investment performance on a regular basis, a standard that may be difficult for some hedge funds to meet.

ERISA plans can invest in hedge funds, and many of them do. But not all hedge funds are willing to take ERISA plans because the fund managers must also follow the requirements of the law.

Transparency in Hedge Funds: Rare but There

Hedge funds are like undercover cops: They don't like to talk about what they do. You can attribute their preference for mystery to a few reasons. They're organized as private partnerships (see Chapter 2); they may not be registered with the Securities and Exchange Commission (see Chapter 3); and they may have figured out proprietary strategies to take advantage of market inefficiencies (see Chapter 6). If they tell the world what they're doing, they risk losing their little money-making secrets.

However, you have legitimate reasons to know what's happening in the fund. Not only are you putting your money at risk, but also you may need to report to others or certify that you've met your fiduciary responsibilities if you work with an endowment or charitable organization, for example (see the section "Figuring Out Your Fiduciary Responsibility"). If you have fiduciary responsibilities, transparency — or the lack of it — may affect your ability to do your job.

In this section, I discuss position transparency, risk transparency, and window dressing and how they affect fiduciary responsibility — a consideration when choosing whether to invest in hedge funds or which hedge funds to invest in. (In Chapter 9, I discuss how transparency can affect asset allocation decisions, which are the choices you make about how to divide your money among different types of securities.)

Reports of a hedge fund's holdings should come from a prime brokerage firm — a firm that handles the hedge fund's trading account — and a bona-fide accounting firm should audit the reports. One recent hedge fund investigation found that a fund's shareholders hadn't received a report for two years (one tip off of trouble), and when they finally saw a partial report of holdings, it was a statement from a discount brokerage firm — a fine company, but not one that handles prime brokerage services for hedge funds. If you find out that a hedge fund doesn't have an audited financial statement and doesn't work through a prime broker (see Chapter 18 for more on due diligence), you shouldn't invest in it.

Appraising positions

When a hedge fund releases a list of the investments it owns, it has *position transparency*. You can look at the list to see what stocks sit in the account, what bonds the fund holds, what currencies it's exposed to, and other information. You can combine this information with any other holdings you have (see Chapter 9 for more information on structuring your portfolio) to ensure that the fund is meeting your overall investment risk and return objectives. Position transparency can also show if the fund is complying with any unique requirements that you may have.

Many hedge funds refuse to release information on their positions out of concern that others could use the info against them. For example, if news breaks that a big hedge fund has a large short position in a particular stock (that is, it has borrowed the stock and sold it in hopes that it will go down in price), other funds may do a short squeeze, bidding up the price of the stock or calling back any stock that their prime brokers may have lent out to other investors. Such a squeeze would force the hedge fund to close the short position at a loss.

Many hedge funds give position information to investors who need it to fulfill their fiduciary responsibilities; however, the funds may make the recipients sign confidentiality agreements. The agreement ensures that a pension fund's trustees have enough information to see that the hedge fund is behaving as a prudent expert and in line with the pension's investment objectives, but it prevents the trustees from giving copies of the fund's investments to employees covered by the pension plan. A hedge fund manager knows if an investor has fiduciary responsibilities because the investor has to tell the manager before making the investment.

Interpreting risk

By using tactics such as leverage (or borrowing, which I discuss in Chapter 11) and agreements such as derivatives (contracts based on the value of an underlying asset; see Chapter 5), a hedge fund may present a different risk level than its holdings list indicates (see the previous section). The risk may be more or less than the investor realizes.

The bad news is that you don't have an easy way to measure the amount of risk in a hedge fund. You can blame it on the fact that risk isn't well defined in finance, despite Nobel Prizes going to men who have done years of research on the subject. Under the Modern (Markowitz) Portfolio Theory (discussed in great detail in Chapter 6), risk is based on the standard deviation of return. Risk measures the likelihood of an investment netting any return other than the return you expect. Most investors wouldn't consider getting a greater-than-expected return to be risky, but it is in theory.

Most investors consider the likelihood of loss to be risky, but likelihood is a lot harder to measure. Some hedge fund managers simply refuse to give investors information on risk, saying that the information is proprietary. But most hedge funds try to give their investors some information that they can use, and if you need to know the risk of the hedge fund that you're investing in, you should deal only with funds that give you risk information. A common measurement is *Value at Risk* (VAR), a single number that gives the likelihood of the portfolio losing a set amount of money over a set period (say, 10 days). One problem with Value at Risk is that the likelihood will never be zero. Another is that the hedge fund manager may give you information on Value at Risk at a given point in time, but that number can change rapidly as market conditions change.

Another technique that some portfolio managers use is *stress testing,* where they run computer models to find out how a hedge fund's portfolio might perform in different economic conditions. What would happen to the portfolio if inflation increases dramatically, or if the government of Thailand collapses, or if the euro falls apart? The results of stress testing give you some parameters to use in determining how much risk an investment has. Keep in mind, however, that stress testing can't test for every possible event. Martians could take over the earth tomorrow — why not? — and you can bet that no one has done a stress test for that.

Avoiding window dressing

Hedge funds rarely give transparency in real time. A hedge fund won't tell anyone what's happening on any particular day. Some hedge fund managers take advantage of this position to make their portfolios look good on the days that they must report. This tactic is known in the investing world as *window dressing.*

For example, say that a hedge fund handles many government pension and university endowment accounts. The trustees for these accounts have made it clear that fund can't invest their money in Sudan, and they want to see a list of positions every six months. One day, the hedge fund manager sees some great opportunities in bonds that will finance an oil project in Sudan. She ignores the accounts' wishes and buys the bonds, and then she sells them the day before she has to report her fund's holdings.

A less-nefarious, and far more common, form of window dressing takes place when a hedge fund manager sells all the positions that turned out to be bad ideas right before the reporting date.

Activists and opponents in the hedge fund world

Not surprisingly, everyone who looks at hedge funds doesn't appreciate the limits on transparency. Some activists groups have formed to demand more information on how hedge funds are investing. Students and faculty at Yale University formed one group, Unfarallon (www.unfarallon.info), to protest the institution's investment in hedge funds managed by Farallon Capital Management. Those who formed the group aren't opposed to hedge funds, per se, but they think that an institution of higher education has a responsibility to make its investments known to its stakeholders.

Unfarallon isn't the only group out there. Trade unions, charitable donors, elected officials, and others who have a say in money that ends up in hedge funds often want more information about how those funds invest their money. To date, no hedge-fund investments have stopped because of activism, but that could change, so keep an eye out for it. If you're handling money that has politically active stakeholders, like students or union members, this may affect you.

Practicing Socially Responsible Investing

Some investors prefer to put their money into investments that reflect their social values. One person may not want to have any holdings in tobacco companies, and another may not want any investments involving pornography.

For other investors, social responsibility isn't a preference, it's a constraint put into the law. For example, a government pension may not be allowed to invest in companies doing business in Myanmar or the Sudan; anyone allocating that pension's money to a hedge fund has to be aware of that policy.

And for a unique set of investors, the law is set by a higher authority than any government. A strict Muslim, for example, has to place investments in accordance with the laws of the Muslim faith. A Muslim investor would no more borrow money than eat pork, for example (see sidebar in this section for more on this topic).

Although the fast-paced, wheelie-dealie world of a typical hedge fund may seem antithetical to any calling except making money, money, and more money, several hedge funds are addressing the preferences of different groups of investors. You can find many funds that are managed to respect the beliefs of Roman Catholics, Mormons, or environmentalists, to name a few. Hedge funds that work with government pension funds, university endowments, and charitable foundations have experience in dealing with constraints placed on those funds. What's the worst that could happen if you ask? If a fund can't respect your particular limits, it will turn down the investment.

Shariah and investing

The Islamic religion has more than a billion adherents in the world, many of whom have money to invest. The religion's Shariah laws not only regulate diet and dress, but also limit how Muslims can handle their money. The world's financial markets evolved in Judeo-Christian cultures in Europe and North America, so many common financial transactions are out of step with Shariah. Under Fiqh Al-Muamalat — the part of Shariah that deals with finance — a devout Muslim must follow some strict regulations:

✔ No paying interest or engaging in speculation.

✔ The return on a financial transaction should be in line with the risk taken, not greater.

✔ No Muslim should profit from investments in such prohibited activities as gambling, drinking, or pork processing.

On a simple level, these prohibitions make it difficult for a Muslim to buy a house in Western countries, although the banks are coming around more these days to meet their needs. Devon Bank, located on the north side of Chicago in a neighborhood that's home to many Pakistani and Indian immigrants, developed residential real estate sale-leaseback arrangements that comply with Shariah laws. People in the neighborhood who had to avoid mortgages can now buy houses.

And what about a devout Muslim who has made millions running a business in Chicago, London, or Dubai? He may want to put some of his money into a hedge fund, but the fund has to be compliant with Shariah. Most hedge funds look to generate a higher level of return for a given level of risk, which Shariah may consider to be undue speculation. Also, many hedge funds rely on leverage and short-selling (see Chapter 11), which require the payment of interest.

Still, a handful of hedge funds are rising to the Shariah challenge. These funds are generally structured as long-short funds that buy shares of stock in companies expected to do well and sell borrowed shares of stocks from companies expected to do poorly (in other words, sell them short). The funds set up the borrowing as repurchase agreements or fee-based arrangements to get around the interest prohibitions. The strategy is that the trades themselves don't involve excessive risk, so the overall risk-and-return profiles of the funds are compliant.

If you want to invest with a social conscious, you should seek out hedge funds that have similar goals. You can find them through online searches, by working with investment advisors who understand your needs (see Chapter 17), or by getting advice from others who share your objectives. It's the same process that you'd go through in order to find any hedge fund.

Fiduciaries debate whether socially responsible investing is appropriate because of some evidence that it may lead to a reduced investment return (see the section "Figuring Out Your Fiduciary Responsibility" for more on the topic). If you're a fiduciary, check to make sure that socially responsible investment decisions are in line with the overall strategy of your fund and that they make sense from a risk-and-return perspective. Otherwise, you may violate your fiduciary responsibilities, no matter how pure your heart may be.

Chapter 9

Fitting Hedge Funds into a Portfolio

*H*edge funds are wildly different from each other. Because hedge funds are simply lightly regulated investment partnerships — and therefore can take advantage of more investment strategies than other highly regulated investment vehicles, such as mutual funds — different funds are bound to invest in different ways. Some managers design hedge funds to be different from other types of investments, and others don't.

Given the limits of the private partnership structure, like restrictions on withdrawals and high fees (see Chapter 2), an investment portfolio is rarely made up entirely of hedge funds. Some investors treat hedge funds as a separate asset class, and others treat them simply as a different forum to hold and manage existing assets.

So, do hedge funds fall in a separate asset class or not? How do you fit a hedge fund into a portfolio? How do you use hedge funds to meet your investment objectives? You've come to the right place for answers. This chapter looks at how you can include hedge funds in your investment portfolio to increase your return for a given level of risk.

Assaying Asset Allocations

A *real asset* is a tangible piece of property that you can own: a factory, a house, a gold mine, and so on. A *financial asset* — also called a security — is a claim on a tangible asset: a piece of paper showing partial ownership of a factory, a loan to the factory owner or bond holder, rights to a share of the production of a mine, and so on.

Different assets have different sources of return and present different tradeoffs, and you want a balance of them in your portfolio. I summarize many types of financial assets in Table 9-1 (see Chapter 5 for more details on these assets).

Table 9-1	Characteristics of Different Financial Assets		
Financial Asset	*Primary Source of Return*	*Relative Level of Return*	*Relative Level of Risk*
Stocks (equities)	Capital gains	High	High
Bonds (fixed income)	Income	Medium	Medium
Cash	None	Low	Low
Real estate	Income, store of value	Medium	Medium
Commodities	Store of value	Low	Low

The chapters of Part III cover the different types of hedge funds and hedge-fund strategies to give you a sense of how they fall on this matrix. Different fund managers have their own techniques for managing risk and return that make the profiles of their funds different than you may think by looking at the holdings.

When choosing a hedge fund (whose manager chooses assets to invest in) to fit into your portfolio, you need to think about how it will act with the other investments in your fund. Will the fund help you reduce risk, increase return, or both? Will it help you reach your investment goals?

Matching goals to money

Asset allocation is the process of matching your investment goals to your money in order to meet your goals with the lowest possible amount of risk (see Chapters 7 and 8 for more about goals and the upcoming section "Diversification, risk, and return: How the asset pros and cons play out"). Do you need to generate $100,000 in pre-tax annual income from your investments? Are current interest rates at 4 percent? If so, you should put $4,000,000 in fixed-income securities with an average coupon (annual interest rate) of 4 percent. Do you need $10,000,000 in 20 years to meet a contractual obligation? Do you think that an 8-percent return is acceptable as long as you experience little variation between your expected return and the return that you get? If so, you should put $2.2 million in a hedge fund with an absolute-return strategy (see the section "Absolute-return funds" later in this chapter).

The exact amounts and investments you choose will vary with your means and your goals. The other chapters in Part II should help you think about what you need. Any professional advisors you work with should take the time to find out what you need, too (see Chapter 17 for info on working with a consultant).

Beware of advisors who try to sell you products without finding out what your needs are. It's no only against regulations (a violation of the know-your-customer and suitability rules), but also bad for you.

Chasing return versus allocating assets

"I don't care what fund you put me in, as long as it performs well. How about this fund that was up 40 percent last year?" Whoa, cowboy! Unfortunately, that's a common strategy among investors, and it's a dangerous one. Known as *chasing return,* this strategy ignores long-term goals, near-term constraints, and good investing principles in hopes of landing the big bucks right now.

Return chasers are doomed to fail in the long run, and often in the short run, too. Markets move in cycles, so last year's hot performer will probably cool off this year. Moving your money around too much leads to plenty of taxes and commission charges that eat into your investment base. And without a sense of how much money you really need, when you need it, and with what degree of certainty you're operating, you risk choosing investments that miss your goals by a mile.

Mathematicians talk about *reversion to the mean.* In mathematical terms, it means that if you have a large set of numbers, the more that one number varies from the average, the more likely that the next number will be closer to the average. Now look at it in investing terms. If mean performance for an asset is 10 percent per year, and the asset earns 50 percent this year, chances are good that next year's performance will not only be closer to 10 percent, but also negative so that the mean doesn't change. Investors who chase return usually suffer the negative effects of reversion to the mean.

Using Hedge Funds as an Asset Class

One of the biggest debates in the hedge-fund world is whether hedge funds represent a separate, new asset class, or whether they simply represent another vehicle to manage the traditional asset classes of stocks, bonds, and cash. The discussion affects the way that people make decisions about their money, some good and some bad.

Asset classes are distinctly different from each other, with unique risk-and-return profiles. For example, bonds are loans; the borrower makes regular interest payments and returns the principal at the end of the loan. Changes in interest rates and the ability of the borrower to make the payments affect the bond price. Stocks, on the other hand, are partial shares of ownership in a company. The company's profits and prospects affect the price of stocks.

I don't think that hedge funds deserve to be treated as a separate asset class, but many reasonable and smart people would disagree with me, so I take this section to look at the arguments in favor of hedge funds being in a separate asset class so that you can make the decision for yourself.

The other side of the argument is that hedge funds are managed uniquely, so they deserve to be thought of as unique assets — even though they're made up of other assets. The problem is that a portfolio may take on the wrong balance of risk and return because it views the hedge-fund investment as an investment in a diversifying asset, when really the investment may intensify risks elsewhere in the portfolio. (See the section "Viewing a Hedge Fund as an Overlay" for more on this side of the argument.)

How hedge funds are assets

The argument for hedge funds representing a unique asset class is rooted in the fact that many hedge fund managers design their funds to post completely different risk-and-return profiles than traditional asset classes. The big idea is that if you have an investment that you design to return, say, 6 percent to 8 percent every year (see Chapter 6 for more) — year in and year out, regardless of how interest rates fluctuate or how the economy shifts — you have an investment that's different from anything else out there. And if your risk-and-return profile is different, you should put it in a different asset class.

Of course, not all hedge fund managers design their funds to perform differently from the financial markets. Hedge funds generally fall into two categories:

✔ Absolute-return funds

✔ Directional funds

The following sections cover these categories in more detail so you can see how these two broad groupings of hedge funds have distinct risk and return tradeoffs, helping you narrow the choices for your portfolio. (See Chapter 1 for more on these two types of funds.)

Following the Modern (Markowitz) Portfolio Theory (MPT; see Chapter 6), you sort out investment return by its source. Most of an investment's return comes from its exposure to the market. This exposure to the market is called *beta.* Some return may come from the investor's skill. Return from the investor's skill is called *alpha.* (By the way, many people argue that alpha doesn't exist, and that if it does exist, it is as likely to be negative as positive.)

Absolute-return funds

The goal of an *absolute-return fund* is to generate a reasonable percentage return each year, regardless of the state of the financial markets. Absolute return funds rarely aim to beat the equity indexes; they instead opt to have a positive return with relatively little risk. These funds are sometimes referred to as "bond-like investments," because a bond that the holder maintains to maturity generates a steady return from the interest, year in and year out.

Investment reports often list hedge funds as *alternative investments* or *absolute-return investments,* not as hedge funds.

An absolute-return fund has another moniker: a *pure-alpha fund.* In theory, the fund manager tries to remove all market risk (in other words, beta risk) in order to create a fund that doesn't vary with market performance. If the manager removes all the market risk, the fund's performance comes entirely from the manager's skill, which in academic terms is called *alpha.*

Many financial types treat absolute-return investments as a separate asset class, and many hedge fund managers and investors prefer to use the term absolute-return strategy when they invest in hedge funds. The term "hedge funds" seems scary and scandal-ridden, they think, although this type of investment is something else entirely. Of course, much hedging of risk is required to get a steady, low-risk return (see Chapter 6), so an absolute-return hedge fund may be the purest example of the genre.

Although the exact definition of hedge fund is vague, the fund widely acknowledged as the original, run by Alfred Windsor Jones, was structured as an absolute-return fund. It bought and sold stocks equally in order to have no market risk (see Chapter 1).

An absolute-return fund comes with its own set of problems; the following list outlines two problems with the strategy:

- ✔ **Determining exactly how to generate a steady target return.** Ideally, an absolute return fund will choose two or three strategies and move among them as market conditions change. With this tactic, the risk and return of the fund will stay steady even as the markets move, without the fund manager going in too many different directions. But what happens if the market enters a period where none of the strategies work? Should the hedge fund manager stick to her guns, or should she try something else to meet investor expectations — expectations that may not have been realistic in hindsight?

- ✔ **Investors may say that they'd be happy with an 8-percent return if they earn it consistently, but in reality, most investors will be unhappy if the Dow Jones Industrial Average goes up 25 percent and their hedge fund investments go up only 8 percent.** What this means is that the fund manager may have an incentive to pursue strategies that will beat the market but that also change the risk profile of the fund to something that it wasn't designed to be. The manager may keep investors happy in the short run, but she's no longer operating the fund as one with a unique risk-and-return profile.

An investment return is a reward for taking risk. The greater the expected return of the investment, the greater the likelihood that the investment may return a different amount. As much as all investors would like tons of return with no risk, you can't entirely eliminate risk, but you can reduce it through diversification (see Chapters 6 and 11 for more).

Directional funds

Fund managers design *directional hedge funds* to return the maximum amount possible. These funds assume a lot of risk and are sometimes called *beta funds* because they maintain some level of market exposure. In fact, a directional fund manager may even increase market exposure through leverage — by borrowing money to take an even larger bet on the market than the amount of assets in the fund (see Chapter 11 for more on leverage). Because directional funds often have beta exposure, they're sometimes considered to have equity-like returns.

A directional fund's return may be disproportionately larger than its risk, but the risk is still there. These funds can also swing wildly, giving a big return some years and plummeting big in others. Longer-term investors may not mind as long as the upward trend is positive. It can be frustrating for the hedge fund manager, however, because he doesn't earn his performance fee when the fund loses money (see Chapters 2 and 4).

Under the Modern (Markowitz) Portfolio Theory (MPT; see Chapter 6), you can diversify beta but not alpha. A fund that has beta exposure probably can't be its own asset class for this reason. Almost by definition, the beta exposure means that the fund is part of the same market as other investments, not standing alone.

Diversification, risk, and return: How the asset pros and cons play out

Does it matter if a hedge fund represents its own asset class or not? Yes, it does, and here's why: An investor should structure his or her investment portfolio to reflect the risk and return that he or she needs. If a hedge fund appears in its own asset class, other assets that the investor selects to offset the portfolio's risk and return characteristics need to appear in the portfolio. After all, some years stocks will be up, and some years bonds will be. A diversified portfolio has exposure to both stocks and bonds, in line with the investor's preferences, in order to meet the investor's needs — regardless of how the market performs. In fact, adding different kinds of assets to a portfolio can reduce risk without affecting expected return (see Chapter 6).

If return is a function of risk, how can adding different assets to your portfolio reduce risk without affecting return? The answer sits in a statistical measure called *correlation*. Correlation shows how much two assets move together. If they move in tandem, the assets are perfectly correlated. If two assets aren't perfectly correlated, some of the movement in one offsets the movement in another. An investment manager can run a computer program that analyzes the correlations of all her assets under consideration and determines how much of an investor's portfolio should be in each in order to generate the *minimum-variance portfolio*. This portfolio has less risk — but not less return — than any of its assets do on their own. See Chapter 6 for more information.

Here's a breakdown of what happens when a hedge fund is in its own class and what happens when it isn't:

- ✔ If a hedge fund is its own asset class, with its own risk-and-return profile, it can diversify the risks of other assets in the portfolio. For this reason, many large pension and endowment funds have been putting money into hedge funds that feature an absolute-return style and listing them as separate asset classes.

- ✔ If a hedge fund isn't its own asset class, it increases the risk in the portfolio. Investors would have to add other assets to offset that risk. For this reason, many hedge fund investors don't break out their investments in hedge funds; they opt to include them with their domestic equity or international markets assets when they report their holdings.

Hedge fund managers have a ton of discretion, and they sometimes change strategies or attempt trades in new areas. You may think you're buying one type of fund but end up in something different. Your hedge fund's investment agreement may specify limitations, but it may not. You can exit the fund if you don't like the new strategy, but only when the lock-up period expires (see Chapter 2).

Viewing a Hedge Fund as an Overlay

Many investors view hedge funds as an *overlay*, not as a separate asset allocation. In other words, an investor makes the asset allocation first (see the section "Assaying Asset Allocations") and then decides if any of the assets should be managed by a hedge fund manager or by another type of investor.

Considering the overlay pros and cons

Investors have two reasons for taking the overlay approach — one good and one not so good:

- ✔ **The overlay thumb's-up:** To think about the portfolio's risk and return as a whole, acknowledging that a hedge fund will have market exposure no matter how much the fund manager wants to talk about pure alpha (see Chapter 6). Overlay lets the investor think about how much exposure the portfolio has to different asset risks instead of placing the risk elsewhere.

- ✔ **The overlay thumb's-down:** To deny an investment in a hedge fund. For every person who wants to invest in a hedge fund, another person is scared off. This person sees something inherently dangerous and evil about hedge funds. A charity may be concerned that listing hedge funds, or even alternative investors, in its annual holdings will scare off donors. A pension-fund consultant may be concerned that worker representatives on the trustee board will panic if they see hedge funds on the list. The solution to this fright is to hide the hedge-fund investments, which isn't quite honest.

Just because a portfolio listing doesn't include hedge funds or absolute-return strategies among its assets doesn't mean it has no investments in them. If you're analyzing the investments of a large pension or endowment plan and you don't see hedge funds listed, chances are good that the fund included them in another asset class. If you need to know, don't hesitate to ask.

Investment reporting: An overlay example

The following tables show a few of the ways that organizations can report investments. The first table shows the investments of a hypothetical charitable endowment:

Investment	Amount
Cash	$5,000,000
U.S. Treasury Bonds Owned Outright	$10,000,000
International Bond Investment	$10,000,000
Shares Donated by Foundation's Founder	$20,000,000
Equity Index Fund Investment	$30,000,000
Real Estate Holdings	$3,000,000
Macro Hedge-Fund Investment	$1,000,000
Absolute Return Hedge-Fund Investment	$1,000,000
Total	$80,000,000

The following table shows the reports of the charitable endowment with the hedge-fund investment broken out:

Cash	$5,000,000
Fixed Income	$20,000,000
Equities	$50,000,000
Alternative Investments	$4,000,000
Absolute Return	$1,000,000
Total	$80,000,000

And this final table shows the reports of the charitable endowment with the hedge fund as an overlay:

Cash	$5,000,000
Fixed Income	$20,000,000
Equities	$52,000,000
Real Estate	$3,000,000
Total	$80,000,000

The cash portion in the previous tables is straightforward. The fixed-income investments, which include U.S. treasury bonds and international bonds, are also straightforward. However, things start to get complicated in the other asset groups. This endowment holds a lot of stock in one company, which isn't unusual in a charitable endeavor, where the founder is sometimes an entrepreneur who wants to turn his stake in the business over to charity. For example, the Milton Hershey School Trust owns 33 percent of The Hershey Company; the chocolate company's founder used his fortune to establish a school for orphans.

Our hypothetical endowment also has money in an index fund, which is an investment designed to match the performance of a stock index, like the Standard & Poor's 500 (www.standardandpoors.com), by investing in all the companies in the index.

Next come the alternative investments, added to the portfolio to bring different risk-and-return characteristics than those of the classic assets — stocks, bonds, and cash. Real estate is a common alternative asset. The charity also has money in two different hedge funds — a macro fund designed to profit from changes in the global economy and an absolute return fund that should generate a steady, low-risk return regardless of market conditions.

Here's how the charity has decided to list the holdings:

✔ **First grouping:** The charity's trustees list the holdings by name.

However, the trustees may not want to be that exact, for all kinds of reasons. For example, the hedge fund manager may not even give them a detailed holdings list with that information. So, their next option is to report the charity's holdings by asset class, handling the hedge funds as alternatives to the stocks, bonds, and cash.

✔ **Second grouping:** The charity's trustees have decided to treat the macro hedge fund as an alternative asset class, so they add it to the real estate holding in the investment report (see Chapter 13 for more on macro funds). They then put the absolute-return fund on a separate line, with the idea that it represents something different from any of the other assets.

> ✔ **Third grouping:** The trustees have lumped the hedge-fund investments into equity holdings, using the logic that the funds have a risk-and-return profile that's more like an equity investment than cash, fixed income, or real estate.

Mixing and Matching Your Funds

When you determine that a hedge fund is right for you (which is the aim of the chapters in Part II, of which this is one), you should take two more steps before you make your investment. First, you need to figure out how much of your portfolio you should put in a hedge fund. Next, you need to determine what types of hedge funds are most likely to help you meet your investment objectives (see Chapters 7 and 8).

One key characteristic of hedge funds is that they're *illiquid* (see Chapter 7). Most hedge fund managers limit how often investors can take their money out; a fund may lock in investors for two years or more. For this reason alone, hedge funds are seldom appropriate for an entire investment portfolio. In almost all cases, hedge funds offer their maximum portfolio benefit in relatively small doses.

But how big or how small an allocation is right for you? The following sections look to help you out (along with the section "Assaying Asset Allocations" earlier in this chapter).

Looking for excess capital under the couch cushions

Hedge funds are mostly designed as investment vehicles for *excess capital* — money that the investor doesn't need now and doesn't need to support near-term spending.

Suppose, for example, that you're in charge of making investment decisions for a trust fund worth $20 million. You need to generate $600,000 in annual income. In most cases, a 5-percent income is reasonable for a minimum long-term return assumption for a mixed stock and bond portfolio. So, you start with the $600,000 income need and divide it by 5 percent to determine how much of the portfolio you should put in stocks and bonds. The answer: $12 million. The remaining amount of the portfolio is considered excess capital. You can lock up and invest this money at a higher risk level than the rest of the portfolio because you don't need it to support your income needs.

Although you don't want to lose that money, losing it wouldn't affect the minimum portfolio objective of generating $600,000 in annual income.

You may not need to generate income right now, but that doesn't mean you should lock all your money away in hedge funds. Instead, you should start by figuring out when you'll need that money and what you'll need it for.

Suppose that you're a professional athlete earning $20 million per year through a combination of salary and endorsements. You don't need to spend all $20 million; in fact, you're able to spend only about $3 million of it this year maintaining your current lifestyle. After you spend 3 of the $20 million that you earned, you have $17 million left that you can invest for the future. You don't know exactly when you'll need the money, though. You probably have several more playing years, but you could have a bad injury next game. And the endorsement market is fickle! If you stop playing, you can sell one of your houses and get rid of your personal jet timeshares, in which case you think you'll be fine with about $1 million in annual income. What if you need that $1 million next year, though?

In this case, one possible solution is to put away $1 million in cash or equivalent securities because you may need that money at any time. In order to preserve capital for future spending, you should put about $10 million into a balanced mixture of stocks and bonds. You may decide to put the remaining $6 million into a hedge fund — especially one following an absolute return objective to increase your portfolio to meet your post-retirement needs, all while preserving capital (see the section "How hedge funds are assets" earlier in this chapter).

And if you don't get injured? Next year, you can allocate your money in a similar fashion.

Taking different funds to the dressing room

After you calculate the maximum amount of money you can responsibly lock up in a hedge fund (see the previous section), your next step is to figure out what type of fund is the best fit for you. Hedge funds fall into two broad categories: absolute-return and directional; within those categories are many different strategies and asset concentrations (see Part III). (See the chapters of Part III for more on researching the types of funds and Chapter 18 for info on doing your due diligence with funds.)

Absolute-return funds or directional funds?

An *absolute-return fund* is designed to produce a steady but relatively low rate of return with relatively little risk. In most cases, the expected return is higher than that of a bond but with less risk. A *directional fund* swings for the fences, aiming for the highest possible return, although with a high level of risk. A directional fund may still have great diversification benefits for its investment portfolio, especially if it invests in assets that are different from the others in the non-hedge-fund portion. (See the earlier section "How hedge funds are assets" for more on the types of funds.)

What type of investment strategy?

Directional *and* absolute-return fund managers use strategies such as short selling and leverage, look for arbitrage opportunities, and pay attention to both corporate and government life cycles. They just trade their assets differently. (In Part III of this book, you can read about several of the strategies that hedge funds follow.)

Different asset classes interact with your other investments differently, too. For example, if you mostly invest in domestic stocks and bonds, you may want to put your hedge fund allocation into macro funds because those will have more international exposure. This strategy will reduce the risk of your overall portfolio better than a U.S. long-short equity fund.

After they decide between absolute-return and directional strategies, some hedge fund investors research the track record and reputation of their hedge fund managers, not the strategies that the managers follow (see Chapter 18). That tactic may work in some situations, especially if the rest of the investment portfolio is so well diversified that the incremental effects of the hedge fund would be small.

Working without transparency

Here's the problem that many investors have when trying to do allocations with hedge funds: Hedge fund managers often don't want to tell investors what strategies they're following or where they invest their money. This secrecy can make it difficult to determine how well a fund is diversifying your other assets.

A manager has some good reasons not to give investors too much information. The biggest is that the fund's investment strategy may be highly proprietary. If other people find out about it, everyone will follow the strategy, and the hedge fund's advantage will be gone. Likewise, if word gets out that certain hedge fund managers have certain positions, others in the market will react to that information, and the value may change.

However, you need to face facts: Some hedge fund managers just like the aura of secrecy, even if they don't need it. And some managers follow really simple investment strategies, but they don't want any investors to know that.

How much disclosure do you need?

Although investors like you prefer disclosure, you don't all need the same amount. Here are three key questions to ask yourself:

- ✔ **Do you have a legal obligation to know what's in the hedge fund?** People in charge of investment portfolios covered by the Employee Retirement Income Security Act of 1972 (also called ERISA — a law that governs pensions and employee benefits) need more disclosure to meet their obligations than other types of investors. Some hedge fund managers refuse to accept ERISA money for this reason.

- ✔ **How big a percentage of your overall portfolio is the hedge fund?** The smaller the percentage, the more likely it is that you can take the risk of not knowing how the manger invests the hedge fund.

- ✔ **How well diversified is the rest of your portfolio?** The greater the amount of asset diversification you have, the less of an effect the hedge fund will have. The fund's performance becomes less important to meeting your overall investment objectives, so it becomes less necessary to know what's in the hedge fund when you adjust your portfolio.

How much disclosure can you demand?

Even if the hedge fund manager has good reasons for secrecy (see the previous section), and even if you don't need to know all the whys and wherefores of the hedge fund's holdings, you still deserve some information about the fund. Turn to Chapter 18, which covers due diligence, for some information on what questions to ask of current and prospective managers.

Part III
Setting Up Your Hedge Fund Investment Strategy

The 5th Wave   By Rich Tennant

"Do I recommend a hedge fund strategy? Let me put it to you this way: I'm a strict Catholic who goes to Temple every Saturday, so 'Yes', I would recommend a hedge fund strategy."

In this part . . .

*I*n investing, return is a function of risk. The greater the return you seek, the greater the amount of risk you'll need to take, and the greater the likelihood of getting a return other than the return you want. The name of the hedge fund game is hedging: reducing risk relative to the amount of return expected. Other than following this mantra, different hedge funds aim for different levels of expected return, leading to wildly different levels of risk. They pursue a wide range of strategies to meet their risk and return objectives, and I look at these strategies in Part III.

I also give you some tips for evaluating the performance of a hedge fund so you can make better decisions before you pick a fund and while you're in a fund.

Chapter 10

Buying Low, Selling High: Using Arbitrage in Hedge Funds

In This Chapter

▶ Knowing how hedge funds use arbitrage to invest

▶ Becoming familiar with the tools of arbitrage

▶ Exploring the many types of arbitrage strategies

An economist and a hedge fund manager are walking down the street. The hedge fund manager looks down and says, "Hey, look, it's a $20 bill!" The economist says, "Don't bother. If it were real, someone would've picked it up already." The hedge fund manager looks at the bill, sees that it's real, and picks it up. He turns to his economist friend and says, "How about if I take this $20 and buy you a free lunch?"

Did you know that financial types were so funny? Really, they aren't. That's the only joke they know. (I'm kidding, I'm kidding.) This joke describes *arbitrage* — the process of buying an asset cheap in one market and selling it for a higher price in another. In the joke, the economist assumes that there's no riskless profit — no $20 bill just lying on the street — or it would've already been taken. The hedge fund manager, on the other hand, sees that the bill is real so he takes it, with no risk. Economists often say that there's no such thing as a free lunch, and they point out that life is full of tradeoffs. To get one thing, you must give up another. But because the hedge fund manager picked up the $20 bill on the sidewalk, he can buy lunch without another tradeoff, except, of course, for giving up the use of the money.

The word arbitrage is from derived from the French word for judgment; a person who does arbitrage is an *arbitrageur,* or *arb* for short.

Applying the arbitrage formula

Benjamin Graham was an economist at Columbia University who wrote extensively about stocks. He developed a formula to determine whether an arbitrage transaction will be profitable. The formula looks like this:

Annual Return = [CG − L (100% − C)] ÷ YP

where

C is the expected chance of success in percentage terms.

G is the expected gain in the event of success.

L is the expected loss in the event of failure.

Y is the expected holding time in years.

P is the current price of the security.

So, according to Graham's formula, if you expect a 50-percent chance (C) of making $100,000 (G) on an investment that currently costs $50,000 (P) — and you'll lose $40,000 (L) if you're wrong — and if you think it will take six months, or ½, of a year (Y) to find out if you're right, your annual return is as follows:

[0.50($100,000) − $40,000(0.5)] ÷ 0.5($50,000) = 120 percent

This particular transaction would be a go.

Many hedge funds use arbitrage as their primary investment strategy. It may be combined with strategies that increase risk and return, such as high levels of leverage (or borrowing; see Chapter 11) to increase returns. In this chapter, I cover the terms and strategies you should know when dealing with hedge funds that engage in arbitrage. I cover the basics of arbitrage and how funds put it to good use. I outline the tools that funds use to employ this tactic. Finally, I list the many types of arbitrage you're likely to see among the hedge funds that you investigate for possible future investment. With this info, you'll have a better understanding of what a hedge fund manager talks about when he or she talks about arbitrage.

Putting Arbitrage to Good Use

In theory, arbitrage opportunities don't exist, because markets are perfectly efficient, right? (I get to the theory on this later.) In reality, arbitrage takes place every single day, which forces markets into efficiency. However, the price differences needed for arbitrage are often small and don't last long. After all, the increased demand in the cheap market forces the price up, while the increased supply in the expensive market forces the price down. In seemingly no time at all, the arbitrage opportunity disappears. For this reason, successful arbitrageurs have to be paying constant attention to the market, and they have to be willing to act very quickly. They have no room for indecision.

People often misuse the word "arbitrage" to describe any kind of aggressive trading. If you hear a hedge fund manager say that his fund uses arbitrage, ask what kind of arbitrage is involved.

Here's a classic arbitrage example: A hedge fund trader notices that a stock is trading at $11.98 in New York and $11.99 in London. He buys as many shares as possible in New York, borrowing money if necessary, and immediately sells those shares in London, making a penny on each one. This type of arbitrage transaction has no risk, so people often describe it as "finding money on the sidewalk."

The following sections dive deeper into the topics of market efficiency and arbitrage.

Understanding arbitrage and market efficiency

Market efficiency, which I cover in Chapter 6, says that market prices reflect all known information about a stock. Therefore, as I state in the previous section, arbitrage simply isn't possible in theory. But keep in mind that academic theory describes some kind of financial utopia. By making one assumption — market efficiency — researchers can test other assumptions — like how much inflation, unemployment, or returns on a market index influence market prices.

In the academic world, market efficiency comes in three flavors, with no form allowing for arbitrage:

- ✔ **Strong form:** Even inside information, known only to company executives, is reflected in the security's price.

- ✔ **Semi-strong form:** Price includes all public information, so it may be possible to profit from insider trading.

- ✔ **Weak form:** Price reflects all historical information, so research that uncovers new trends may be beneficial.

Someone who believes in market efficiency would say that arbitrage is imaginary because someone would've noticed a price difference between markets already and immediately acted to close it off. That's why, in the joke at the beginning of the chapter, the economist says that the $20 on the street can't be real, or "someone" would've taken it already.

People with a less-rigid view of the world would say that arbitrage exists, but the opportunities for taking advantage of it are very few and far between. An investor who wants to find opportunities and exploit them better pay close attention to the markets to act quickly when a moment happens.

Finally, people who don't believe in market efficiency would say that not only do arbitrage opportunities happen all the time, but also they're not just weird, one-off price discrepancies. These people believe that someone in one of the markets knows something, and if you can figure out what that person knows, you may have a solid advantage in the marketplace.

Factoring transaction costs into arbitrage

What goes into the cost of trading? First, the fund manager must deal with all the overhead of having traders on staff, including salaries, bonuses, and benefits. The fund also has the cost of having the information systems in place to monitor several markets in real time. The free quotes that investors can find online through such sources as Yahoo! Finance (`finance.yahoo.com`) are delayed for 15 to 20 minutes, depending on where the security trades. Real-time quotes are expensive. Not to mention the connection between the hedge fund and a broker has to be fast enough to execute an arbitrage trade almost instantaneously.

On most exchanges, the fund manager has to execute the trade through a broker authorized to handle the transaction, and these brokers charge commissions for their services. Commissions are negotiable; managers rarely pay higher than $0.03 per share, but the cost is never $0.

In addition to commissions, brokers quote most securities on a *bid-ask basis.* The *bid* is price that the broker will pay a seller for a security, and the *ask* is the price that the broker charges an investor who wants to buy it. The difference is the broker's profit. For example, if the bid is $12.98, and the ask is $13.01, the broker buys stock from the seller at $12.98 and sells it to an investor for $13.01, making a profit of $0.03 per share. In the United States, the minimum spread is $0.01, but it can be quite a bit higher. It isn't as big a trading cost as it once was, but you still have to take it into consideration.

In the United States, stocks now trade in decimal amounts (dollars and cents). They used to trade in ⅛ of a dollar, and many bonds still do trade that way. The use of the ⅛ method dates back before the American Revolution, when the dominant currency in financial markets was the Spanish doubloon. To simplify trading in those days, people often cut large coins into halves, quarters, or eighths. In later years, the government minted coins in smaller denominations, but the money was based on the idea of eight bits to a whole. In Robert Louis Stevenson's book *Treasure Island,* the parrot keeps cawing, "Pieces of eight! Pieces of eight!" Now you know where that comes from!

What these trading costs mean is that arbitrage may exist, but it only takes place if the *arbitrageur* — the person who does the arbitrage transaction — can make enough of a profit to cover the costs involved. In the example that kicks off the chapter, the difference in share price between the two markets is only $0.01. The cost of trading has to be below a penny a share if you have any hope of making a profit.

Because of transaction costs, hedge funds tend to either commit heavily to arbitrage or avoid it entirely. A successful arbitrage strategy requires the following with respect to cost:

- Dedication to cover the high fixed costs of real-time quotes in several markets
- Bandwidth to handle large trades
- Purchasing power to bring down commissions
- Compensation for traders who know what they're doing

If you plan on investing in a hedge fund that expects to generate most of its profits from arbitrage, be sure to ask about these factors during due diligence. See Chapter 18 for more information on that.

Pitting true arbitrage versus risk arbitrage

True arbitrage is riskless trading. The purchase of an asset in one market and the sale of the asset in another happen simultaneously. The fund manager can count on profit as long as the trades go through immediately. True, riskless arbitrage is possible, but rare. No hedge fund that pursues only riskless arbitrage will stay in business for long.

Most arbitrageurs practice *risk arbitrage,* which is similar to true arbitrage in that it seeks to generate profits from price discrepancies; however, risk arbitrage involves taking some risk (go figure!). Risk arbitrage still involves buying one security and selling another, but an investor doesn't always buy the same security, and he doesn't necessarily buy and sell at the same time. For example, a fund manager may buy the stock of an acquisition target and sell the stock of an acquirer, waiting until the acquisition finalizes before closing the transaction, making (he hopes) a tidy profit in the process.

In many cases, the risk taken is that of time. The trade may work out but not as soon as the hedge fund manager hopes. In the meantime, his portfolio's performance may suffer or loans taken to acquire the position may be called in. It's one thing to be right; however, it's another thing entirely to be right in time for the decision to matter.

Cracking Open the Arbitrageur's Toolbox

Riskless opportunities where a fund manager buys a security at one price in one market and sells the exact same security at a slightly higher price in another market — at the exact same time — are very few and far between. Therefore, to find risky arbitrage opportunities, hedge funds look at similar securities, and they look for ways to profit from price discrepancies while offsetting much of the risk. I cover a few of the arbitrageur's favorite tools for offsetting risk in this section before I describe different arbitrage strategies in the next.

Drawing upon derivatives

A *derivative* is a financial instrument (like an option, a future, or a swap; see Chapter 5 for more information) that derives its value from the value of another security. For example, a stock option is a type of derivative that gives you the right, but not the obligation, to buy shares of the stock at a predetermined price. Whether or not you can get a good deal depends on where the stock is trading.

Because derivatives are related to securities, they can be useful in risk arbitrage. A fund manager may see a price discrepancy between a derivative and an underlying asset, creating a profitable trading opportunity.

With their value so closely liked to the value of other securities, derivatives offer many opportunities for constructing risk arbitrage trades. And with a wider range of low-risk arbitrage opportunities, a fund stands a better chance of making money. For example, a fund manager could trade options on a stock rather than the stock itself when setting up arbitrage on a merger. And if arbitrage trade takes time to play itself out, using interest-rate or currency futures can offset some of the risk that goes along with waiting. The more ways a hedge fund can structure a trade, the more arbitrage opportunities it can grab.

Using leverage

Leverage, which I discuss in detail in Chapter 11, is the process of borrowing money to trade. Because a hedge fund puts only a little of its own capital to work and borrows the rest, the return on its capital is much greater than it would be if it didn't borrow any money.

Because leverage allows a hedge fund to magnify its returns, it's a popular tool for arbitrage. After all, many price discrepancies between securities are small. If a hedge fund borrows money for a trade, the profit it sees as a percentage of its assets is much larger than it would be if the fund didn't use any borrowing.

However, leverage has a downside: Along with magnifying returns, it magnifies risk. The fund has to repay the borrowed money, no matter how the trade works out.

Short-selling

Short-selling, a topic I cover in Chapter 11, gives fund managers a way to profit from a decline in a security's price. The short-seller borrows the declining security (usually from a broker), sells it, and then repurchases the security in the market later in order to repay the loan. If the price falls, the profit is the difference between the price where the fund manager sold the security and the price where she repurchased it. If the price goes up, though, that difference is the amount of the loss.

Short-selling allows an arbitrageur more freedom in choosing how to buy securities low and sell high. By shorting an asset, the seller gives up the risk of the price going down, which can offer both a way to exploit a price discrepancy and a way to manage the risk of the transaction.

The opposite of *short* is *long.* When an investor owns a security, she's said to be long.

Synthetic securities

A *synthetic security* is one created by matching one asset with a combination of a few others that have the same profit- and loss-profile. For example, you can think of a stock as a combination of a *put option,* which has value if the stock goes down in price, and a *call option,* which has value if the stock goes up in price. By designing transactions that create synthetic securities, a hedge fund manager can create more ways for an asset to be cheaper in one market than in another, thus increasing the number of potential arbitrage opportunities. Many of the arbitrage styles that you can read about later in this chapter involve the creation of synthetic securities.

A typical arbitrage transaction involving a synthetic security involves shorting the security itself and then buying a package of securities that mimic its payoff.

Flipping through the Rolodex of Arbitrage Types

Arbitrageurs use the tools of arbitrage (see the previous section) in many different ways. Most arbitrage funds pick a few strategies to follow, although some may stick to only one and others may skip from strategy to strategy as market conditions warrant. Most hedge funds use some forms of arbitrage, and some may use arbitrage as their primary source of investment returns.

The following sections outline all the varieties of arbitrage transactions that a hedge fund may use as part of its investment strategy, arranged in alphabetical order for your reading pleasure. The strategies vary in complexity and in how often a fund can use them, but all are designed to take advantage of profits from security price discrepancies. Armed with the information here, you'll have a better understanding of how hedge funds try to make money, and you'll be in a better position to evaluate any funds that you consider investing in.

You may come across other types of arbitrage out there, but that doesn't mean that people who have found profitable strategies will talk about what they're doing. Wherever people still watch markets intently and collect data on price behavior, the search for small price differences that investors can turn into large, low-risk profits will continue.

Capital-structure arbitrage

The *capital structure* of a firm represents how the company is financed. Does it have debt? How much? Does it have stock? How many classes? Many companies have only one type of stock that trades, but other company portfolios can be quite complicated. General Motors, for example, has one class of common stock and 13 different debt securities for its parent company and its finance subsidiary. (This situation is actually simpler than in years past, when the company also had different classes of common stock for its different business units.)

When a company has many different securities trading, arbitrageurs look for price differences among them. After all, if all the securities are tied to the same asset — the company's business — they should trade in a similar fashion. You can't count on it, though.

Say, for example, that the MightyMug Company has common stock outstanding, as well as 20-year corporate bonds at 7.5 percent interest. The stock price stays in line with market expectations, but the company bonds fall in value more than expected given changes in interest rates. An arbitrageur may buy the bonds and short the stock (see Chapter 11 for more on short-selling), waiting for the price discrepancy between the two securities to return to its normal level. That means that the bonds will have increased in price, so he can sell them at a profit, and the stock will have fallen in price, so he buys it back to cover the short and locks in a profit.

Convertible arbitrage

Some companies issue *convertible bonds* (sometimes called a *convertible debenture*) or *convertible preferred stock.* The two types of securities are very similar: They pay income to the shareholders (interest for convertible bonds and dividends for convertible preferred stock), and they can be converted into shares of common stock in the future.

For example, say a $1,000 convertible bond pays 5.5 percent interest and is convertible into 50 shares of stock. If the stock is less than $20 per share, a holder can collect the interest income. If the stock appreciates above $20, the holder can convert, giving up the interest but getting stock cheap. The interest rate is usually below the rate on a corporate bond or the yield on a similar preferred stock offering. The convertible buyer is okay with that because she has the right to convert.

Convertible securities generally trade in line with the underlying stock. After all, the securities represent options to purchase the stock. If the convertible gets out of line, an arbitrage opportunity presents itself.

Here's an arbitrage example: An arbitrageur notices that a convertible bond is selling at a lower price than it should be, given the interest rates and the price of the company's common stock. So, she buys the bonds and sells the stock short (see Chapter 11 for more information on short-selling). The trade cancels out the stock exposure, reducing the transaction risk and leaving only the potential for profit as the bond's price moves back into line.

Fixed-income arbitrage

Fixed-income securities give holders a regular interest payment. Some people like to buy them just to get a check deposited every quarter. These securities may seem safe because the money just keeps rolling in, but they have enormous exposure to fluctuating interest rates.

In fact, if you've read through Chapter 6, you've heard me say (or read me saying, I suppose) that interest rates — the price of money — affect the value of many kinds of securities. Bonds have a great deal of interest-rate exposure, and so do some stocks. Currencies are highly exposed to changes in rates between different companies. Derivatives are valued in part with interest rates.

Because interest rates affect so many different securities, they're a common focus for arbitrageurs. With *fixed-income arbitrage,* the trader breaks out the following:

- ✔ The time value of money
- ✔ The level of risk in the economy
- ✔ The likelihood of repayment
- ✔ The inflation-rate effects on different securities

If one of the numbers is out of whack, the trader constructs and executes trades to profit from it.

Imagine that a hedge-fund trader tracks interest rates on U.S. government securities. He notices that one-year treasury bills are trading at a higher yield than expected — especially relative to two-year treasury notes. He shorts the two-year treasury notes (see Chapter 11) and buys the one-year treasury bills until the price difference falls back where it should be, given the expectations for interest rates in the economy.

Index arbitrage

A *market index* is designed to represent the activity of the market. It can be designed a few different ways, which I cover in Chapter 14, but an index is always based on the performance of a group of securities that trade in the market.

Futures contracts are available on most indexes, for example. These are derivatives based on the expected future value of the index. Sometimes, the value of the futures contract deviates from the value of the index itself. When that happens, the arbitrageur steps in to make a profit.

Here's an example: An arbitrageur notices that the S&P 500 futures contract is looking mighty cheap relative to the S&P 500 index. He shorts all 500 stocks in the index and buys the contracts to profit from the difference.

Most indexes have many securities, so buying a load of them can be expensive. The S&P 500 index has 500 stocks in it! That's why only the largest hedge funds are active in index arbitrage, and they use plenty of leverage out of necessity (as well as the profit motive). Only a few funds are able to buy enough stocks in the index to make the investment matter, and even fewer can do it with cash on hand!

Liquidation arbitrage

Liquidation arbitrage is a bet against the breakup value of a business. An arbitrageur researches a company to see what it would be worth if it was sold. Many businesses own real estate, patents, mineral rights, or other resources that their market values don't reflect, so selling a company piece by piece can be profitable. (This strategy is very similar to the bottom-up fundamental research I describe in Chapter 5.)

Here's one way to look at liquidation arbitrage: A hedge fund manager looks at the business of Giant Sloth Industries. The company's stock has been beaten up badly because its core chemical business has large environmental liabilities. The company has a subsidiary that owns a patent for a weight-loss drug, but everyone has overlooked its value. It also owns prime real estate in Silicon Valley that could be developed for housing, as well as an incredible corporate art collection. A fund manager realizes that the value of all these parts, net of the liabilities, is greater than the current market value of the company's stock. She buys shares of the company in anticipation that someone will come along and take over the company at a price that reflects its value.

Back in the 1980s, some huge insider-trading scandals that involved arbitrageurs took place. A handful of people (Ivan Boesky? Dennis Levine? Do those names ring a bell?) found that they could make even bigger profits from liquidation arbitrage if they knew before everyone else which companies were being acquired for breakup purposes. Needless to say, this strategy is illegal. Liquidation arbitrage itself is a fine and legal practice, as long as it's based on publicly available information.

Sometimes, liquidation arbitrageurs acquire so many shares in a company that they can influence whether or not a merger takes place. When this happens, the arbitrageurs become known as *corporate raiders*. You can find out more about the role of hedge funds in corporate finance decisions in Chapter 12.

Merger arbitrage

Liquidation arbitrage is about doing research in order to be ahead of an acquisition (see the previous section); *merger arbitrage* is about profiting from a company's acquisition after the merger has been announced. A merger announcement includes the following:

- ✔ The name of the acquiring company
- ✔ The name of the company being taken over (and no matter what PR people say, there are no mergers of equals)
- ✔ The price of the transaction
- ✔ The currency (cash, stock, debt)
- ✔ The date the merger is expected to close

Any of these variables can change: The acquiring company may decide that the deal is a bad one and walk away, for example; maybe the target company finds a buyer offering more money. The list goes on. All those variables create trading opportunities, although not all are riskless.

Consider this example: The management of Instruments R Us announces that it plans to acquire Violet Violins for a total price of $150 million in Instruments R Us stock, which works out to $25 per share. The deal is expected to close in three months. The Instruments R Us stock trades at $40 per share. Violet Violins was trading at $20 per share when the merger was announced. After the news hits the tape, Violet Violins shares jump to $24.75. An arbitrageur swoops in and sells shares of Instruments R Us and buys shares (*goes long*, in trader-speak) of Violet Violins. If the merger holds up, the arbitrageur locks in the $0.25 per share difference between the current $24.75 price of Violet Violins and the $25.00 merger price. If the deal doesn't go through, Violet Violins stock will fall and Instruments R Us stock will go up.

When companies announce a big merger, traders sometimes get caught up in the mood of the moment and engage in *garbatrage*. That is, everyone gets so excited that even businesses with no real connection to the merger become part of the speculation. For example, if a drug company buys a shampoo manufacturer, the shares of any and all beauty-products manufacturers may go up. This may cause folks to pay too much money because not all the shares will be worth their newly inflated price.

Option arbitrage

Options come in many varieties, even if they exist on the same underlying security. They come in different types, *puts* (bets on the underlying security price going down), and *calls* (bets on the underlying security price going up). They have different prices, where a holder can cash the option in for the underlying security, and different expiration dates. You can exercise some options, known as *European options,* at any time between the date of issue and the expiration date, and you can exercise others, known as *American options,* only at the expiration date. (American and European options can be issued anywhere; see Chapter 5 for more info on options.)

Needless to say, having so many securities that are almost the same creates plenty of opportunities for a knowledgeable arbitrageur to find profitable price discrepancies.

For example, say a hedge fund's options trader notices that the options exchanges are assuming a slightly higher price for a security than in the security's own market. She buys the underlying security and then buys a put and sells a call with the same strike price and expiration date. The put-call transaction has the same payoff as shorting the security, so she has effectively bought the security cheap in one market and sold it at a higher price in another.

Pairs trading

Pairs trading is a form of long-short hedging (which I describe in Chapter 11) that looks for discrepancies among securities in a given industry sector. If one security appears to be overvalued relative to others, a savvy arbitrageur will short that security; the arbitrageur then buys another security in the group that seems to be undervalued.

Say, for example, that a hedge fund's analyst is studying companies in the grocery business. He notices that the stock of Chubby Cubby markets, which is taking market share in the industry, is trading at a lower price/earnings ratio than it usually does. Meanwhile, shares in the Gems Market look relatively expensive. The analyst figures that other investors will come to their senses soon; when that happens, he hopes to profit by shorting shares in the Gems and buying shares in Chubby Cubby, betting that Chubby Cubby increases in value and the Gems decreases.

Scalping

Scalping is a form of arbitrage that takes advantage of small price movements throughout the day — an especially common practice in commodities markets. In most cases, scalpers look to take advantage of changes in a security's bid-ask spread. The *bid-ask spread* represents the difference between the price that a broker will buy a security for from those who want to sell it (the *bid*) and the price that the broker will charge those who want to buy it (the *ask* — also called the *offer* in some markets).

For many securities, the bid-ask spread stays fairly constant over time because the supply and demand should balance out. If everyone has the same information (the old market-efficiency situation), their trading levels are in balance and the broker-dealers can maintain a steady profit.

Sometimes, however, the spread will be just a little out of balance compared to normal levels. A scalper can take advantage of that situation by buying the security, waiting even a minute or two for the spread to change, and then selling it at a profit. Or, the scalper can buy the security, wait a few minutes for the price to go up a small amount, and then sell it.

The scalper has to work quickly to make many small trades. He has to have a low commission structure in place, or else transactions costs will kill him. He also has to be careful to get out of the market as soon as a news event comes along that causes the security's trading to become more volatile, because scalping becomes a high-risk proposition when market prices are changing quickly. This is why some folks describe scalping as "picking up nickels in front of a steamroller."

Scalping probably isn't a primary strategy for any hedge fund, but the strategy may give a trader profit opportunities on a slow day.

Imagine that a security has a bid-ask quote of $15.12–$15.17. The scalper buys 1,000 shares of the security at the ask, $15.17. He waits a few minutes until the price changes to $15.18–$15.22. He sells his position at $15.18, making $10. A few minutes later, the price quote becomes $15.15–$15.22. He buys another 1,000 at $15.22. A few minutes later, the price quote changes to $15.18–$15.23, so he sells at $15.23, making another $10.

The scalping I describe in this section is perfectly legal. One of my friends has a husband who scalps corn at the Chicago Board of Trade, an occupational description that always cracks me up. But the word "scalping" is also used to describe the illegal practice of promoting a security in public and then selling it in private. If a hedge fund manager goes on a cable finance news show, talks about how great a stock is so that the price goes up, and then sells it during its rise, she commits the crime of scalping. Be careful not to confuse the two strategies!

Statistical arbitrage

Statistical arbitrage is a popular hedge fund trading strategy that involves the use of complex mathematical models to determine where a security should be priced. Have you read the discussion of the random walk in an efficient market in Chapter 6? That theory says that price changes are random. And when you talk about the normal distribution of returns, a series of random events converges on a mean.

For example, a standard die has six sides. If you roll it, any one of those six results is equally likely. If you roll the die 100 times, the average of the results should be close to 3.5, which is equal to $(1 + 2 + 3 + 4 + 5 + 6) \div 6$. If the average deviates from 3.5 a significant amount, rolling the die several more times should give you results that begin to close in on the mean. If not, you can conclude that your die is loaded.

In statistical arbitrage, the trader works off of huge databases of securities prices that indicate where securities should trade, on average. In most cases, the trader is looking for an average price relative to a trend, like interest rates or the prices of a peer. When a securities price deviates from the norm, the trader enters into a position to take advantage.

Here's an arbitrage example: A hedge fund has data that shows for the past 15 years, electric utility companies have moved in a fixed percentage relative to interest rates. The fund analyst notices that the relationship has diverged, with the stocks having increased in value more than expected relative to rates. The fund sells short a large group (also called a *basket*) of utility stocks, expecting that the prices of the utility stocks will fall so that the normal relationship continues to hold. (See Chapter 11 for more information on short-selling.)

Warrant arbitrage

A warrant is similar to an option, but a company issues it rather than an options exchange. A *warrant* gives the holder the right to exchange it for shares of the company's stock at a predetermined price. Not many companies issue them, but those that do usually issue warrants along with debt as a way of giving holders the right to convert into stock or to sell that right to someone else. As with options and converts, warrant values sometimes differ from the value of the stock that they can be converted into.

Say, for example, that warrants on CupCakeCo seem to be trading on the assumption that CupCakeCo's shares are more valuable than they are right now. An arbitrageur can short the warrants and buy the underlying shares to turn a quick profit.

Chapter 11

Short-Selling, Leveraging, and Other Equity Strategies

*E*quity-based hedge funds, which are hedge funds that invest in equities, start with the same investment strategies as mutual funds, brokerage accounts, or other types of investment portfolios that invest in equities. However, equity hedge funds use two unique strategies — short-selling and leveraging — to change the risk profiles of their investments in stocks. Depending on your hedge fund's strategy and market expectations, it may have greater or less risk than the market, in part because of the use of these strategies (see Chapter 6 for more on risk and return). And you can assume that most hedge funds are using some leverage and some short-selling to reach their risk and return objectives.

You can find out about the basics of equities and other types of investment assets in Chapter 5. In this chapter, I show you how hedge funds invest in equities. They rarely buy and hold stocks in the way that traditional investments do (although they will if they see the right opportunities). Instead, hedge funds use techniques like short-selling and leveraging to reduce the risk of their portfolios while increasing return — or so you hope! In this way, hedge funds feature a different way of thinking about stock investing. If you're investigating hedge funds, you'll likely come across these types of funds. The more you know about them, the better equipped you'll be to make good decisions with your money.

Here's one other thing to note about hedge funds: Fund managers can mess around with the risk-and-return profiles of their portfolios by using a wide range of strategies. Unlike mutual funds, hedge funds have no hard and fast rules about what type of investment strategy is best for any given type of investor. When researching hedge funds, you need to know more than just whether the fund manager prefers big-cap stocks or small-cap stocks and whether she prefers to manage risk through short-selling or through derivatives. You also need to know what her risk and return targets are and whether they make sense for your investment objectives. (You can discover more about setting investment objectives in Chapters 7, 8, and 9.)

Short-Selling versus Leveraging: A Brief Overview

Short-selling and leveraging, two investing strategies, are fundamental to the operations of a hedge fund. They're widely associated with equity trading, although they can be used with other types of securities and derivatives. In fact, almost all hedge funds use some short-selling and leverage in order to increase return for a given level of risk. Therefore, if you're interested in hedge funds, you should find out as much as you can about short-selling and leverage so that you have a better understanding of what hedge funds do. The following list introduces these topics to begin your learning process:

✔ **Short-selling:** Borrowing an asset (like a stock or bond), selling it, and then buying it back to repay the loaned asset. If the asset goes down in price, the hedge fund makes the difference between the price where it sold the asset and the price where it repurchased the asset. Of course, if the asset appreciates in price, the hedge fund loses money. The opposite of short is long, so an investor who is *long* is an investor who owns the asset.

If much of your portfolio sits in an S&P 500 index fund — a fund that invests in all the securities in the S&P 500 in the same proportion as the index in order to generate the same return — you have significant exposure to the stock market, which means you have market risk. One way to reduce that risk without giving up your expected return is to seek out equities with a different risk profile. Short-selling gives you more places to look.

✔ **Leverage:** Borrowing money to invest, often from brokerage firms. Leverage increases your potential return, but also increases your risk. Hedge funds use leverage, but so do other types of accounts, and many individual investors use it, too.

You can find more coverage on leverage and short-selling in Chapter 6.

Strutting in the Equity Style Show

In this section, I talk about some different investment styles used by long equity managers, or those equity investors who don't short stocks (and thus are rarely hedge fund managers, although a small number of hedge fund managers are long-only). With this information, you'll have a sense of how a hedge fund manager may start the hedging process; at the least, you'll understand how some hedge fund strategies are different from the strategies used by other types of investment accounts.

Long equity managers fall into several broad categories and employ several styles, often called *style boxes*. Fund managers use these categories to guide their choices for the long portions of their portfolios (the securities that they own, not those that they short) or to determine the risk that they can reduce with hedging strategies. At a minimum, you want to recognize the terms I cover in this section when they come up in conversation.

Few hedge funds use the strategies in this section exclusively. Hedge fund managers are in the business of using exotic investment techniques in order to beat the market — and to justify their high fees.

Trying on a large cap

A *large cap fund*, which may be a hedge fund, a mutual fund, or another type of investment portfolio, invests in companies with a market capitalization (shares outstanding multiplied by current price) of $5 billion or more. These companies tend to be multinational behemoths with steady performance and fortunes tied to the global economy. You can find these companies in the S&P 500, the Fortune 500, and on every other 500 list, save the Indy 500.

Many large cap managers engage in a strategy called *closet indexing:* They buy shares in the largest companies in the S&P 500 in more or less the same proportion as the S&P index. The result is that the portion of the portfolio containing the large cap shares has almost identical risk and return as the index but for the higher fee that an active manager receives. A hedge fund manager who does closet indexing isn't hedging, so she isn't doing what you pay her to.

Fitting for a small cap

A *small cap stock* is a share of a company with a market capitalization of under $1 billion. These companies tend to be growing faster than the market as a whole, and they aren't as closely covered by investment analysts as larger companies, so their shares may not be as expensive as those in similar but better-known companies.

Some fund managers concentrate on investing in company stocks with a market cap of under $100 million, believing that's where the real money-making opportunities lie because these stocks are even less covered than small cap stocks, so the managers may be getting in on the ground floor. This style of investing, known as *micro cap,* is similar to venture capital and requires that the fund manager do careful research, because other investors may be showing little interest in the company.

What's in between $5 billion and $1 billion? Mid cap investments, which have characteristics of both large cap and small cap stocks. Easy, huh? Some small and mid cap companies will grow and graduate to the next level. However, some mid cap companies used to be large cap companies before they ran into trouble, and some small caps are former mid caps whose growing days are over.

Note that the industry has no standard cutoff for small, mid, and large cap stocks. Different analysts and money-management firms set their own parameters, and the parameters tend to go up when the market goes up and come down a little bit when the market comes down. So, if you come across a hedge fund manager who defines companies with a capitalization of $2 billion as small cap stocks, she isn't doing anything wrong; she's just using a cutoff that works with what she sees in the market at that point.

If a hedge fund manager mentions capitalization as a style, you should certainly ask about how the fund defines the cutoffs.

Investing according to growth and GARP

A *growth fund* looks to buy stock in companies that are growing their revenue and earnings faster than the market as a whole. Hedge funds expect these equities to appreciate more than the market and to have some life to them, making them longer-term holdings.

Because markets are structured to be reasonably efficient, growth stocks tend to be more expensive than stocks in companies that are growing at a normal rate. For this reason, many fund managers try to find cheap growth stocks, following a strategy called *Growth At the Right Price* (or *Growth At a Reasonable Price [GARP]*). The fund manager attempts to combine growth with low price-to-earnings ratios in order to earn a greater-than-market return for a market rate of risk.

So, what's cheap and what's expensive? Professional investors look at the stock price relative to a company's earnings and assets, not the absolute stock price, to determine the value of a stock. A stock priced at $5.00 per share may be expensive if the company is losing money, and a stock priced at $350.00 per share may be a bargain if the company has $400.00 per share in real estate that other investors are overlooking. You can certainly ask a hedge fund manager about the fund's valuation methods used to determine whether a stock is cheap.

Swooping in on lowly equities with value investing

Value investors are the most traditional of equity investors. Guided by the classic text *Security Analysis* (McGraw-Hill), written by Benjamin Graham and David Dodd in 1934 and updated frequently since then, hedge fund managers who consider themselves value investors look for stocks that are cheap based on accounting earnings or asset values. They shoot for companies that have solid assets, plenty of cash, and inferiority complexes because the market doesn't recognized them. Value investors care more about what a business would look like dead, with the assets sold and the proceeds distributed to shareholders, than what it would look like if it grew in the future.

Sometimes, when a stock takes a hit on a bit of bad news, a hedge fund manager will swoop in and buy shares from panicking sellers. Even if the stock never recovers its old high-flying price, it may recover slightly after investors digest the news, allowing the value manager to make a quick profit. On the other hand, value investors sometimes fall into value traps when stocks keep getting cheaper and cheaper. They buy all the way down until the companies end up in bankruptcy and the investments are worthless.

Alpha is a rate of return over and above the market rate of return, but for the same amount of risk. Hedge fund managers are on an endless search for alpha, and many think that buying into unappreciated or unrecognized companies may be one way to capture their elusive quarry (see Chapter 6 for more on the topic).

Keeping options open for special style situations

Many hedge fund managers avoid certain style boxes for their portfolios. They may label themselves *special-situations investors* or say that they like to take an opportunistic approach. A sharp manager may want to keep his options open, especially at a larger firm that can afford investment analysts and traders who have their own investment niches. Other managers may want flexibility to move between styles whenever the current en vogue style isn't working out. A cynic may say that this is why fund managers are often so secretive about their strategies (see Chapter 8 for more on transparency).

A special-situations investor doesn't like to declare allegiance to any one style of equity investing; he prefers to look at stocks that seem likely to appreciate, for a variety of reasons:

- ✔ Because they're cheap
- ✔ Because they're going to grow
- ✔ Because of a takeover battle (see Chapter 12)

Although it seems like a novel idea to keep all investment options open, special-situations investors can end up chasing ideas all over the place. With no discipline to help them determine valuation, these investors may end up buying high and selling low, which is a sure path to ruin. If you interview a special-situations fund manager because you're interested in his fund's ability to handle your money, ask how he makes his investing decisions (see Chapter 18 for more on doing your due diligence).

Market Neutrality: Taking the Market out of Hedge-Fund Performance

Wouldn't it be great to receive a market return on an equity investment without exposing yourself to market risk? When you or your hedge fund buys a stock, you buy some exposure to the risk-and-return performance of the market as a whole, which may not be your intention. A typical, fully diversified equity portfolio looks a lot like an index fund (an investment fund that seeks to duplicate the performance of a market index). The more securities you hold, and the more diversified your portfolio, the more your portfolio's performance will mirror that of the market, and you'll be compensated for market risk that you take.

But here's the thing about equity investing: With a typical, diversified equity portfolio, you can earn only the market rate of return. Although you take on the same amount of risk as the market, that may be more risk than you want. For these reasons, many hedge funds have a market-neutral strategy. You expect a *market-neutral portfolio* to generate a positive return, regardless of what the market does. This doesn't mean that a market-neutral portfolio will generate a higher return than the market, although it should when the market loses money.

Whatever you do, you don't want to give up all risk on your investments. Without risk, your investments have no potential for return (see Chapter 6 for more on risk and return).

Of course, even Switzerland has its biases. A fund manager has to tweak a market-neutral portfolio to maintain its neutrality, so the manager needs a system for the tweaking process. The three common styles of market-neutral investing are creating beta-neutral, dollar-neutral, and sector-neutral portfolios.

Being beta neutral

Many hedge fund managers go back to academic theory and use beta as the neutral point when figuring out ways to make their portfolios market neutral. A *beta-neutral portfolio* is made up of securities that have a weighted average beta of 0 — in other words, the portfolio has no market exposure (see Chapter 6 for more on beta). This strategy encompasses what a traditional hedge fund is all about: generating an investment return that isn't exposed to market risk.

Under the Modern (Markowitz) Portfolio Theory (MPT), which I discuss in detail in Chapter 6, the market has a beta of 1, and a stock that's correlated with the market also has a beta of 1. A security that's negatively correlated with the market has a beta of –1, and a security that features no correlation with the market has a beta of 0.

A beta-neutral sample trade

A portfolio manager is considering three stocks for her portfolio: one with a beta of 1.50, one with a beta of 0.40, and one with a beta of –0.75. She wants to figure out what percentage of her fund she should put in each security in order to achieve a beta of 0 (for more on balancing a portfolio, see the section "Rebalancing a Portfolio" later in the chapter). If she meets her goal, she can eliminate her fund's exposure to the market, which will help her reduce the overall risk in her portfolio. She calculates the weighted average by multiplying the beta of the stock times its portfolio percentage, as shown in the following table.

Stock	Beta	Portfolio Percentage	Weighted Beta
A	1.50	20.5%	30.8%
B	0.40	25.1%	10.0%
C	(0.75)	54.4%	–40.8%
		100.0%	0.0%

Few 0-beta securities exist in the market, because if a security is part of the market, it almost definitely has some bit of exposure to it. The closest asset to a 0-beta security is a short-term U.S. treasury security, which has a very low return. A beta-neutral hedge fund has to generate a return greater than treasuries in order to attract assets! Otherwise, investors will simply buy low-returning, 0-beta treasuries directly from the U.S. government (www.savingsbonds.gov), saving all commissions, fees, and performance bonuses.

In order to maintain 0 beta while maximizing return, a fund manager can run a program that comes up with optimal portfolio weighting (for more on this topic, see the section "Rebalancing a Portfolio" later in this chapter). In some ways, a beta-neutral portfolio is as much about programming as it is about picking stocks, because the weightings are very difficult to calculate by hand. Finding negative-beta stocks, on the other hand, is easy. Shorting a stock is the same as reversing its beta, so a fund manager can generate negative-beta securities by taking short positions in stocks with positive betas (see the section "Short-Selling versus Leveraging: A Brief Overview").

This tactic is a relatively simple weighted-average strategy that a fund can undertake by using spreadsheet software, especially with the help of the goal-seek function. A hedge fund that has many positions probably uses optimization software to improve the speed of the calculations.

Beta is the relationship of a security to the market as a whole. Firms that rely heavily on beta for their investment-management decisions calculate beta in-house, although they can find research services that publish versions of beta. Services or brokerage firms often give beta with a detailed stock-price quote — Yahoo Finance, for example. The beta given by these services may not be accurate or up-to-date, however.

Establishing dollar neutrality

Another basis for market neutrality is the amount of money under management. In a *dollar-neutral portfolio,* the hedge fund manager holds the same amount of money in short positions — that is, in securities that he borrowed and then sold in hopes that they would go down in price so that the fund could repurchase them at a lower price to repay the loan — as in long positions — securities that the fund owns outright. With this strategy, the portfolio's expected return isn't highly exposed to the market, because the portfolio should benefit no matter what direction the market moves. An investor follows this strategy to eliminate market risk from a portfolio. Of course, if you want to have market risk, this feature would be a disadvantage. It all depends on your point of view.

A dollar-neutral sample trade

A dollar-neutral fund manager receives $1 million from an investor to put to use. The following list shows the steps he goes through to establish a dollar-neutral portfolio:

1. The fund manager goes through the list of stocks in a market index and identifies undervalued securities that he expects to do as well as or better than the market; he also looks for overvalued securities that he expects to do worse.

2. He takes the funds received from the investor and establishes long positions (buys) in the undervalued basket of stocks.

3. He borrows $1 million worth of the overvalued stocks (known as *leveraging*) and sells them short (see the section "Short-Selling versus Leveraging: A Brief Overview").

On paper, the fund manager has a portfolio worth nothing because he bought and sold an equal amount. However, he expects the long portfolio to generate a market return plus some additional return from the selection of undervalued stocks. He expects the short portfolio to lose the market return but gain some additional return because the shorted, overvalued stocks should either go down more than the market or at least not appreciate as much as the market. The market returns cancel each other out, leaving the excess return from the identification of the overvalued and undervalued securities.

Staying sector neutral

Aside from beta neutrality and dollar neutrality, a hedge fund manager can achieve market neutrality through the sectors in market indexes, which aren't exactly neutral. Certain industries represented in the investment indexes perform differently than others, which can make index performance more volatile than a true market investment should be. (This is a relative measure and can vary from industry to industry and time to time. For example, sometimes technology companies are volatile; at other times, utility companies are volatile.) In fact, the people who select the stocks for the indexes have been known to make additions and subtractions that make the indexes perform better, even if the indexes become less representative of the market and the economy.

A hedge fund manager has a chance to structure his or her portfolio free of political influences, generating less risk than may be found in an index fund in the process. The manager can do this by weighting each industry sector equally so that Internet stocks don't crowd out automaker stocks, for example. This is called *sector neutrality*. This strategy doesn't eliminate market risk, but it does reduce it. Many hedge fund managers combine sector neutrality with other portfolio strategies, such as arbitrage or leverage (see Chapter 10).

A sector-neutral sample trade

A hedge fund manager receives a $1 million investment for a portfolio that the investor wants to be sector-neutral relative to the S&P 500 index. The fund manager invests the money equally in nine S&P 500 industry groups: Basic Materials, Conglomerates, Consumer Goods, Financial, Health Care, Industrial Goods, Services, Technology, and Utilities. In the process, she buys more securities in the undervalued sectors and less in the overvalued ones, reducing the risk of the portfolio relative to the market. The portfolio still has market exposure, but the exposure is less than it may be with other types of investments.

When Chrysler merged with Daimler-Benz, the company was removed from one index, the S&P 500 (www.standardandpoors.com), because it was no longer a company in the United States. The S&P replaced Chrysler with Yahoo!, which I'm sure had nothing to do with the fact that the year was 1998, the dot-com stocks were booming, and the S&P 500 received a nice performance increase from the switch. Yes, I'm being sarcastic. Just remember, in the market, as in life, it's almost impossible to be completely neutral all the time.

Rebalancing a Portfolio

When structuring a portfolio, a hedge fund manager starts out by calculating how much money to put into different investments — in other words, how to weight the portfolio. After the investments hit the books, some of the securities go up, some go down, and all the manager's hard work goes right out the window! For this reason, it's imperative that the fund manager rebalances to maintain the fund's (and its investors') desired risk-and-return profile. The hedge fund manager monitors the portfolio, buying and selling securities as necessary to maintain the fund's desired characteristics and to get back to the starting point, wherever it may be.

Any fund manager who wants to maintain a set beta position (see the section "Being beta neutral") has to rebalance. For that matter, any investor who wants to maintain a target risk-and-return profile should rebalance his or her portfolio periodically.

Naturally, this give and take comes with a catch — buying and selling is expensive. The person who does the trading will have to pay commissions and may create tax liabilities (see Chapter 8). Some hedge-fund positions sit in illiquid securities, so the fund can't easily add to or reduce the securities held without causing big price changes. Options and futures may help the situation. For example, to reduce exposure to certain stocks owned outright in the portfolio, a portfolio manager can write a put, giving the manager the right but not the obligation to sell the stock at an agreed-upon price. This tactic reduces the amount of exposure, but the manager doesn't have to sell the underlying security.

I cover options and futures in great detail in Chapters 5 and 12, but here's a quick reminder of the difference between a put and a call. A *call* gives you the right, but not the obligation, to buy a security, so calls make money when the security goes up in value. A *put* gives you the right, but not the obligation, to sell a security, so puts make money when the security goes down. Want an easy memory trick? "You call up your friend to put down your enemy."

A savvy hedge fund investor needs to know how the hedge fund rebalances its portfolio and how often it performs the task. Otherwise, the risk in the portfolio will be all wrong for the investor. You should ask about this during due diligence (see Chapter 18).

Rebalancing your portfolio is a good practice to ensure that you continue to meet the investment objectives that you set out with initially. It's also a way of forcing you to buy low and sell high. Here's what you do:

1. **Set your objectives.**

   Start your portfolio with your investment objectives in place. How much risk do you want? How much exposure to different asset classes? How much cash flow do you need to generate, and when do you need it? Part II of this book has extensive information on how to set investment objectives.

2. **Develop a portfolio that meets your objectives.**

   This process is a little more involved than a line on a checklist. Chapters 7 and 9 can help you out.

3. **Run the portfolio for a set time period.**

   Some people make a practice of rebalancing once per year, some once per quarter. What's right for you depends on the portfolio strategy and the trading costs incurred during the rebalancing.

4. **Evaluate the portfolio's performance.**

   At the end of the time period, see where your portfolio stands relative to your objectives. Is your portfolio still in proportion? Probably not.

5. **Evaluate your objectives.**

   Does your portfolio still meet your needs? Maybe. Have your needs changed? Maybe, maybe not.

6. **Update your asset parameters.**

   The risk-and-return profiles of different assets change over time. Beta is fickle (see Chapter 6 for more information on beta). Your objectives may stay the same, but the asset allocation you need to reach them may be very different after six months or a year (see Chapter 9 for more on asset allocation).

7. **Buy and sell assets to meet the ideal portfolio proportions.**

   Armed with all this information on your portfolio's performance, asset parameters, and your needs, sell off enough of the over-weighted assets to bring that class back into proportion. Use the proceeds you generate to buy more of the under-weighted classes.

Putting rebalancing into practice: A sample trade

A beta-neutral portfolio manager (see the section "Being beta neutral") started out with 20.5 percent of his funds in stock A, 25.1 percent in stock B, and 54.4 percent in stock C. His allocation created a 0-beta portfolio. Each of the stocks performed differently, and at the end of the month, the portfolio had 20.9 percent of funds in A, 24.3 percent in B, and 54.8 percent in C. At that point, the portfolio had a beta of –0.01 — close to zero, but not precisely market neutral. The portfolio manager decided to sell some shares in stocks A and C and buy more B stocks in order to restore his fund's 0-beta position. See the following table for an illustration of this process.

The Initial Position

Stock	Beta	Portfolio Percentage	Weighted Beta	Initial Price per Share	Shares Purchased	Initial Value
A	1.50	20.5%	0.31	$20.00	10,250	$205,000
B	0.40	25.1%	0.10	$20.00	12,550	$251,000
C	–0.75	54.4%	–0.41	$20.00	27,200	$544,000
		100.0%	(0.00)			$1,000,000

How It Looks after a Month

Stock	Stock Price, 30 Days Later	Position Value, 30 Days Later	Portfolio Percentage	Beta	New Weighted Beta
A	$20.40	$209,100	20.7%	1.50	0.31
B	$19.00	$238,450	23.7%	0.40	0.09
C	$20.60	$560,320	55.6%	–0.75	–0.42
		$1,007,870			(0.02)

Bringing It Back into Balance

	Desired Portfolio Percentage	Desired Position Value	Desired Shares Held	Shares Bought (Sold)
A	20.5%	$206,613	10,128	(122)
B	25.1%	$252,975	13,314	764
C	54.4%	$548,281	26,616	(584)
		$1,007,870		

Long-Short Funds

A *long-short fund* is actually a traditional hedge fund (see Chapter 1); it buys and sells stocks according to its risk profile and market conditions. A long-short manager probably doesn't worry about market neutrality (see the section "Market Neutrality: Taking the Market out of Hedge-Fund Performance"), assuming that her short positions are enough to offset the general risk of the market. The fund's investors probably aren't looking for market neutrality, either. They may want market risk, particularly if they have reason to expect that the market will be going up.

Some long-short managers match stocks in a given industry, like technology or healthcare. Some look for interesting opportunities to buy and sell, regardless of market conditions or industry sectors.

Nowadays, people apply the term "hedge fund" to any unregulated investment partnership. Although the first hedge funds were long-short funds, not all hedge funds follow this strategy.

A long-short fund manager looks for overvalued assets to sell and undervalued assets to buy. The valuation may be relative to the current assets and earnings of the securities or relative to the future prospects for the companies. Matching the two allows for reduced risk and increased returns — the very stuff of the hedge-fund game.

Some hedge fund managers allocate parts of their portfolios to pure short-selling. (The other part of the portfolio is long but not matched to the short assets, so this is a type of long-short fund.) These managers want to increase their risk (and thus their expected returns) by finding overvalued securities in the market and then selling them short. This strategy isn't for the faint of heart, because the most a stock can go down is 100 percent, to 0, but the most it can go up is infinity. If the economy grows, the stock market should grow, too, so short-selling can be a bloody, quixotic quest. That's why most hedge fund managers view short-selling as part of a hedged portfolio, not the centerpiece of it.

Long-short funds: A sample trade

Your hedge fund manager tells you that he has reason to believe that WidgeCo will take market share in the widget industry, which is growing at a good rate. WidgeCo's competitor, Acme Widgets, doesn't seem to be doing as well and is losing its share of the market to WidgeCo. So, your manager buys shares of WidgeCo and sells shares of Acme Widgets. If WidgeCo grows faster than the industry by taking shares from Acme Widgets, you maximize return as WidgeCo goes up and Acme Widgets goes down. If both WidgeCo and Acme do well, your fund won't make much money, but you won't lose much, either — your gain on WidgeCo helps offset your loss on Acme Widgets. And if your savvy fund manager is wrong and both stocks go down, your gain on Acme Widgets will offset your loss on WidgeCo. The only bad scenario is if WidgeCo goes down while Acme Widgets goes up; this puts you in trouble because you would lose money on both your long and your short positions, with no offsetting gains.

The trade described here — buying WidgeCo and shorting Acme — gives the portfolio exposure to the widget industry. The short position reduces risk while increasing the potential for return. What's not to like about that? The following table illustrates this long-short example.

If Both WidgeCo and Acme Widgets Go Down

	Share Price	Number of Shares Held	Total Value
WidgeCo	$10.00	40,000	$400,000
Acme Widgets	$5.00	(100,000)	$(500,000)
			$(100,000.00)

If WidgeCo Goes Down and Acme Widgets Goes Up (the Worst-Case Scenario)

	Share Price	Number of Shares Held	Total Value
WidgeCo	$10.00	40,000	$400,000
Acme Widgets	$15.00	(100,000)	$(1,500,000)
			$(1,100,000)

The flip side of this is a long strategy called a *short squeeze,* in which a hedge fund or other portfolio manager looks for stocks that have been shorted. At some point, all the short-sellers have to buy back the stocks to repay the lenders. This means that someone can buy up enough of the stock to push the prices higher, causing investors on the short side to start losing money. As the shorts lose money, the managers can buy shares to cover the loans and get out of the positions; their buying drives the prices even higher.

Most short-sellers do excellent research. An unscrupulous few have been known to drive asset prices down by starting ugly rumors and spreading outright lies. As a result, short-selling isn't a game for the faint of heart.

The Modern (Markowitz) Portfolio Theory (MPT; see Chapter 6) assumes that investors trade both long and short, using no-cost borrowing and lending. Most investors can't do that; in the real world, lenders charge borrowers interest, which many see as a flaw in the ivory-tower approach. But many hedge funds can come close.

Making Market Calls

A traditional hedge fund — namely, a long-short hedge fund (see the previous section) — hedges risk. A modern, lightly regulated partnership may enlist all sorts of risky strategies to increase return. As long as the fund doesn't closely correlate the risk with the other holdings in the portfolio, it can meet its goal of reducing risk. What's more, a strategy keyed off of market performance doesn't require the portfolio manager to determine how the market is moving.

But some investors want more. They want return tied to the market in one form only — a return that beats the market handily. But here's the thing: How do you call the market? In other words, how do you foresee the future? Anyone who can call the market consistently is retired to a beachfront estate in Maui, not running a hedge fund. Some hedge fund managers are close to affording a beach hideaway, but others are still trying to beat the market in order to get there. But how? How can a fund manager call the market in order to figure out how to position her portfolio? Magic? Tea leaves? Astrology? Or hardcore analysis? Maybe a little of each strategy, and it's a perilous enterprise.

Predicting the market is nearly impossible to do in the long run. Money managers try to predict the future all the time, but almost all fail, whether they're running hedge funds or other investment portfolios. Don't expect a hedge fund you're interested in to beat the market, and be leery of a fund manager who claims to be a seer. Instead, think about how the hedge fund will help you manage risk.

In this section, I describe some of the things that hedge fund managers look for when they make decisions about buying and selling securities.

Investing with event-driven calls

An *event-driven* manager looks at situations he expects to happen in the market, guesses how the market will react, and invests accordingly. A manager always has two moving pieces when making event driven calls: predicting the event and determining what the market expects the event to be.

For example, say a country has an election coming up, and political pundits (and your fund manager) expect the socialist candidate to lose. If that happens, financial experts expect the currency to appreciate and the stock market to rally. Two predictions are at play: the outcome of the election and the market's response to that outcome. Both have some probability of happening, but neither is 100-percent certain. The fund manager has a few choices. She can analyze the current situation and make a bet based on her conclusions. For example, if she thinks that the socialist candidate will lose, she can buy stock traded in that country in advance of the election. Or she can design trades based on either election outcome — one long, based on the socialist candidate losing, and one short, based on the socialist candidate winning — and then hold them until the news is announced, acting on them only at that point.

Taking advantage of market timing

A hedge fund manager who *times* the market allocates different portions of his portfolio to different asset classes (see Chapter 9 for more on asset classes). The exact proportion for each class varies with different market indicators. The idea is to have plenty of money in assets that the fund manager expects to do well and to put less money in assets that aren't supposed to do as well. The difference between a market-timing strategy and an event-driven strategy (see the previous section) is that an event-driven manager looks for individual securities that he expects to do well based on specific events; the market timer looks for changes in general economic trends, such as inflation and unemployment — often signaled by technical indicators — which would show up on stock trading charts analyzed by using technical analysis (see Chapter 5 for more information on technical analysis).

Market timing can be used long or short. Some long-short hedge fund managers decide what portion of their portfolio they'll invest outright and what part they'll short, based on their analysis of where the market will go.

Technical analysis doesn't necessarily involve computers, although funds often use technology. Technical analysis is more accurately an examination of recent market prices. Technical analysts believe that past price behavior signals upcoming changes in price trends.

Market calls: A sample trade

A hedge fund's portfolio manager allocates 10 percent of the fund's holdings to euro-denominated cash equivalents, 40 percent to U.S. stock, and 50 percent to Japanese stock. As a part of technical analysis, the portfolio manager uses a complex econometric model that signals an upcoming decline in economic conditions in Japan, which would cause the value of the Japanese stocks to go down and the euro to become more valuable against the yen. The manager sells the equivalent of 60 percent of the portfolio as Japanese stock, shorting some of the fund's position, and invests the proceeds into euros.

Putting the Power of Leverage to Use

Even a simple investing strategy — such as buying stocks in the S&P 500 index in the same proportion in order to replicate the index's performance (the classic index fund) — can take on new risk and return levels through the use of *leverage*. Maybe you've heard the phrase "using other people's money"; that's what leveraging is. An investor borrows money to make an investment, getting maximum return for a minimal amount of cash up front. Of course, this strategy can also lead to a maximum loss.

The following sections show you how to use leverage in an equity portfolio to maximize return. But be forewarned: It's a strategy that also increases your risk.

Buying on margin

The simplest way to use leverage is to borrow money from the brokerage firm that holds the investment account — called buying securities *on margin*. (**Note:** You should never invest with a fund that doesn't use a brokerage firm; see Chapter 18 for more on due diligence.) The Federal Reserve Board sets the amount that a hedge fund can borrow (the margin requirement is one of the Fed's many tools for maintaining financial stability). As of press time, the Board requires individual investors to have 50 percent of the purchase prices on account at the time they place their margin orders; they may borrow the rest of the money from their brokerage firms. Hedge funds and other large investors are often allowed to borrow more. You should ask about how a hedge fund manager uses leverage as part of your due diligence (see Chapter 18).

Many brokerage firms set house limits on the total amount that hedge funds can borrow from them, even with 50 percent of their purchase prices on account. The house limits protect the firms from the collapse of their larger borrowers.

After the leverage takes place, the margin borrower must meet ongoing margin requirements. As the security bought on margin fluctuates in price, the 50-percent purchase-price level kept on account may fall to only 30 percent of the money owed. In this case, the borrower gets a margin call and has to add money to the account to get it back to the minimum maintenance level. If not, the brokerage firm will cash out the borrowed position. The New York Stock Exchange (NYSE) and National Association of Securities Dealers (NASD) set minimum margin requirements, although many brokerage firms have the ability to set higher levels based on their risk-management requirements and their comfort levels with the clients.

Leverage through margin: A sample loan

A certain hedge fund buys $10,000 worth of MicroWidget shares with $5,000 of its own cash and with $5,000 leveraged. MicroWidget trades at $25 per share, so the fund purchases a total of 400 shares. The interest rate on the margin loan is 10 percent. The following table shows what happens as the stock price changes.

Ending Price	Ending Value	Loan Value	Net Equity	Maintenance Margin	Interest Expense	Rate of Return	% Change in Stock Price
$40	$16,000	$5,000	$11,000	69%	$500	110%	60%
$25	$10,000	$5,000	$5,000	50%	$500	−10%	0%
$15	$6,000	$5,000	$1,000	17%	$500	−90%	−40%

Notice that if the stock goes up from $25 to $40 — an increase of 60 percent — the rate of return on the investor's money goes up 110 percent. That's because much of the money is borrowed. But note that interest still has to be paid, which means that if the stock price is flat, the investor is out the interest. And if the stock goes down? The investor loses money from the stock price and has to pay interest, dragging a 40-percent decline in stock price down to a 90-percent loss on investment.

In other words, leverage increases potential return but also potential risk.

As long as a borrowed security appreciates by more than the cost of the borrowing, the margin position makes money. But, because the borrowing fund has to pay interest, margin buying is a money-losing proposition if the security doesn't go up.

Gaining return with other forms of borrowing

A hedge fund has other tools besides its brokerage firm to lift potential return — and potential risk. Larger hedge funds can find banks, financial institutions, and even other hedge funds willing to lend them money that they can use to buy securities. If you're investing in a hedge fund, you should expect that the fund has more sources of funds than just margin accounts.

Long-Term Capital Management, a hedge fund that notoriously collapsed in the summer of 1998, followed a relatively conservative investment strategy — other than the fact that it relied almost entirely on borrowed money. The money was borrowed from many different banks and brokerage firms. When the loans were called for repayment, the firm had to sell its underlying securities at low prices, which caused the fund to fall apart. The borrowing turned a conservative investment strategy into one with high risk (see Chapter 1 for more on this hedge fund).

Private banks often loan hedge fund investors money to get into a fund or a fund of funds (see Chapter 15). In this case, the investor's personal wealth is leveraged over and above whatever leverage the fund has. The same risks apply: If the investment goes up, the loan leads to a greater rate of return, but if the investment heads south, the investor still has to repay the loan.

Chapter 12

Observing How Hedge Funds Profit from the Corporate Life Cycle

In This Chapter

▶ Breaking down the corporate structure

▶ Taking advantage of the corporate life cycle

C ompanies form, grow, slow down, and eventually die, and investors often take advantage of the steps in this process. Start-up companies need venture capital and loans; mergers need financing and offer arbitrage situations (see Chapter 10); savvy investors can short ailing stocks (see Chapter 11); and the assets of bankrupt companies can be liquidated at a profit for people who buy at the bottom (see Chapter 10).

As you may be able to tell from the terminology I use in the previous list, hedge funds play a huge role in the life cycle of companies. Many hedge funds have plenty of money to invest; they have the ability to borrow even more; they don't have to fund regular cash withdrawals, which means they can make longer-term investments; and they sometimes take big risks in the hope of generating even bigger returns.

In this chapter, I lay some groundwork by showing you, briefly, how companies are structured, and then I explain how hedge funds make money off the corporate life cycle. If you want to invest in a hedge fund, you need to know about these strategies so that you have a better understanding of what a particular hedge fund may be doing. The more you know, the better your questions will be, and you'll make better decisions with your money.

Examining the Corporate Structure (And How Hedge Funds Enter the Picture)

Hedge funds buy and sell securities based on corporate assets, and they participate in corporate finance activities as companies move from start-up to bankruptcy. But what does that mean? Well, allow me to get a little corporate-finance information out of the way first. Companies have *assets,* which are the goods they use to generate profit. Assets can be classified as

- ✔ **Tangible assets:** Like real estate, machine tools, and computers. Some tangible assets are listed on the company's balance sheet at the prices that the company paid for them, even if the company purchased the assets decades or centuries ago. Other assets are adjusted for ongoing depreciation, leading to an accounting value that may be very different from the actual value.

- ✔ **Intangible assets:** Like trademarks, patents, and secret formulas. Intangible assets aren't valued at all unless the company purchased them from someone else.

Because of accounting practices, a company's balance sheet may have no relation to what its assets are actually worth. Coca-Cola's secret formula, for example, has no value as far as Generally Accepted Accounting Principles (GAAP) are concerned. (The GAAP are the accounting policies used by American corporations that must report to the U.S. Securities and Exchange Commission.)

Companies use assets to generate revenue — to produce goods or services that people are willing to pay for. To buy assets, a company's management team has two choices: equity or debt. If the company issues equity, such as shares of common stock, it takes in other owners, but it has no obligation to repay them. If the management team decides to take on debt, such as bonds, it takes out a loan that it must pay back.

In an efficient market, security prices should reflect all known information about a company's value and its prospects. But, as you may be able to attest from your battles with work productivity, there are limits to efficiency, and these limits create opportunities for investors. (You can find out more about market efficiency in Chapter 6.)

Investors, such as hedge funds, buy stocks and bonds in order to make money. If an investor buys enough stock in a company to take control, the investor or investment team may be able to convince the company's management to make changes that would make more money for the investor(s). If an investment fund owns a lot of the company bonds, and the company misses a payment, the fund becomes the owner and has a say in the way the company is shut down or turned around. The following sections dig deeper into the corporate structure and show how investment decisions factor into company proceedings.

Observing the relationship between owners and managers

The owners of a large company — the people who have stock — elect a board of directors, which in turn hires the company's management team. The board and the management team are expected to act as agents for the owners, but they don't always have the same incentives to behave. The resulting issue is known as the *principal-agent problem*. Some hedge fund managers look for corporate situations where managements don't act on the shareholders' behalf; the fund managers can try to make changes — if the funds own enough stock in the companies — that will create profits for the funds.

For example, as of press time, Carl Icahn owned approximately 3 percent of Time-Warner through his hedge fund. He was pushing with the company's CEO, Richard Parsons, to break up the company in hopes of raising the stock price, which would generate a big profit for Icahn and the other investors in his fund.

Obviously, the owners and managers of a company don't have a marriage made in heaven. Owners and managers have conflicting interests. The agents, or management, want to maximize their personal pay scales and prestige levels, even if their goals cause them to make decisions that aren't in the owners' best interests. For example, Enron's executives made a ton of money before that company's stock tanked.

However, owners aren't always looking out for the best interests of the company, either. Bondholders want paid, and they put pressure on the company to improve cash flow now instead of investing in the future. Shareholders often want to maximize short-term profits, so they pressure the company to hit a quarterly earnings number, even if it means destroying the long-run viability of the business. For example, Enron's shareholders didn't complain about the company's behavior when its stock price was going up, even though many of the company's shenanigans were disclosed in its Securities and Exchange Commission (SEC) filings.

Pitting business skills versus investment skills

Many fund managers try to make changes within companies (provided they own enough stock in the companies) to create profits for their funds. This strategy introduces quite a wrinkle: The skills required to run a business are very different from those required to make investment decisions. This could create problems for the hedge fund manager who succeeds in taking over control of a business.

Management decisions versus investment decisions

Folks in the investment business tend to be decisive. If they see a problem with a position, they sell it. Boom! Out of there and on to the next trade. They don't worry much about history, looking instead to today's opportunities and tomorrow's possibilities.

People operating a company, on the other hand, have to concentrate on keeping the team motivated, along with the following responsibilities:

- They have to keep customers happy.
- They have to think through problems, because the people associated with the company have to live with the effects of management's decisions for a long time.
- They have to worry about the reputation of the business and the strength of the brand.

Hedge funds as business managers

So, what does the difference between management decisions and investment decisions have to do with hedge funds and you? Well, in some cases, hedge funds are taking large enough positions in companies that they assume management roles.

For example, in 2004, Kmart announced its acquisition of Sears. ESL Investments, a hedge fund managed by Edward Lampert, controls Kmart, and Lampert is now calling the shots at Sears. He has improved the company's profitability by cutting costs and closing stores, but sales have declined under his watch. Is that good or bad? What does it mean for the short run and the long run? Hard to say. A company can't stay in business if it keeps losing money, but it also can't stay afloat if it has no customers.

Given that the skills needed for running a business and making an investment are very different, be sure you check out the skills of a hedge fund manager who shows interest in operating a company owned by the fund! You can check a manager's skills during a due-diligence meeting with a prospective fund (see Chapter 18).

From Ventures to Vultures: Participating in Corporate Life Cycles

For many years, money managers would raise money from investors with a specific type of investment strategy in mind. For example, they would invest only in start-up companies, in distressed debt of companies near bankruptcy, or in mergers and acquisitions. The problem with this dedicated investment strategy is that markets run in cycles.

When the economy is strong, entrepreneurs are more likely to start their own companies, so they need venture capital. When the economy is in trouble, existing companies are more likely to have financial problems, so investors can find more distressed debt in the marketplace. The managers of funds dedicated to one strategy would have to return money to their investors because they had no place to invest it, and the investors would be disappointed because they didn't get the risk and return that they wanted in their overall portfolios.

This is where hedge funds come riding in on the white horse. Hedge funds can offer investors a level of expected return for a given level of risk, but they rarely lock in to just one kind of investment strategy. Rather than being a venture-capital-only fund, a manager may set up a hedge fund to invest in publicly traded or private-equity companies, either long or short (in other words, either owning securities or selling borrowed shares in hopes that the prices will fall; see Chapter 11), by using derivatives or leverage (see Chapters 5 and 11). That type of investment policy still sets limits for the fund manager, but the limits aren't so narrow that the fund can't meet its investor's objectives.

Given the inherent flexibility and current popularity of hedge funds, it's no surprise that they're taking on a big role in corporate transactions — ranging from venture capital and project finance to takeovers. What this means for you, a prospective investor, is that the hedge fund you're interested in may be taking roles in corporate transactions. In the following sections, I describe these transactions so you'll understand what a hedge fund that follows this type of strategy is doing with your money.

The many stages of the corporate life cycle give hedge funds plenty of opportunities to make money. Some funds concentrate on corporate finance transactions, and others view that strategy as one of many ways to make money. Hedge funds aren't mutual funds. No one type of fund is suitable for all investors, and no one type of investor is suitable for any given type of fund.

Identifying venture capital and private equity as hedge-fund investments

Venture capital, sometimes known as *private equity,* is money given to entrepreneurs to fund new companies — money that comes with strings attached. An investor who gives the money wants to ensure that the business succeeds. For example, it isn't uncommon for venture capitalists to make their investments on the condition that the founders leave their companies so seasoned managers can replace them. Hedge funds often invest in venture capital.

Although their styles may seem pushy, venture investments can help a company grow faster than it could otherwise, and investors can bring expertise — and potential clients — to the start-ups. Some of America's biggest technology companies, like Intel, Oracle, Apple, and Google, were started with venture capital. The payoff to those investors (and investors in those investors) was huge, which is the attraction of the investment.

Return is a function of risk (see Chapter 6). Venture investors count on acquiring some companies that will fail in their portfolios, offset by the few companies that hit it big.

Venture capital comes in different forms. Investors from a hedge fund may give the money to a young company as equity, making the hedge fund one of the owners of the company. The capital can also be debt that converts into equity if the company goes public or sells out to a larger company. The structure depends on the start-up company's business and state of profitability.

Venture-capital investors need a liquidity event to make money. This event occurs when a company is sold to a larger one or when it issues stock through an Initial Public Offering, or IPO. Until that event happens, the venture investor won't make much money.

The following list presents the most common forms of venture capital that you're likely to encounter when scoping out hedge funds (including private equity, which deals with established companies, making it not quite venture capital, but close):

> ✔ **Late-stage venture.** After a new company gets over the initial hurdles of setting up the business and attracting customers, it becomes a lot more interesting to investors, who see a little less risk with some huge upside. The company still needs more money to grow, and it still isn't ready to go public or to be acquired. Investing at a later stage makes a lot of sense for hedge funds that want to make private equity investments, but not as primary business strategies.

✔ **Mezzanine capital.** When a young company needs just enough financing to move it to the stage where it can go public or be an attractive acquisition, it needs *mezzanine financing*. Mezzanine capital is the least risky stage of venture capital (although it's still riskier than investing in a public company) because a company's management has proved that the business is viable. The company just needs a little more time before it can appear on the stock markets because the current market conditions would limit how much money the company could make. Returns are likely to be higher with a company at this stage than with public companies, though, so this stage of venture investing is interesting to hedge funds.

✔ **Private equity.** Many established companies choose not to be publicly traded; other companies are publicly traded but can't raise money efficiently through a public offering. These companies turn to *private equity deals,* often with hedge funds on the other side. These transactions carry lower potential returns than venture capital because they carry less risk (the company is established), but they often carry higher returns than shares of common stock in similar companies because it's harder to sell private equity.

Private investments in public equity, deals that sometimes go by the acronym PIPE, are less common than conventional private equity deals because companies that are already publicly traded issue them. Issuing public stock is expensive, though, and it's sometimes prohibitive for a public company to raise more money that way. A private investment in public equity allows a company to sell more stock, but only to accredited investors (including hedge funds) who agree not to sell for at least two years. This is just one of many types of offbeat investments that you may come across while you're investigating hedge funds.

✔ **Seed capital.** Money used to take an idea and turn it into a business is called *seed capital.* Some hedge funds provide seed capital, but only if they know the people and technology involved. For the most part, entrepreneurs have to fund companies themselves or with money from friends and family (sometimes called *angel investors*). With that money, they can prove their concepts to be sound and get their companies running before they turn to other investors for expansion funds.

Few hedge funds do seed capital deals. Because they aren't in the primary business of venture capital, most hedge funds prefer to wait to see if a company has a chance of surviving.

Project finance: Are hedge funds replacing banks?

When a company needs to borrow money, it can go to a bank, or it can go to an investment fund that has money to lend and that's looking to make a return on it. On the flip side of the coin, when a company has excess money and wants to make a return on it, it can deposit the money at a bank, or it can loan the money to an investment fund that needs it.

Hedge funds may have money to lend, or they may need money to invest. When it comes to short-term transactions — sometimes as short as overnight — hedge funds often replace banks in the role of taking deposits and lending money. When they lend money, hedge funds are paid interest, which contributes to the return of the fund.

Corporations may turn to hedge funds rather than banks for all sorts of reasons, including the following:

- ✔ A company may need to borrow money for a day or two in order to meet payroll until its customers pay their bills.

- ✔ Company executives may need funds for a specific, risky project, and a hedge fund manager may be more willing to take on the risk than a bank's loan officer.

- ✔ In the event of a corporate takeover — especially a hostile one (see the section "Investing in troubled and dying companies with vulture funds" later in this chapter) — the buying group needs to raise a lot of money.

- ✔ Commercial or investment banks may not have the money to lend, or they may not be able to lend because they have relationships with the target companies. Hedge fund managers can turn over their funds at prices that make the deals worthwhile for them.

Hedge funds borrow money from banks, and they compete with them at the same time. It's unclear if the banks will let this situation go on forever, but for now, you may well be able to take advantage of it through your hedge-fund investment.

Borrowing

Most hedge funds use *leverage* to increase their potential return, which means that they borrow money to buy securities, increasing the amount of money that they can make relative to the amount of money actually in the funds. Hedge fund managers are always looking to make the largest possible amount of money at the lowest possible rate. They borrow from other hedge funds, from banks, from brokerage firms, and sometimes from large corporations (see Chapter 11 for more on leveraging).

Many corporations have money sitting around that they won't need for a few days. A company's executives want to get the maximum possible return on their funds, so they lend the money out, often only overnight. But for the hedge fund on the other side of the transaction, overnight may be exactly enough time to take advantage of a profitable price discrepancy between two securities. The borrowed funds may allow for a small profit in percentage terms to become a large profit relative to the fund's total size. Because it's unlikely (but not out of the question) that the borrower will go out of business in such a short period, this type of transaction carries very little risk.

Lending

One way a hedge fund manager tries to generate a high rate of return relative to a given level of risk is to keep the fund's holdings earning returns at all times. Therefore, if he sees money in one account that isn't being used for one of the fund's investments, he may decide to loan it out, even for a short period, to get some amount of return. Hedge funds receive interest when they loan out money; of course, the funds take on the risk that the borrowers won't repay the money.

Some hedge fund managers are willing to loan out money for longer periods of time — even a few years — to corporations or governments that need money. They can do this by buying bonds (as can any investor, because bonds are simply tradable loans), or they can make loans through private transactions. They can create all kinds of risk and return combinations by lending money, depending on the funds' goals and the market opportunities.

Gaining return from company mergers and acquisitions

Companies are bought and sold all the time. Certain companies decide to join forces with other companies instead of going it alone. Large companies buy smaller companies in order to build market share, add links in the supply chain, or expand internationally. In other words, a *merger* is a combination of equals, and an *acquisition* is the purchase of a smaller business by a larger one.

Acquisitions take place all the time. Most big mergers, on the other hand, don't work out over the long run, but that doesn't mean they don't happen. And no matter the long-term prospects of a merger or acquisition, in the short term, there's money to be made. Hedge funds, which are in the business of making money, are often players in mergers and acquisitions by providing funding and speculating on the outcomes. The following sections outline certain situations funds look for and the strategies they use to increase return and put money in your pocket.

Leveraged (management) buyouts

Sometimes, a company's management group becomes fed up with its share-holders and the hassles of having publicly traded shares. The members of the group have reason to believe they could make more money if they ran the company themselves, so they decide to raise the money to take over. Because it involves heavy borrowing, this type of transaction is called a *leveraged buyout* (LBO) in the United States; because the management group is doing the buying, the transaction is called a *management buyout* (MBO) in Europe.

Many hedge funds invest in LBO debt because it tends to be riskier than most corporate debt. The risk comes from the management group's decision to borrow most or all of the money needed for the acquisition.

Buyout funds

Buyout funds are investment pools formed by hedge fund managers and other private investors for the express purpose of funding leveraged buyouts (see the previous section) and business expansions. Like venture capital funds (see the section "Identifying venture capital and private equity as hedge-fund investments"), buyout funds tend to go in and out of fashion, and funds often see mismatches between the amount of money raised to invest in buyouts and the need for buyout capital.

Some hedge fund managers consider investing in buyouts to be one of many strategies at their disposal for generating alpha (the excess return that hedge funds seek to generate due to manager performance; see Chapter 6 for more information). They can provide funding in buyout situations, invest in junk bonds (which offer higher returns than regular bonds; see Chapter 5), and then move on to other strategies when market conditions change. The new strategies may be related to buyouts — a fund manager who invests in buyouts will probably be interested in other forms of corporate finance and debt rather than currency transactions or commodity pools — but they'll help the funds meet their return objectives regardless of the business cycle. It's unlikely that you'll come across a hedge fund dedicated solely to buyouts; instead, it will be one of many strategies that a hedge fund manager may use.

Bridge lending

Hedge funds that want to loan money may work with companies that are looking to acquire other companies. At least in the short run, a company looking to acquire may need some financing to acquire shares in the market or otherwise support its bid for another company. A loan from a hedge fund in this situation is called a *bridge loan* or *bridge financing*. Bridge loans usually have terms of less than one year and carry higher interest rates than other forms of short-term financing not available to the company, for whatever reason. A bridge loan is one of many investments that a hedge fund may consider to meet its risk and return objectives.

Merger arbitrage

Merger arbitrage is a low-risk trading strategy designed to profit after a corporate merger or acquisition is announced (see Chapter 10 for more on the topic). In general, the shares of the company about to be acquired trade at a discount to the offer price because you take on some risk that the deal won't go through. A hedge fund trader buys the stock of the target company and sells the stock of the acquirer, waiting until the deal is announced for the gap to close at a nice profit.

Investing in troubled and dying companies with vulture funds

Insiders often use a slang term for investment pools that seek out troubled businesses and troubled countries — *vulture funds.* In some ways, vulture funds are the opposite of venture capital funds: The venture funds profit as the companies get going, and vulture funds are there to profit at the end of the corporate life cycle.

Many hedge fund managers run their funds as vulture funds at least some of the time, but they probably don't like that label for their strategy. If a fund's traders see that a nation's currency has weakened or that some bonds are in risk of default, they swoop in, buy as much as they can, and then use their positions as negotiating leverage to get a profit for the fund. Fund traders may also take large positions in the equity and debt of a troubled company and then force management to sell off divisions and other assets.

Other hedge funds inadvertently take on the vulture-fund role. For example, a fund may have a large stake in the debt of a company that goes bankrupt, giving the fund manager a stake in the proceedings. Naturally, his goal is to get the maximum possible return (which may be the smallest loss).

Several investment strategies prey on troubled businesses, including hostile takeovers, liquidation arbitrage, and shareholder activism, to name a few. I cover these strategies and more in the following sections.

Hostile takeovers

A *hostile takeover* occurs when a company or an investment group acquires enough common stock in a company to get control of its board of directors. In some cases, the company or investment group believes that it can operate the business more profitably. In other cases, the acquirer simply wants to sell off the company's assets at a profit.

A hedge fund may offer financing to another takeover group, or it can buy enough stock to be a part of one. Both strategies can be profitable, so I discuss some of the nuances of takeovers in the following subsections.

Hostility is in the eyes of the beholder. Employees of the doomed company may see a takeover bid as hostile, but the management group sees a payout and the shareholders see a nice profit.

Section 13(d) filings

Under Section 13(d) of the Securities Exchange Act of 1934, an investment group has to file a notice with the United States Securities and Exchange Commission as soon as it acquires 5 percent or more of a company's stock. A filing investor needs to indicate if the holding is for investment purposes (in which case the filing falls under Section 13[g]) or is part of an attempt to influence a company's management or to seek control (a 13[d] filing).

After a hedge fund manager files a 13(d) statement, he makes his fund's intentions public, and the stock price of the company to be taken over will react. The news reaction may put pressure on the company's management, so the fund manager may try to negotiate with management before he files the paperwork. He can take a couple different paths here:

- ✔ He may ask the company to buy back stock in the open market, pay a dividend, or sell off a division to increase the value of the stock.

- ✔ He may make an offer for the rest of the shares, which management and the board of directors may accept on their behalf (see the following section).

In some cases, a 13(d) filing inspires other investors to come forward and identify themselves if they have opinions on the validity of the hedge fund manager's request. If the stock has been underperforming the market, for example, other investors will probably side with the fund, putting more pressure on management to make changes. One example of this happened with Pep Boys, the auto-service company. In August 2006, a group of four hedge funds got together to force the company to add more directors to its board and make changes to its shareholder-rights policies.

Tender offers

If negotiations with a company's management group fail, the investment group organizing the hostile takeover turns to a tender offer. A *tender offer* is a legal offer to buy shares, usually at a price above the current market price. The offer is distributed to all shareholders, and they can decide if the tender is a good deal or if they'd rather stay put.

A hedge fund may be behind the tender offer, or it may provide funding to a hostile bidder so that she can buy the shares that are tendered to her. Another option is that the fund could engage in arbitrage between the tender price and the current market price (see Chapter 10). Tender offers are rare, but they present a range of money-making opportunities for hedge fund managers who want to pick them up.

Liquidation arbitrage

Liquidation arbitrage is an investment technique that looks to profit from the breakup of a firm (see Chapter 10 for more on the topic). An investor does careful research to determine exactly how a company's market value differs from the value of the sum of its parts. The investor seeks to find out certain pieces of information, such as the following:

- ✔ Are people overlooking the value of the firm's real estate?
- ✔ Does the company have an art collection that could fetch a fancy price at auction?
- ✔ Does the company have patents that could be really useful to another company?
- ✔ Does the corporation hold mineral rights in a region where oil has just been discovered?

And so on. If the investment fund, often a hedge fund, finds an opportunity where the actual value of the company looks very different from the market value, the fund can acquire enough shares to force management to break the company up or at least sell off some of the assets at a gain for shareholders.

Liquidation arbitrage is perfectly legal as long as it isn't based on material nonpublic information. Many analysts rely on what's called the *mosaic theory,* which holds that small pieces of immaterial nonpublic information can be pieced together to make a legal investment decision. The problem is how to define materiality. The courts have generally defined *material information* as information that would make a rational investor buy or sell a security. In practice, most insider-trading cases — some of which have featured merger and liquidation arbitrageurs — involve plea bargains before trial or charges on provable information. Martha Stewart, for example, went to prison for obstruction of justice, not for insider trading.

Activist investing

Many hedge fund managers who work in supposed "vulture funds" prefer to be known as *shareholder activists,* which are investors who push management groups to make changes for the good of the businesses, the employees, and the shareholders. Both true activists and raiders who don the activist guise are in the news a lot these days.

The leader in activist-investing circles is the California Public Employees Retirement System, also known as CalPERS. It controls $207 billion in assets, which it uses to provide pensions to 1.4 million people who work for state and local governments in California. Outside money managers oversee most of the money, including investors at several different hedge funds, but CalPERS executives keep close watch on where the money goes. Starting in 1987, CalPERS created an annual list of six or so companies that had poor performances, due in large part to problems with management and corporate governance. CalPERS executives made it clear to these companies that they expected changes or they'd put their votes to work. Many others in the investment world are willing to align with CalPERS against management teams because CalPERS has a reputation for being credible and effective.

Proxy battles

A public company is structured as a democracy, at least in theory, with each share of stock representing a vote in the company. Companies send ballot statements called *proxies* to their shareholders each year, giving shareholders the opportunity to vote on the members of the boards of directors, executive compensation plans, and certain other matters. The members of the boards then determine other aspects of running the businesses, including hiring management, developing long-range strategies, and approving acquisitions.

In practice, a public company isn't very democratic. If an outsider, such as a hedge fund, acquires enough shares in the company, it can often have proposals added to the proxy and can present its own slate of candidates for the board of directors — candidates who presumably would push for big changes upon election. The outside fund that takes this course has to convince folks who hold a majority of the shares to vote with it. Proxy battles rarely succeed in getting new directors elected, but they often push management to make needed changes in the running of the company.

Chapter 13

Macro Funds: Looking for Global Trends

. . . .

. . . .

*O*ur big world is constantly changing. Nations develop their economies, and nations decline. Interest rates go up in some places and down in others. Currency prices change, commodity prices fluctuate, and governments are overthrown. The one thing that remains constant is that many hedge fund managers want to profit from all the upheaval.

When looking at the way nations function, economists talk about *macroeconomics*. Macroeconomic factors include prices, employment, inflation, industrial production, corporate profits, tax receipts, imports, and exports. Funds based on macroeconomic factors are known as *macro funds*. (For whatever reason, everyone likes the slang term better; you hear "macro" more than "macroeconomic," so that's what I use here.)

Some of the biggest and most glamorous hedge funds are macro funds. Good macro funds tend to be huge because they need a lot of capital to take positions all over the world, and they need to generate high fees to cover their operating costs. Because of their size, macro funds tend to deal mostly with the largest investment institutions and the wealthiest individuals. Examples of macro funds include funds run by such legendary managers as George Soros and Julian Robertson, whose returns drew people's attention to hedge funds. Macro funds such as these are the funds that dictators complain about, that traders want to work for, and that end up in the headlines.

By looking at securities around the world, hedge fund managers can often increase returns relative to domestic stocks, with an entirely different risk profile. Macro funds invest in the markets, currencies, and commodities that the world market expects to do well and sell short those securities that have a less-than-rosy outlook (see Chapter 11 for more on shorting). Some macro funds have had an enormous effect on exchange rates in certain developing countries. Because of that, a macro hedge fund is often reviled in the popular media. Is that fair? That's for you to decide.

In this chapter, I discuss how fiscal and monetary policy affect investment values, highlight the issues that are unique to macro funds, and talk about currency and commodity investments, which are especially popular with macro investors. After reading this chapter, you'll have a better understanding of what macro funds do to reach their risk and return goals.

Fathoming Macroeconomics

Macroeconomic factors play together in different ways, and a fund can't look at a single factor alone. For example, when employment is low, so is inflation, in general. After all, workers don't have money to buy anything if they're not working. High levels of industrial production are great, unless the workers are producing items that people don't want. Low taxes may stimulate businesses to produce more profits and give individual consumers more money to spend, or they may deprive a government from the money it needs to function or lead to government employees who demand large bribes to offset paltry salaries.

 Political decisions that have nothing to do with how markets function can muddy macroeconomic analysis. Watch out for a hedge fund manager who applies the conventional wisdom of his home country or his favorite political party; he may make really bad decisions overseas.

An analysis of macroeconomics can bring the expectations of a given country's economy to light, possibly pointing a hedge fund manager toward money-making opportunities. An analysis can also drop hints about how a government may respond to different economic events. And yes, governments have a few tools at their disposal, too — namely fiscal policy and monetary policy. I cover these topics in the sections that follow.

Focusing on fiscal policy

Governments collect taxes to spend on running their countries and on infrastructure investments, such as highways, airports, and sanitation systems. As much as some idealists like to believe in free and unfettered capitalism, some of these functions are necessary. For example, a country with a government that enforces intellectual property is a better place for a technology business than a country where piracy is rampant. Also, a nation without good public schools won't have a large number of highly productive workers.

The key for an administration is to balance taxes with the needs for government services. If taxes are too high, businesses won't invest. If taxes are too low, governments can't provide necessary services.

If a government doesn't raise enough money from taxes, however, it can borrow from investors, including hedge funds, by issuing bonds. If the borrowed money goes into good infrastructure investments, the country's economy will be better off. Just as many individuals borrow money to buy houses that will provide years of shelter for their families, governments borrow money to build highways and modernize airports. On the other end of the spectrum, just as some individuals charge their credit cards up to the limits rather than cut back or find jobs that pay more, some governments borrow money when their politicians lack the will or the ability to increase taxes or cut spending. Government borrowing affects the supply of securities for investors to buy, the level of interest rates in an economy, and the infrastructure in a country.

Making moves with monetary policy

National governments have one huge tool for influencing the economy: the printing press. As long as it's willing and able to print money, a government can meet payments on all its debt. Monetary policy is a government's strategy for managing the money supply.

Hedge funds have other considerations when it comes to monitoring monetary policy across the globe. The following sections dive into these considerations.

Governments with too much money

The more money a government has in circulation, the more prices will rise because more money is chasing a smaller amount of goods. At an extreme, people need huge amounts of paper money to meet everyday expenses. After World War I, Germany was ordered to pay reparations to the countries that it targeted. Germany's leaders decided to print enough money to meet the payments, which drove down the value of all the money in the country. The result was hyperinflation, which drove prices higher. No wallet was big enough; people took sacks and wheelbarrows full of money to shops to buy groceries.

Many investors hold onto the belief that governments never default on their bonds because they can always print money to meet their loan payments. However, because printing extra money leads to high inflation at home, not all governments are willing to go this route. In the summer of 1998, Russia decided to default on its debt rather than print more money, which proved disastrous for Long-Term Capital Management, a hedge fund that had borrowed money to acquire exposure to Russian bonds and related securities (see Chapter 1 for a full rundown of this infamous hedge fund).

Governments with too little money

If too little money is circulating in a nation's economy, its banks and investors have no funds to give to businesses and individuals with worthwhile projects. Prices keep falling to levels where people can afford to buy goods, and in some cases, prices fall so low that companies can't stay in business. This economic state is called *deflation,* and the effects are more punishing than those of any increase in price levels (see Chapter 6 for more on the topic). The United States suffered from deflation in the 1930s, leading to a long period of high unemployment. Japan also had a long deflationary era in the 1990s and into the 21st century. Japan has avoided anything on the scale of the Great Depression, but the country has seen little economic growth or investment for years.

Money is more than currency

Because money comes in the form of credit cards, checks, electronic transfers, and paper and metal currency, the total amount of money in an economy can be very different from how much the Treasury prints up. This is one reason why hedge fund managers and other investors have so many securities available for investing.

Here's an example of how non-paper money works. As I write this book, I turn in the chapters to my editor. Whenever I hit a certain number of chapters, the folks at Wiley cut a paper check toward my advance and send it to my agent. My agent puts the money in her bank and then sends me a paper check for the advance less her fees. I take the paper check to my bank. Later in the month, I make several electronic transfers from my checking account to my credit card company, my utility companies, and the mutual fund company that holds my SEP-IRA account. I take out only a small part of the check in the form of cash for incidental expenses. If you look only at how much money I have in my wallet, you'd have a very bad idea of how much money I actually have.

Non-currency money and interest rates

One way that a government can influence all its non-currency forms of money is by manipulating interest rates. Some governments can do this by decree; others, like the United States, do it in more subtle ways. In the United States, the Federal Reserve Bank (often called the Fed) requires that all member banks keep a certain percentage of their total deposits in the form of currency. If a bank needs more currency, it borrows from the Federal Reserve Bank; the rate charged is the *Fed discount rate*. If a bank has too much paper money and coins on hand, it deposits the excess money with the Fed; the rate paid on this is the *Fed funds rate*. The Fed generally meets every six weeks to discuss the levels of these rates, a process that investors follow closely.

The Fed manipulates the economy by putting businesses, consumers, and investors on puppet strings, so to speak:

- ✔ If the Fed wants businesses, consumers, and investors to take money out of the economy and into savings, it raises the Fed funds rate. Banks, seeing that they can get better returns, raise the rates they pay on savings accounts to encourage customers to bring money in and put it on deposit.

- ✔ If the Fed wants businesses, consumers, and investors to spend more money, it raises the Fed discount rate, which encourages banks to lower their costs by lending out money rather than keeping funds in deposits.

The Fed sets the Fed funds rate and the Fed discount rate to move the economy in the direction that its Board of Governors thinks is most appropriate. Many other nations have central banks that behave in a similar way. A hedge fund manager who correctly anticipates central-bank movements can make a lot of money.

Here's an example: A manager sees that a nation's economy is growing really fast and predicts that inflation will become a factor in the future. She suspects that the nation's central bank will use its tools to increase interest rates in order to encourage people to save more and spend less, thus bringing prices down. If interest rates go up in the nation, bond prices will go down. Therefore, she decides to borrow money to buy put options on the bonds — a highly leveraged transaction that pays off when rates go up (see Chapter 5 for more on options and Chapter 11 for more on leveraging).

Taking Special Issues for Macro Funds into Consideration

Hedge fund managers consider several factors unique to macro funds, as well as some that apply to the asset classes (especially currency) most used by macro funds (see Chapter 9 for more on asset classes). The following sections cover the most common issues that funds are likely to encounter.

Diversified, yes. Riskless, no.

One of the best ways to hedge risk is to diversify (see Chapter 6 for a detailed discussion of risk). A macro fund does just that by investing in many different markets and by using many different asset classes to profit from expected changes in the global macroeconomy.

However, although a macro fund may hold a mix of currencies, commodities, index derivatives, and bonds, it retains exposure to the one or two factors that the hedge fund manager identifies as important. If a fund manager expects a shift in European interest rates, for example, his portfolio will reflect that position, and if the rates don't move as expected, the fund's performance can suffer (causing suffering for investors' wallets).

Global financial expertise

A macro fund manager needs to know a lot about many different places in the world. These managers tend to be steeped in practical economics — what drives inflation, what moves exchange rates, what trade deficits mean, and so on. They tend to have highly quantitative approaches to the market, caring more about raw numbers than the stories behind them. Macro managers are world travelers, but not always; they still have to love sitting on trading desks and making bets on market movements. A money manager with a statistics PhD who has never been out of the country may be a better macro manager than a polyglot with a worn-out passport. These are some things to think about during your due diligence (see Chapter 18).

Subadvisers

Some savvy macro hedge funds subcontract to local advisers in foreign markets to get on-the-ground perspectives. For example, an American may not understand the Mexican market as well as a Mexican who works in Mexico City, so a macro fund manager who wants to invest in that market may subcontract some of the money-management duties to a local investment company. This strategy may lead to higher fees for the fund, but you'll see the benefit when the fees are offset by higher returns.

The multinational conundrum

One of the more interesting aspects of the global economy is how few companies or countries operate in isolation. For example, the largest U.S., European, and Asian companies operate around the world. Shares of Coca-Cola, Unilever, and Sony are almost equally exposed within the economies of the United States, Europe, and Japan. American retailers depend on sourcing from China, and Chinese investors buy American government bonds.

This makes it tough, but not impossible, for a macro fund manager to isolate exposure to only one part of the world's economy. The trick is to carefully weight the fund and use derivatives (see Chapter 9). As often happens, the fund manager starts by running a regression model, which is a statistical analysis of how a security's price moves relative to other factors in the economy.

Here's an example: A macro fund manager believes that the European economy is going to improve, which will drive up prices of European stocks. She buys shares in the biggest companies on the continent and then runs a regression analysis to see how much exposure these stocks have to the U.S. and the Japanese stock markets. She sells futures on U.S. and Japanese market indexes to remove those risks from the portfolio (see Chapter 5 for more on futures and options).

Widening or Narrowing Your Macro Scope

Macro hedge fund managers look for opportunities at home and abroad. They don't like to be limited to any one asset class, as long as they can profit from fundamental economic changes. But the world is a big place, so many macro funds try to narrow their focus in the hopes that familiarity will help them identify opportunities before other market participants do. Many hedge funds that adopt the label "macro fund" are really somewhere between macro and micro.

When you research macro and other international funds, you may gain the following bits of knowledge:

- ✓ **Global funds invest everywhere.** A global fund is open to all markets in the world, including the fund's home market. A global fund based in the United States, for example, invests in U.S. assets as well as assets elsewhere in North America, South America, Europe, Africa, and Asia. This strategy gives the global fund manager the freedom to choose whatever markets present the best opportunities. On the flip side, it may not give you, the fund investor, the best diversification — especially if the rest of your portfolio concentrates on domestic assets.

✔ **International funds invest outside the home market.** Hedge funds that invest everywhere in the world but in the funds' domestic markets are known as *international funds*. These funds offer more diversification benefits for home-market investors, but they give the fund managers fewer options for investing.

✔ **Regional funds look at specific markets.** Many macro fund managers believe the investing world is too big, even when they exclude their domestic markets. These funds choose to pursue macro strategies, but they limit investments to only a few of the world's markets. Some of these funds are obvious in their intentions — Asia-Pacific funds invest in markets located in Asia and on the Pacific Ocean, for example — but others are less obvious, so I define them here (no need for thanks . . . I'm here for you!):

- **BRIC — Brazil, Russia, India, China:** BRIC funds are all the rage these days because Brazil, Russia, India, and China offer a combination of large and relatively well-educated populations, a move toward modernization from relatively undeveloped bases, and relatively stable governments that seem to be supporting capitalistic endeavors. Yet, these four nations are at early enough stages in development that investors have high growth expectations, and high premiums are paid in return for taking on the risk of investing in these markets.

- **EAFE** (pronounced EEE-fah): Short for Morgan Stanley Capital International's Europe, Australasia, and Far East index, EAFE captures the performance of the most developed markets in the world, making it a widely used approach to international investing. The approach leaves out many emerging markets, so an EAFE portfolio may limit growth opportunities.

- **Eurozone:** The definition of Europe seems obvious, but it isn't always. Some nations are physically located in Europe, some nations are members of the European Union, and some nations use the euro for currency. There's some overlap. The *Eurozone*, however, is a narrow definition that applies only to nations that use the euro, notably excluding the United Kingdom and Switzerland.

Big returns in foreign currency sometimes disappear when converted back to the home currency. The problem compounds if your home currency is different from the macro fund's. A macro hedge fund based in London that makes a killing in yen, for example, may not have such a stellar return for a U.S. investor after the yen convert to pounds and the pounds convert to dollars.

Coming to terms with currencies

Macro funds use *currencies* to capture the underlying economic changes in countries without creating too much of a ripple in the prices. They can follow this strategy because the currency markets dwarf the markets for other asset classes. As of press time, Microsoft's market capitalization is $280 billion; marketable U.S. government bonds total $4.3 trillion; but the U.S. money supply is $6.7 trillion.

This section discusses the trading of currencies and the factors that affect their values so you can better understand how hedge funds may use currencies to meet their risk and return goals.

Trading currencies

Hedge funds that want to make money from currencies can do it a few different ways, depending on market opportunities and the structure of their portfolios. For example, a fund can buy a currency straight up or it can work with derivatives. The following list outlines some options that macro funds have:

- ✔ **Spot:** If a fund pays the going price for a security and gets it immediately, this means that it has bought it in the spot market. The spot market for sandwiches is whatever the local sub shop charges you today for a sandwich today. The spot market for yen is whatever a bank charges you to exchange your dollars for yen today.

  Hedge funds buy and sell currencies in the spot market, often by transferring money between bank accounts in different markets. They can keep the money in those accounts and hold it until its value changes, or they can use the money to make other investments in the markets. Hedge funds can also borrow money in different markets (or *leverage* money; see Chapter 11); if they get their loan proceeds today, they've made *spot-market transactions*.

- ✔ **Derivatives:** *Derivatives* are contracts that draw their value from the value of underlying assets (you can find a description of derivatives in Chapter 5).

- ✔ **Options:** Currency options give a buyer the right, but not the obligation, to buy or sell a currency at a set exchange rate at some point in the future. These options allow macro fund managers to profit from changes in exchange rates without committing capital. They also allow funds to set up complex trades, which are the stock-in-trade of most macro funds.

- ✔ **Swaps:** A *swap* is an exchange of interest-rate payments in two different currencies. A swap allows you to better match your income with your expenses in a given currency, or it can allow you to increase your portfolio's exposure to a given currency, if that's feasible.

Exchange rate regimes

Much of my discussion in the section up to this point assumes that currencies are freely floating; however, they aren't in many markets. A *free-floating currency* goes up or down in value with supply and demand. If consumers want more of a currency — to buy a country's goods or to invest in that country's market — they're willing to pay more of their home currency to get the foreign currency they need. They can go this route only if the currency floats. The dollar, the euro, and the yen are among the largest free-floating currencies in the world.

Other currencies are *fixed* — a county's government sets the exchange rate and its central bankers are instructed to buy and sell securities and set interest rates as necessary to maintain the relationship. The Chinese yuan trades at a rate of eight yuan to one U.S. dollar, for example, and the rate barely fluctuates.

Some governments allow their currencies to fluctuate, but only within narrow bands. Of course, if investors have reason to believe that a government will allow its fixed-rate currency to float, or if investors believe the pegs used to set the exchange rate may change, they have the potential to make some handsome profit. For example, many people think that the yuan is grossly undervalued relative to the dollar as of this writing. The question is, how long will you have to wait until the Chinese government allows the exchange rate to go to six yuan per dollar?

Markets seem global in nature, but they aren't as closely linked as you may think. Many nations don't fully participate in world markets — ranging in size from China, where the currency doesn't freely fluctuate, to underdeveloped countries with painfully small and impoverished economies. On occasion, trades take place involving unusual assets, but these trades are usually negotiated (sometimes under the table) or come with high transaction costs. If a hedge fund manager tells you about great arbitrage opportunities (see Chapter 10) between the Malawi kwacha and the Chinese yuan during a discussion or due-diligence interview (see Chapter 18), you should be suspicious.

Determining exchange rates

An *exchange rate* is simply the price of money, and like all prices, supply and demand determines the rate. Simple enough, but what determines how much money is supplied and how much money is demanded? That's where things get a little more complicated. A hedge fund manager can use several different approaches to find out if exchange rates are out of line. If exchange rates are slightly off where they should be, a manager can engage in arbitrage, for example (see Chapter 10); if the rates are way off, she can take large speculative positions and wait for the necessary events to pass.

The more home currency it takes to buy a foreign currency, the more valuable the foreign currency is. If the foreign currency starts to cost less relative to the home currency, the foreign currency is said to be depreciating in value. For example, if 1 U.S. dollar buys 117 yen today, and if it can buy 125 yen a year from now, the price of yen has depreciated.

Interest-rate parity

Interest-rate parity says that you can explain the difference between two currencies with the difference in the market rate of interest in each country (which is the rate of interest that's currently quoted in that market). The ratio of the future rate (the rate for currency traded in the future) to the spot rate (the rate for currency traded today) should be the ratio of the home interest rate to the foreign interest rate. If an investor sees a difference, he can take advantage of an arbitrage opportunity (see Chapter 10 for more on arbitrage). And if a fund manager has reason to think that interest rates are going to change, he can use the relation between the future rate and the spot rate to take advantage by investing in currencies.

Here's an example of this process: Suppose you have $100,000 to invest for one year. You have two choices: You can invest the money at home at the current interest rate, or you can trade your money for foreign currency, invest in that country at its interest rate, and then hedge your exchange-rate risk by selling forward the future value of the foreign currency investment. Because both of these investments have the same risk, they must have the same future value, which means that the difference in the exchange rate is the difference in the interest rates.

Table 13-1 shows how this process works. In an efficient market (see Chapter 6 for more on efficiency), exchange rates should be set so that it doesn't matter what country you borrow from or lend money to; your proceeds should be the same after everything converts back.

Table 13-1	How Interest-Rate Parity Works	
	Canada	*United Kingdom*
Interest rate	5%	8%
Spot exchange rate	$1.00	£1.50
Forward exchange rate	$1.00	£1.48
Amount borrowed	$1,000,000	
Amount to be repaid in one year	$1,050,000	
Amount of currency purchased with the money	£666,667	
Amount after one year	£720,000	
Amount of Canadian dollars bought forward with U.K. money	$1,050,000	

The last figure is the £720,000 due at the end of the year, multiplied by the £1.48 forward rate.

Macro fund managers look for situations where interest rates and exchange rates differ. If the Canadian/U.K. exchange rate doesn't quite reflect expected differences in interest rates, a fund manager can convert Canadian funds to pounds and invest them in the U.K. and then exchange the proceeds at the forward rate to lock in a riskless profit. Sure, this strategy produces a small percentage gain, but if the manager couples it with a leverage strategy (the use of borrowed money to conduct the transaction; see Chapter 11), returns can be much greater. Table 13-2 presents this example.

Table 13-2	Using Interest-Rate Parity for an Exchange-Rate Arbitrage Play	
	Canada	*United Kingdom*
Interest rate	5%	8%
Spot exchange rate	$1.00	£1.50
Forward exchange rate	$1.00	£1.48
Amount borrowed	$1,000,000	
Amount to be repaid in one year	$1,050,000	
Amount of currency purchased with the money		£666,667
Amount in one year if invested in the U.K.		£720,000
Amount of Canadian dollars bought forward with U.K. investment proceeds	$1,065,600	
Profit on the transaction	1.49%	

The amount of Canadian dollars bought forward is the £720,000 due at the end of the year, multiplied by the £1.48 forward rate.

Purchasing-power parity

Purchasing-power parity is a weird concept. It says that a particular good made and sold in one country should cost exactly the same as the same good made and sold in another after the currency is translated.

For example, the Icelandic krona price of a sweater made in Iceland and sold in Iceland should be equal to the Icelandic krona price of a sweater made in Ireland and sold in Ireland. Otherwise, a savvy retailer would buy sweaters in a cheap market to sell them in a more expensive market. As you shoppers out there in reading land may know, these two sweaters could be very different — different styles, different grades of wool, different dye techniques, different brand names or logos, and so on. So, in the real world, it doesn't make much sense that these two sweaters should be the same sweaters, let alone trade at the same price.

There are two refinements of the basic concept of purchasing-power parity. The first looks at a list of goods rather than one specific item. You draw up a list of goods and services and shop around in Iceland in Icelandic krona and in Ireland in euros. If the Icelandic krona price of the Irish items is the same as the Icelandic krona price of the Icelandic items, purchasing-power parity holds up.

Editors at *The Economist,* a British newsweekly with an international reader base, have come up with a model of purchasing-power parity by using the McDonald's Big Mac, which is sourced locally, using local labor, but which is made to the exact same specifications everywhere in the world. If purchasing-power parity holds, a Big Mac in Boston should cost the same as a Big Mac in Bangkok. If not, there may be a discrepancy in the exchange rates that will correct over time. The Big Mac index isn't perfect, but it does point to gross inconsistencies in exchange rates that seem to correct over time. You can find a detailed explanation of how the Big Mac index works and historical records on its performance on the magazine's Web site, www.economist.com/markets/Bigmac/Index.cfm.

Of course, each market has its own culture and quirks. Some products simply aren't available in some places, and a staple in one place is a gourmet food in another. Therefore, researchers took the analysis of the parity concept a step further and looked at relative price levels between markets. This research led to the next refinement in purchasing-power parity: that exchange rates move by the expected difference in purchasing power, as measured by the difference in inflation between two countries.

Purchasing-power parity is one relationship that a macro hedge fund manager thinks about when looking at two markets. If a manager has reason to believe that price levels are going to change in a country, he knows that the changes will affect wages and employment, how much consumers will buy, and the price of the country's export goods. And all these factors end up affecting exchange rates.

For example, say an analysis of consumer-price indexes in Japan and Thailand indicates that the yen is overvalued relative to the Thai baht. A macro hedge fund manager takes advantage by short-selling yen and using the proceeds to buy baht (see Chapter 11 for more on short-selling).

The International Fisher Effect

Irving Fisher, an economist who studied the role of interest rates in economies, decided that because interest rates include levels of risk to an economy and a component for inflation, traders don't need to worry too much about what's causing changes in interest rates or price levels; they just need to make sure that the difference in rates is properly taken into account. He deduced that the difference in interest rates between two countries is the amount by which spot exchange rates are expected to change (see the section "Trading currencies" for more on spot rates).

The International Fisher Effect works like this. Say country A's interest rates fall from 5 percent to 4 percent. Country B's interest rates remain at 8 percent. Under the International Fisher effect, a 20-percent decline in country A's rates should cause country A's currency to increase by 20 percent relative to country B's currency. If this doesn't happen, a hedge fund manager could take advantage by acquiring country A's currency and shorting country B's (see Chapter 11).

Contemplating commodities

Commodities are the basic goods of life — natural resources and agricultural products that feed people and animals, fuel vehicles, go into manufactured items, and store value for future use. Some commodities are incredibly plentiful, and others draw their value from their scarcity. Commodities are popular with macro fund managers because their prices are set at the most basic level of supply and demand in an economy. The fact that one bushel of wheat is the same as another means that price fluctuations for commodities have less extraneous noise than for stocks and bonds. An investor can buy oil to get exposure to positive economic fundamentals in Nigeria without taking on the unique and messy political risks of that nation, for example. What's more, derivatives on many commodities are readily available for trade, giving fund managers more ways to structure profitable transactions (see Chapter 5 for more on derivatives).

On the exchanges, currencies and interest-rate derivatives are classified as *commodity derivatives*. In actual use, currencies and interest rates are considered to be in different categories.

Financing

Professionals who deal in commodities sometimes need financing to cover the cash-flow gap between when they have to acquire raw material and when they can sell the finished goods. Hedge funds are in the business of making money rather than making goods, so this mismatch is a great opportunity. A macro hedge fund can lend money to a business that needs to acquire commodities. Depending on the structure of the deal, the fund may be able to make money on the commodity-price fluctuations and on the interest for the use of the money.

For example, say that Refine Co. is an oil-refinery business that converts oil into gasoline. It needs help buying the oil because prices keep going up. A hedge fund swoops in and buys the oil and transfers it to Refine Co. When Refine Co. sells gasoline to retail stations, it pays the hedge fund the current spot price plus an interest factor. Refine Co. still makes money on its refining services, and the hedge fund makes money on the financing — as long as oil prices stay flat or go up.

Currency crises: Are hedge funds to blame?

Macro fund managers often take huge bets on government policies and institutions. If a bet is right, and if it involves profiting from bad news, the hedge fund is left with big gains, and the government officials are left looking bad. What does any good politician do in this situation? Place the blame on someone else, of course! No hedge fund manager has taken more blame for economic events than George Soros. In 1997, he and other hedge fund managers had reason to believe that, given certain economic indicators, the currencies of Thailand, Indonesia, Malaysia, and the Philippines were overvalued relative to the dollar and other world currencies. Therefore, they shorted huge amounts of the currency (borrowing the currency and selling it, hoping to repay the loan when the borrowed currency depreciated; see Chapter 11). The managers borrowed so much money that there was no one left to buy any of the currency. And when it became clear that the currencies in question were, indeed, overvalued and that everyone was short, the currencies entered into a freefall, and the hedge funds posted huge profits.

But while the fund managers toasted champagne, the people in these countries suffered. Suddenly, goods were so cheap that it was hard to make a living. These nations had been trying to modernize, and the currency decline set back the process. The resulting economic pain led to political unrest.

The fact that George Soros funds a think-tank called the Open Society Institute, which promotes democracy and human rights around the world, only compounded the conflict. His work may seem like a good thing, unless of course you happen to be a corrupt politician in an authoritarian regime. Indonesian president Suharto accused Soros of manipulating currency to destroy his political power. Suharto was forced to resign in 1998. He may have had a strong case against Soros if rumors of corruption and political mismanagement hadn't dogged him throughout his reign.

Speculating

Not all hedge fund managers have the patience to wait around to get paid, and not all managers want to have business partners. But if a manager so much as sniffs a profit opportunity, you can be sure that he'll want a piece of the action. To gain some profit without undue hassle, macro hedge funds *speculate* on the value of commodities by buying at one price in the hopes of selling higher, but they rarely want to take physical custody of the assets. Seriously, if you had an expensive and tasteful office in Greenwich, Connecticut, would you want cattle running around the courtyard and wheat stacked up in the lobby?

To avoid befriending a cow named Betsy and feeding her grains in the lobby, a hedge fund manager buys commodities through derivatives. He may buy futures contracts to lock in exposure and sell futures to give up exposure. This strategy gives the manager all the economic interest without the hassle of storage. (If you want to find out more about derivatives, check out Chapter 5.)

Chapter 14

But Will You Make Money? Evaluating Hedge-Fund Performance

Calculating investment performance seems easy: You take your balance at the end of the year, divide it by your balance at the start of the year, subtract 1, and voila! For example, $1,100,000 ÷ $1,000,000 – 1 = 10 percent. But what if you add to your investment in the middle of the year in order to net a bigger return? What if your hedge fund manager had to cash out other shareholders? Quickly, you're left with algebra unlike any you've seen since high school. Because of all the possible complications, many researchers in the investment industry are trying to standardize calculations, and others are asking pointed questions to make solid comparisons.

This chapter looks at how a hedge fund measures and evaluates its performance, as well as what questions you need to ask your prospective fund partners about performance calculation. Evaluating a hedge fund's performance helps you determine if the fund is the right fit for your investment objectives. It also tells you if the hedge fund manager is doing well relative to the risk taken, which is why you invest in the fund in the first place.

Measuring a Hedge Fund's Risk and Return

Risk and return are measures of how a hedge fund performs. In general, less risk is preferable to more, and more return is preferable to less. Some people invest in hedge funds to reduce risk, preferring *non-directional* or *absolute-return funds* (see Chapter 1); other investors aim to increase return regardless of risk by investing in *directional funds.* These funds maintain exposure to the market rate of return, and you have no guarantee that the direction of the return will be up. (In Chapter 6, you find a big discussion of how risk and return affect the assets that a hedge fund selects for its portfolio; the other chapters of Part III cover different strategies that hedge funds can use to manage risk and return.)

No type of hedge fund is better than another, as long as the fund that you invest in suits your investment objectives. (You know what your objectives are, don't you? If not, head to Chapters 7, 8, and 9 for a crash course.)

The following sections give you the methods used to measure return and risk within a hedge fund. I present the different forms of return and factor in fees, and I explain how risk factors into performance.

Unlike mutual funds, hedge funds don't have to publish their performance numbers. And even if they do, they don't have to follow a set methodology. You have to ask questions about the numbers that you see.

Reviewing the return

Return is an estimate that investors can manipulate. The price of a security tonight won't be the price you'll get if you sell in the morning, but it may be the best you get. Return is a measure of past performance, not a predictor of future results. It doesn't matter what a hedge fund did last year; this year is an entirely different ballgame. Whether you're a current or a prospective investor, past return numbers are only rough indicators of what you can expect.

However, I can't say that return figures are worthless. If you're already in a fund, return measures tell you how you did over a time period, which is important information. You may get a different return when you cash out of the fund, but the fund manager still posted a set of investment gains or losses over a specific time period. You can compare that number to your expectations and your needs.

What muddies the picture is that a hedge fund manager may have been lucky or unlucky, or he may have an investment style that does very well in some market conditions and not so well in others. That's why return is only one piece in the evaluation of a portfolio's performance.

Without further ado, the following list gives you the steps taken to calculate investment return:

1. **Valuing the assets.** A hedge fund has to know what it holds and what its holdings are worth. The best method is to use market value — what the security would sell for on the market today — but some funds use their initial costs instead (especially for assets, like real estate, that don't trade easily; see Chapter 5). Sometimes, a hedge fund will estimate the value of an illiquid asset (see Chapter 4). The estimate may be close to reality, or the fund may use it to make itself look good.

   Many securities pay off some income. Certain bonds make regular interest payments, and some stocks pay dividends. Funds should value securities that pay income with an accrual for any upcoming payments.

2. **Choosing the dates.** A year has 365 days (366 in leap year) and ends on December 31. It has 12 months of 28, 29, 30, or 31 days. At least, that's how a year runs on a regular calendar. In an accounting calendar, years may be a little different. A year may be 360 days long and have 12 months of 30 days each. Each month could end on the last day on the calendar (the 28th, 29th, 30th, or 31st), or a month may end on the last business day or the last Friday.

   It doesn't matter how a hedge fund's manager sets the fund's time periods as long as she discloses the beginning and ending dates and applies the method consistently. Just make sure when you're doing comparisons that you compare numbers for the same time periods. A shady fund manager may change the ending date for a quarter in order to avoid a big market decline on the last calendar day, for example (see Chapter 18 for more on due diligence).

3. **Calculation methodology.** Give someone with a numerical bent a list of numbers and a calculator and she can come up with several different relationships between numbers. After investors determine the asset values for certain time periods, they can calculate rates of return. But how? And over how long a time period? The process gets a little more complicated at this stage. Even though the fund may hand over the work to accountants or even actuaries, you should still understand the differences in the methods.

The following sections take you inside this third step by giving you different calculation options. I also show you how fees enter the scene — about as anticipated as a trip to the dentist (unless you're the fund manager).

Time-weighted returns

The most common way to calculate investment returns is to use a *time-weighted average* — also called the *Compound Average Growth Rate* (CAGR). For one time period, the calculation produces a simple percentage:

$$\frac{EOY - BOY}{BOY}$$

EOY stands for "end of year asset value," and *BOY* is "beginning of year value." The result is the percentage return for one year. Simple arithmetic!

Now, if you want to look at your return over a period of several years, you need to look at the compound return rather than the simple return for each year, because the compound return shows you how your investment is growing. You're getting returns on top of returns, which is a good thing, but the math gets a little complicated because now you have to use the root function on your calculator. The equation looks like this:

$$\sqrt[N]{\frac{EOP - BOP}{BOP}}$$

EOP stands for "end of the total time period," *BOP* stands for "beginning of the total time period," and *N* is the number of years that you're looking at.

Table 14-1 shows a time-weighted return over a four-year period.

Table 14-1	Calculating a Time-Weighted Return			
	Year 1	Year 2	Year 3	Year 4
Beginning-of-Year Asset Value	$100,000	$123,456	$156,030	$145,683
End-of-Year Asset Value	$123,456	$156,030	$145,683	$158,966
Annual Percentage Return	23%	26%	–7%	9%
Four-Year Time Weighted Return				15%
	Year 1	Year 2	Year 3	Year 4

Dollar-weighted returns

The *dollar-weighted return* — also called the *internal rate of return* (IRR) — is the rate that makes the net present value of a stream of numbers equal to zero. You find the number through an iteration that almost always has to be done on a calculator or a computer. You use the IRR to determine the return for a stream of numbers over time; it's also widely used to value bonds.

Table 14-2 shows a comparison of year-by-year dollar weighted returns with a cumulative dollar-weighted return over a five-year time period.

Table 14-2	A Dollar-Weighted Return Example				
	Year 1	Year 2	Year 3	Year 4	Year 5
Beginning-of-Year Asset Value	$100,000	$123,456	$156,030	$145,683	$158,966
End-of-Year Asset Value	$123,456	$156,030	$145,683	$158,966	$175,620
Incremental Gain	$23,456	$32,574	$(10,347)	$13,283	$16,654
One-Year Dollar-Weighted Return	23%	26%	–7%	9%	10%
Five-Year Cumulative Dollar-Weighted Return					16%

I'm convinced that this method became popular in the 1970s, when Hewlett-Packard introduced its HP12C financial calculator, the first of its kind that could find internal rate of return easily. The calculator was also relatively expensive when it came out, making it a big status symbol. Many financial types started using internal rate of return so they could show off their fancy calculators. Even today, IRR requires more computing power than most calculators have because it's the result of a series of calculations, not the solution to a single equation.

The calculation for IRR simply doesn't work well for everything. The dollar-weighted method can overstate returns, and it can occasionally show nonsensical results if too many negative returns appear in a series. (As much as investors don't like it, a long-running hedge fund may have a year or two of losses and still be a good investment.)

Because of the problems with dollar-weighted returns, most people who analyze investment returns prefer to use a time-weighted, compound average approach (see the previous section). It isn't as flashy — you can do it with the same cheap scientific calculator you used in high-school chemistry — but it gives you a more precise way to figure out how a fund performs over a range of market cycles.

Gross of fees

One big nuance with return calculations is whether or not you include fees. And fees can be hefty — a typical hedge fund charges a 1- or 2-percent management fee and takes a 20-percent cut of profits (see Chapter 2). Other funds take much more. If the return the fund achieves is high enough, the fees may be worth it. On the other hand, you may be subsidizing the fund manager's art collection rather than getting the investment return that you're expecting.

A gross-of-fees arrangement allows investors to evaluate a manager's performance so they can decide if it's worth the fund manager's price. If a fund manager reports returns *gross of fees,* that means he hasn't taken out most of the fees. Trading costs should be removed because those commissions and fees are necessary to building the portfolio. However, the manager shouldn't remove the investment management fees and cuts of profits. Trading costs should be relatively small, but they can be high if the fund makes many small, frequent trades or if it uses unusual strategies that carry high commissions.

Table 14-3 shows a gross-of-fees, time-weighted performance calculation, where the trading costs barely amount to a rounding error.

Table 14-3	Gross-of-Fees, Time-Weighted Performance				
	Year 1	Year 2	Year 3	Year 4	Year 5
Beginning-of-Year Asset Value	$100,000	$122,839	$154,474	$143,509	$155,896
End-of-Year Asset Value (Before Trading Costs)	$123,456	$155,250	$144,230	$156,679	$172,228
Trading Costs	$617	$776	$721	$783	$861
Net End-of-Year Asset Value	$122,839	$154,474	$143,509	$155,896	$171,367
Annual Percentage Return	23%	26%	–7%	9%	10%
Five-Year Time-Weighted Return					14%

One reason to report numbers gross of fees is that different investors may be paying different fees. A hedge fund may agree to reduce the profit fee charged to a fund-of-funds (which invests in several different hedge funds; see Chapter 15) or a single large investor in exchange for its investment. So, although most investors may have an arrangement for a 2-percent management fee and a 20-percent share of profits, some may be paying only "1 and 18."

Net of fees

In a *net-of-fees* performance calculation, you remove all the fees charged by the fund. This method may not reflect the return that any one investor receives, because different investors may have different fee schedules.

Anyone evaluating a net-of-fee rate of return has to ask if different investors pay different fees, because any one investor's realized returns may be higher or lower.

Table 14-4 shows the effect of the standard 2-and-20 fee arrangement on a hedge fund's time-weighted returns

Table 14-4	Net-of-Fees, Time-Weighted Performance				
	Year 1	Year 2	Year 3	Year 4	Year 5
Beginning of Year Asset Value	$100,000	$116,765	$140,358	$127,307	$137,346
Increase in Assets	$ 23,456	$ 32,411	$(10,244)	$ 13,170	$ 16,332
2% Asset Management Fee	$ (2,000)	$ (2,335)	$ (2,807)	$ (2,546)	$ (2,747)
20% Profit Share	$ (4,691)	$ (6,482)	$ -	$ (585)	$ (3,266)
End-of-Year Asset Value	$116,765	$140,358	$127,307	$137,346	$147,665
Annual Percentage Return	17%	20%	-9%	8%	8%

This table shows you how expenses will reduce your investment return. If the hedge fund manager's skills are adding value, then it's worth the cost.

Sizing up the risk

An investor must consider return relative to what a manager had to do to get it, which is why you have to compare return to the amount of risk taken. (Chapter 6 contains an in-depth analysis of risk, but I cover some of the basics here as they relate to measurement.)

The problem is that measurements of risk are inherently subjective. What's risky to one investor may not be risky to you. For example, I have a weird phobia about scuba diving, but I'm willing to sell stocks short. Plenty of people have completely opposite views of the world, and that's okay.

In finance, the dispute over how exactly to define risk has led to a range of measures. I present what goes into each measurement in the following sections so that you can judge for yourself how appropriate each method is for your needs.

Standard deviation

In finance, risk is usually considered to be a function of standard deviation — a statistic that shows how much your return may vary from the return that you expect to get.

Say, for example, that you expect a security to have an average return of 10 percent over two years. If it returns 10 percent the first year and 10 percent the second year, no deviation exists between any one return and the average return. But if the security returns 20 percent one period and 0 percent the next, it still returns an average of 10 percent but with big deviations from the 10-percent mean. The more a security swings around the expected return, the riskier it is. (You can see all the math in Chapter 6.)

Some hedge funds are designed to have low standard deviations. Funds of this structure are *absolute-return funds,* which aim to post returns within a narrow range (often 6 to 8 percent). *Directional funds,* on the other hand, try to maximize returns, so they sometimes take on very high levels of risk, creating a high expected standard deviation (see Chapter 6 for more). When looking for a prospective fund, you can compare how much the return varies from year to year to give you a ballpark idea of how risky it is.

In the Modern (Markowitz) Portfolio Theory (MPT; see Chapter 6), standard deviation is the basic measure of risk. It tells how likely you are to get any return other than the average return. The more the return varies from year to year, the more likely the fund is to be risky.

By the way, a fund with a high standard deviation can post mediocre returns, and a fund with a low standard deviation can post stellar investment performance. Most situations are entirely possible. That's the risk you take for investing in a hedge fund!

Beta

A refinement of the standard deviation measurement is *beta,* which compares the standard deviation of an investable asset or fund to the standard deviation of the market itself. (See Chapter 6 for more information and the entire math.)

In most cases, the performance of an index measures the "market" (in the sense that the index is a sample of investable assets, not an agglomeration of all the possible assets that you can invest in), like the S&P 500 in the United States or the Nikkei in Japan.

If a fund has a beta of 1, it should move right in step with the market itself. If it has a beta greater than 1, it should move more sharply up or more sharply down — whichever way the market goes. If it has a beta of less than 1, it should move in the same direction as the market, but less sharply. If the beta is negative, it should move in the opposite direction of the market.

Peak-to-trough ranges

A simple way to look at the volatility of a long-standing hedge fund is to compare the distance between the peak — the year with the highest return — and the trough — the year with the lowest return. The greater the distance between the peak and the trough, and the closer together the two are, the riskier the fund is. For example, if a fund's peak return was 80 percent, followed by a loss of 35 percent the next year, the peak-to-trough distance is 115 percent (80 – (–35)) over two years. If another fund had a peak return of 15 percent, followed by a return of 10 percent the next year, its peak-to-trough distance is 5 percent (15 – 10) over two years. The first fund is much riskier than the second fund.

For a hedge fund with a short operating history, you can look at the peak and trough months rather than years.

Stress tests

Standard deviation and beta (see the previous two sections) are nice shortcuts, but they don't answer one question that may be on a worrisome investor's mind: How much money will I lose if things go terribly wrong? A *stress test* solves this problem. The test is a computer simulation that models what could happen to a hedge fund's portfolio under a variety of different scenarios, like a dramatic increase in interest rates, the Euro falling apart, or the government of Mexico defaulting on its bonds. Based on the sensitivity that the different fund investments have to the tested factors, the stress test shows how much the factors may affect the portfolio's return. The less effect the events have, the less risky the fund — assuming that the right stresses have been tested.

Stress tests are expensive to run, and even the best are based on guesses about the future. They are mostly performed by actuaries working with investment consultants (see Chapter 17). Investors often feel the effects of economic changes that seem to come out of nowhere. Still, the information from a test can be useful — especially for a fund that intends to retain exposure to a certain set of market factors. For example, a macro hedge fund that concentrates on emerging Asian-Pacific markets could undergo a test for exposure to those currencies and interest rates (see Chapter 13 for more on macro funds).

Mathematically, a difference exists between risk and uncertainty. *Risk* is the possibility of an event happening that you can describe and quantify. Someone can study a situation and set odds on the likelihood of it happening. After you describe and measure risk, it becomes possible to set insurance or a hedge against it. *Uncertainty* is an event that may happen, but you have no way to quantify it. The possibility of a hurricane destroying the downtown section of a major city is an example of risk. The possibility of aliens landing on Earth and taking control is an example of uncertainty. The latter could happen, but can you set a probability and limit on it?

Value at risk

Value at risk (VAR) is a single number that represents how much you can expect a portfolio to lose over a given time period. The value is a statistical calculation involving several equations, so it is very difficult to calculate by hand. You see it quoted with similar margins of error that you see with political polls.

For example, a hedge fund may say that it has a 95 percent confidence level that its portfolio has a 10-day VAR of losing $10 million. This translates to the following: Based on the securities held in the portfolio and on market conditions, the fund manager is 95 percent certain that the most the fund could lose over the next 10 days is $10 million. Events could take place over the next ten days that fall into the 5 percent uncertainty level, but more likely than not, the most the fund will lose is $10 million.

In most cases, you will have to rely on the hedge fund for VAR information. The number can change with the fund's holdings and overall market conditions, so it can change over time.

Benchmarks for Evaluating a Fund's Risk and Return

Investment performance is relative — relative to your needs and expectations and relative to what your return would've been had you invested your money elsewhere. That's why you have to compare your return and risk numbers to something. But what? In many cases, hedge-fund investors compare performance to a market index. Some compare performance to that of similar hedge funds or to an expected return based on the fund's style. All these types of comparisons have their advantages and disadvantages, which I go into here in this section.

An old doctor's joke focuses on an operation that was a success even though the patient died. The same basic concept can be true with investment performance. A fund can beat its benchmarks and all its peers and still lose money. The fund manager may be happy; the consultants and brokers who recommended the hedge fund may be happy; but the investors who put money into the fund may be fuming.

Looking into indexes

The most common way to compare investment performance is with a market index. *Market indexes* are the measures of the overall market that you hear quoted all the time in the news, like the Standard & Poor's 500 (S&P 500) and the Dow Jones Industrial Average. Not only are these widely reviewed, but also widely mimicked: Many mutual funds and futures contracts are designed to mimic the performance of market indexes. What this means is that investors can always do at least as well as the index itself if their investment objectives call for exposure to that part of the broad investment market.

Indexes aren't perfect for comparison purposes. One big problem is that investors often look at the wrong indexes for the type of investments that they have. For example, an investor may compare the performance of a macro fund that invests all over the world to the S&P 500 when he or she should use a global index that includes a range of securities (see Chapter 13 for more on macro funds).

In many cases, you should compare a fund to a mixture of indexes. For example, you should compare a macro fund that invests

> 30 percent in international equities
>
> 30 percent in international bonds
>
> 40 percent in currencies

to

> 30 percent of the return on an international equity index
>
> 30 percent of the return on an international bond index
>
> 40 percent to a currency index

Preparing indexes is a big business. In many cases, indexes are designed and calculated by newspapers that want to keep their names in front of investors, so the different companies that calculate and maintain indexes put different conditions on their use. Anyone offering an S&P 500 index fund has to pay a fee to Standard & Poor's. Hedge funds and performance-consulting firms may have to pay index companies for detailed information about the securities in the indexes. When a hedge fund presents its results relative to a given index to you, a prospective investor, it may do so for different reasons:

- Because that index is the best choice
- Because the index's performance makes the fund look good
- Because another index service was too expensive for it to use

A hedge fund should use the same benchmarks every time it reports. If it changes its benchmarks, that may mean that the fund is trying to make its performance look good or is changing its investment style so that it no longer matches the profile of the fund you need in your portfolio.

Different indexes show different results, even if they are calculated using the same securities. There are several different ways to calculate indexes, and understanding them can give you a sense of why a fund manager might choose one over the other.

Market-capitalization-weighted index

Market capitalization is the total value of a security. For example, the market capitalization of a common stock is the total number of shares outstanding multiplied by the price per share, and the market capitalization of a bond issue is the number of bonds issued multiplied by the price of each bond. In a *market-capitalization-weighted index,* different securities are entered in proportion to their total market value. One example of a market-capitalization-weighted index is the Standard & Poor's 500 Index (S&P 500).

A market-capitalization-weighted index is a good representation of how the market as a whole trades, but it may place too much emphasis on the price fluctuations of the largest companies. The NASDAQ Composite Index, which represents the value of all the companies traded on NASDAQ, is disproportionately exposed to the trading of Microsoft and other huge high-tech and biotech companies. Those huge technology companies are mainstays on NASDAQ, but most of the companies on that exchange are quite small.

Price-weighted index

A *price-weighted index* includes one of each security from the group being measured. For example, a price-weighted stock index includes one share of each of the companies it tracks, and a price-weighted bond index includes one share of each of the bonds it tracks. The Dow Jones Industrial Average is an example of a price-weighted index.

The price-weighted index is independent of the total capitalization of the included securities, so securities with a high price may be overweighted.

Differing results for different indexes

Even if they include the same securities, price-weighted and market-capitalization indexes can post different results. Table 14-5 shows how this can happen.

Table 14-5	Price-weighted versus Market-Capitalization-Weighted Index Comparisons			
	Stock A	Stock B	Price-Weighted Index Value	Market-Capitalization-Weighted Index Value
Total Shares Outstanding	1,000,000	10,000,000		
Beginning-of-Year Price	$10.00	$10.00	$20.00	$110,000,000
Market Capitalization	$10,000,000	$100,000,000		
End-of-Year Price	$14.00	$16.00	$30.00	$174,000,000
Market Capitalization	$14,000,000	$160,000,000		
% Change			50%	58%

Picking over peer rankings

If you just want the risk and return that comes with an index, you wouldn't be considering paying a hedge fund's high fees. And if you've made the decision that a hedge fund is the appropriate way to go with your money, you'll want to know how your fund does against other hedge funds that you could've invested in instead.

That's why you look at peer group rankings. Many hedge funds report their results to services, like Morningstar (www.morningstar.com), where the analysts rank funds based on their risk-and-return parameters (see the section "Hiring a Reporting Service to Track Hedge-Fund Performance"). For example, the service ranks arbitrage funds against other arbitrage funds, and long-short funds against other long-short funds. With the information from the services, you can see if your fund is one of the better or worse ones within a specific style. Unlike Morningstar's mutual fund information, you have to pay to see these rankings.

One problem with peer rankings of hedge funds is that reporting is optional, which makes the picture you see less rounded. A fund that doesn't do so well is less likely to report its numbers for a ranking, so the average performance may have an upward bias. A fund in the bottom half of a published ranking isn't in the bottom half of all hedge funds within that style; it's just in the bottom half of funds that reported. You can bet that plenty of funds in that style are worse; they're just in hiding.

Standardizing performance calculation: Global Investment Performance Standards

As you read through this chapter, you may be surprised at just how arbitrary some of the performance information is. Hedge fund managers have many options to use when calculating and comparing risk and return, and they have an incentive to choose the methods that make them look better than the alternatives. In 1996, the Association for Investment Management and Research, now known as the CFA Institute (www.cfainstitute.org), introduced its Performance Presentation Standards to help U.S. investment advisors present their numbers fairly and to make it easy for investors to compare the performance of different firms. In 2006, the CFA Institute adopted a revised standard, the Global Investment Performance Standards (or GIPS) that applies to money managers around the world.

Compliance with the standards is voluntary, but it allows fund managers to market their results to current and prospective investors as being "GIPS Compliant" or "GIPS Verified."

The Global Investment Performance Standards include the following:

- ✔ Accurate data collection, with records to support the information
- ✔ Market-value accounting
- ✔ Accrual accounting for the value of any assets that generate income
- ✔ Monthly portfolio valuation, ending on the last business day or last calendar day of the month
- ✔ Time-weighted returns
- ✔ Results that are net of investment expenses
- ✔ Results shown for the last five years (or from the fund's inception if it's less than five years old), with annual results given for each year

Some hedge funds ignore GIPS, and sometimes for good reasons:

✔ It can be expensive to calculate results in the correct manner in order to qualify for the GIPS label.

✔ The CFA Institute designed the methodology for investment-management firms that handle several different portfolios in-house, but many hedge funds are one-portfolio operations.

✔ Not all investors are aware of GIPS or even care, something that the CFA Institute hopes to change.

Putting Risk and Return into Context with Academic Measures

It isn't enough to have the return and risk numbers and comparisons with indexes or other funds (of course!). You have to put the performance figures into context to figure out what the portfolio manager did to get those numbers.

Given that hedge funds have huge minimum-investment requirements (see Chapters 1 and 2), investors have a lot of money at stake. Many hedge-fund investors, like employees of pension funds or charitable endowments, have responsibilities to the people who rely on their funds. These factors are the reasons why investors need to know what the risk-and-return numbers mean and how they reflect on hedge fund managers' performances. Several equations developed in ivory towers can help you figure out why a hedge fund did as well as it did, and this section shows you what they are.

Academic approaches to finance have their problems because they're based on the assumption that rational investors are trading in efficient markets (see Chapter 6 for more on this topic). You may be tempted to laugh off the whole idea of academic theories, but that leaves you with nothing to determine how a hedge fund performed. Look at the approaches in this section with the limitations in mind If you're taking an MBA-level investments course, these approaches will show up on the midterm — it doesn't matter if I'm teaching or not!

Sharpe measure

William Sharpe is another of the many Nobel-Prize winners that figure into the hedge-fund world. (You may remember him from such equations as the Capital Assets Pricing Model, described in Chapter 6.) His equation, the

Sharpe measure, is the amount of performance that a fund earns over and above the risk-free rate of return (which, for investors based in the United States, is the interest rate on Treasury bills) divided by the standard deviation of returns. (Standard deviation is a mathematical measure of how much one number in a set varies from the average of all the numbers in the set.)

You're dying to see the equation, right? Here's what it looks like:

$$\frac{r_p - r_f}{\sigma_p}$$

In English, the Sharpe measure shows whether the portfolio's return for taking risk (the return minus the risk-free rate) came by increasing the amount of risk in the portfolio or from the fund manager's skill (known as *alpha;* see Chapter 6), which allowed her to get a better return than expected from the amount of standard deviation in the securities held by the portfolio. A higher number is better than a lower one, because a higher number indicates that the hedge fund manager is getting more return for the risk that she's taking.

For example, if the fund returned 15 percent, the risk-free rate was 5 percent, and the fund's standard deviation was 20 percent, the Sharpe measure would be (15 – 5)/20, or 50 percent. This would be better than a fund with a Sharpe measure of 40 percent, and worse than a fund with a Sharpe measure of 75 percent.

Treynor measure

Jack Treynor developed a refinement of the Sharpe measure (see the previous section) that looks at how a hedge fund performed for the risk it took over and above the risk of the market as a whole — not just at how it performed relative to the risk-free rate of return.

The equation is

$$\sigma_p$$

After all, people take risk when they invest, but they can put their money into a low-fee index fund (a fund invested in the same securities as a broad-market index, like the S&P 500, with the goal of generating the same return) instead of paying a hedge fund manager fees for 2 percent of the assets and 20 percent of the profits.

For example, if the fund returned 15 percent, the market rate of return was 10 percent, and the fund's standard deviation was 20 percent, the Treynor measure would be (15 – 10)/20, or 25 percent. This is better than a fund with a Treynor measure of 15 percent, and worse than a fund with a Treynor measure of 35 percent.

Jensen's alpha

Michael Jensen, a professor at the Harvard School of Business, decided that investors should just use the Capital Assets Pricing Model (CAPM; see Chapter 6) rather than Sharpe's or Treynor's measures of performance. The CAPM involves alpha. Hedge fund managers love to talk about alpha. The word derives from the CAPM; it measures how much an investment returns over and above its beta (its exposure to the market).

Here's the equation (with A representing alpha):

$$E(r) = B(r_m - r_f) + A + r_f$$

If a portfolio has a positive alpha, the portfolio manager did a good job. If the portfolio's alpha is zero or negative, maybe the manager's fees weren't deserved.

The appraisal ratio

Some performance analysts use a fourth measure to evaluate a hedge fund's performance: the *appraisal ratio,* which divides the fund's alpha by the non-systematic risk of the portfolio. Although the equation is simple, you more or less need a computer to generate the statistics involved in this calculation.

The *non-systematic risk* is risk that the manager could've diversified by adding more securities to the portfolio but didn't. The return from the risk isn't so much due to the portfolio manager's skill as to the portfolio manager's decision not to diversify the portfolio.

Suppose, for example, that a hedge fund manager decides to invest only in oil-company stock. Beta isn't the best comparison (see Chapter 6), because the fund's portfolio is far narrower than the entire investment market. Some of that risk is unnecessary, and the manager could remove it through diversification. The appraisal ratio is an attempt to separate the diversifiable risk from the true alpha — the true extra performance due to a portfolio manager's skill.

Many experts who study the market say that alpha doesn't exist; that the hedge fund manager has made a decision to take extra risk. After that risk is correctly described, alpha may disappear.

Serving Yourself with a Reality Check on Hedge-Fund Returns

One reason that so many investors are interested in hedge funds is because they think hedge funds are raking in enormous investment returns that other investors can't get. Certainly, some hedge funds bring in enormous investment returns, and the nature of a hedge fund's structure supports the idea that other investors are shut out (see Chapter 2 for info on the structure of hedge funds). But the reality is that many hedge funds don't perform in the stratosphere, which is why you need to know what you want from your investments before you commit. The following sections aim to put you in touch with your investment needs by bringing to light many facts about hedge-fund returns.

The Credit Suisse/Tremont Hedge Fund Index, a leading measure of hedge-fund performance, reported that the average hedge-fund return (at least, among those funds that submitted return data) was 7.61 percent for 2005. The NASDAQ Composite Index returned only 1.37 percent for the same period, but the Morgan Stanley Capital International World Index was up 10.02 percent.

Risk and return tradeoff

Some hedge funds post poor results relative to a stock-market index because they're designed to perform very differently. Investment return is a function of risk; the more risk a fund takes, the greater its expected return. A hedge fund's goal is to post a return that's greater than expected for a given level of risk. Some funds choose high risk levels in the hopes of even higher returns, and others maintain very low risk levels and generate relatively low returns.

Many investors are content with an 8 percent return year in and year out, but others would find this incredibly disappointing. Before you commit to a hedge fund, you need to know your investment objectives inside and out. (Chapter 6 gives you the lowdown on many risk and return topics.)

Survivor bias

Many hedge fund managers limit how often investors can make withdrawals, but they can't lock up an investor's money forever. A fund may require that an investor keep money in for two years, but if performance is bad in both years, you can bet that the investor will yank the money as soon as the time period expires.

In addition, hedge fund managers charge high fees, but they can collect a profit payout only if the funds show a profit (see Chapter 2 for more). If a fund isn't doing so well, its investors will go, and the fund manager will want out, too, so they can make some money elsewhere. Hedge Fund Research, a firm that tracks hedge funds, estimated that 11.4 percent of hedge funds folded in 2005.

When looking at long-term results for hedge funds, remember that the worst performing funds all probably dropped out of the game after two years, which means funds that are still in business have less competition. They already have better-than-average status because they're still in business. However, unless they're looking for new investors, they'll force you to invest in a newly formed fund. Will it be a survivor or one of the ones that eventually shut down?

Performance persistence

One huge problem for any hedge fund and its investors is following one good year with another. Is a great number the result of luck, or is it due to the portfolio manager's skill? Will the manager's luck hold out next year? Will a skilled portfolio manager face bad luck next year? It's really hard to post good performance year after year — a problem known as *performance persistence.*

A study published in 2000 by Vikas Agarwal of Georgia State University and Narayan Naik of the London Business School found no evidence of persistence in the funds that they studied. One year's performance wasn't an indicator of the next year's, and the relationship between performance one year and the next weakened as more time periods were included in the study.

What does this mean? If a hedge fund has the kind of extraordinary return that grabs headlines this year, it probably won't bring in those spectacular returns the next year. This is a phenomenon known as *reversion to the mean.*

Style persistence

The problem of a fund manager changing style to get performance is called *style persistence*. If a fund keeps changing its investment strategy, it may post good numbers, but consultants, academics, and others who evaluate returns may not know what to do with the fund.

Academic performance studies in particular control for different risk measures, which affects the performance persistence that they report (see the previous section). Some funds show persistence, but that's because the fund changes its investment style with the market. Some investors may want a hedge fund that's flexible and can post a consistent return no matter what. Other investors may need a fund to limit its investments or maintain a consistent risk profile so that it complements other parts of their portfolios.

Hiring a Reporting Service to Track Hedge-Fund Performance

Given all the information-collecting options I've covered in the pages of this chapter, how in the world are you supposed to keep track of everything to find out how a hedge fund actually performs? Some people require help in this area, and help is available. Along with the numbers that the fund manager presents, you can find several consulting firms and reporting services that monitor how hedge funds perform, analyze their results, and evaluate their risk and return based on the styles that the fund managers follow. The following list is by no means exhaustive and doesn't represent an endorsement. My only goal is to give you some ideas of where to start if you want to enlist some help to evaluate hedge-fund performance.

Most of these companies charge for their services — and charge a lot.

Greenwich-Van

Greenwich-Van (www.vanhedge.com) is one of many hedge-funds services that operates in two businesses:

- ✔ A consulting firm that advises investors on hedge-fund investments
- ✔ A hedge fund performance-analysis service

Some information on the performance of broad categories of hedge funds is available for free from the Web site, but other information is available only to institutional investors (pensions, endowments, and foundations) that pay the firm for its services.

HedgeFund.net

HedgeFund.net maintains a database of quantitative and qualitative information about hedge funds, submitted by the funds themselves. The site also carries news and information about the industry (even offering a free daily report) and offers both free and paid services; however, all subscribers must be accredited investors (see Chapter 2 for more on this topic).

Hedge Fund Research

Hedge Fund Research (www.hedgefundresearch.com) compiles detailed databases of hedge fund performance and administration. It has at least some information on 9,000 funds and detailed information on 5,800 of them. This helps people determine how many funds are being formed, how many are being disbanded, and what kind of returns are being generated for investors. Full access is available to accredited investors for a fee.

Lipper Hedge World

Lipper (www.lipperhedgeworld.com) made its name in mutual-fund performance reporting, and it now offers hedge-fund performance services as well. The company, owned by Reuters, offers a variety of free and paid reports on performance. How much access you get depends on whether you're accredited (see Chapter 2) and how much you're willing to pay.

Managed Account Report

Managed Account Report (www.marhedge.com) collects news and information on the hedge-fund industry, organizes conferences, and reports on hedge-fund performance. The firm collects its data from fund managers and reports it to subscribers on its Web site and print publication. It compares results to indexes of hedge-fund performance prepared by the Barclay Group (www.barclaygrp.com). Subscribers don't have to be accredited investors.

Morningstar

Morningstar (www.morningstar.com) is a dominant firm for mutual-fund performance analysis, and it's building a niche in hedge funds. Funds report their own performance numbers each month. The database was started in January 2004 and currently holds information on 3,000 hedge funds, funds of hedge funds, and commodity trading advisors. Subscribers, who must be accredited investors (see Chapter 2), can access the site's information to get a sense of how a fund's risk and return compares to other hedge funds following the same investment style.

Part IV
Special Considerations Regarding Hedge Funds

Defining your investment risk with the:
TOAST RETRIEVING RISK TOLERANCE TEST

LOW RISK | Waits for toast to pop up even though it's burning.

MODERATE RISK | Goes after toast with wooden toast prongs.

HIGH RISK | Goes after toast with all metal butter knife.

ULTRA HIGH RISK | Goes after toast with metal butter knife wearing a wet swim suit and a stainless steel colander on head.

In this part . . .

After reading up on hedge funds to this point and set-tling on your investment objectives, you may find that a traditional hedge fund just isn't for you. However, that doesn't mean hedge funds aren't useful to you any-more. You can hook onto different types of hedge funds, or you can use hedge-fund strategies for other types of investments. Find out how in Part IV.

Whether you're dead set on entering a hedge fund or not, you need to do your due diligence on a fund before you invest, because a hedge-fund investment often involves large amounts of hard-earned money. Chapter 18 shows you the way.

Hedge funds are private partnerships, however, so you'll have a difficult time finding out much information about a fund before you invest — but the task isn't impossible. Many investors find it worthwhile to hire consultants or other advisors to help them investigate funds and their appropriateness for the investors' needs. Chapter 17 gives you some advice on how to do that.

Chapter 15

Hooking Onto Other Types of Hedge Funds

*O*ne problem with fund strategies is that they're sometimes too specialized for a hedge fund investor. Even an accredited investor — one with a net worth of $1 million or an annual income of at least $200,000 ($300,000 with a spouse; see Chapter 2) — may not have the resources to take advantage of a diversified range of hedge-fund strategies. Likewise, some hedge fund managers don't like to limit themselves to a single investment strategy when one strategy is temporarily out of market fashion. Other hedge fund managers like to diversify their market approaches so that they can have even performance no matter how the market is doing.

In this chapter, I introduce several types of hedge funds that cover a range of investment strategies. I examine the aptly named multi-strategy fund, and I present the world of fund-of-funds investing; I also look at some niche hedge funds and related investments to show you what your options are. If you're interested in hedge funds that invest in a range of investment styles, you can use the options I present in this chapter to discover more about them.

Multi-Strategy Funds: Pursuing a Range of Investment Strategies

The problem with any investment strategy is that it will work better in some years than in others. It can be really hard to sit through a down year, no matter how much the manager believes in the strategy. A lot of smart people identified the dot-com bubble and predicted its collapse, but most of them were way too early in their predictions. They lost investors who thought they were out of touch — wasn't it obvious that Webvan and Pets.com were the waves of the future?

To circumvent the bad years, some managers want the right to change their strategies. Others, especially those with very large funds, handle several investment strategies in-house, with different staff members getting different amounts of money to manage based on market conditions. *Multi-strategy funds* are hedge funds that pursue several different investment strategies instead of focusing on any one investment style. In the following sections, you find out more about multi-strategy funds.

The advantage of a multi-strategy fund is that a variety of different investment styles all mesh under one roof. The hedge fund investor has more diversification benefits and more consistent performance than with hedge funds that are organized to follow a single investment strategy.

A multi-strategy focus may be just an excuse for posting mediocre performances year in and year out. The best hedge fund managers tend to be disciplined, even when the markets are turned against them; they know that buying low is the best assurance of some day selling high. Other hedge fund managers drift from strategy to strategy, hoping that something will stick for this year, instead of generating value for investors. If a fund you're interested in pursues multiple strategies, find out how the manager determines those strategies and how the fund moves money among them (see Chapter 18 for more on due diligence). A multi-strategy fund is still a hedge fund, so buying into it calls for the same research as any other hedge fund.

Determining the strategies

A multi-strategy hedge fund is usually set up in one of two ways. First, you have the top-down strategy:

1. The hedge fund manager starts with a top-down analysis of market conditions and expectations. (For an in-depth discussion of top-down analysis, see Chapter 5.)

2. The manager works out what sectors and strategies are likely to do well.

3. The manager uses the sector and strategy information to guide the fund's allocation of money.

This may well be a messy process, with plenty of smart people arguing over what these investment traders, analysts, and portfolio managers see ahead in the markets. The goal of the process for the traders, analysts, and portfolio managers involved isn't to get a consensus; the goal is to be right about the direction of the market, or at least make enough of a case to get an allocation of capital to invest. The advantage is that members of the hedge fund's staff have to think through their arguments in order to get them past everyone else, so the best ideas survive. As a result, multi-strategy funds may have some internal tensions and employee turnover. These factors don't necessarily make for a bad fund, although internal turmoil can be disconcerting to hedge fund investors.

The second setup involves the diverse strategies. At many multi-strategy funds, the hedge fund manager hires sub-managers who concentrate on specific market sectors, derivates, arbitrage, or other trading strategies (see Part III for discussions of these strategies). Each sub-manager starts with a set amount of money to manage. If a sub-manager does well, she'll receive more money. If she doesn't do well, she may see her money cut — or she may lose her job. This setup can be a great way to ensure that sub-managers who can make money get to make a lot of it for the fund. However, markets run in cycles. If the hedge fund manager isn't careful, he may give a sub-manager too large a percentage of the fund just as the sub-manager's investing style falls out of favor, while he asks other sub-managers to give up money just as their investment styles come back in fashion.

Dividing in-house responsibilities

After the hedge fund manager(s) determines the allocation of the money (see the previous section), he or she gives the money to different people in the firm to manage. In essence, a multi-strategy hedge fund is a group of little hedge funds clustered under one roof. Two traders may handle the currency; two analysts may work on emerging market equities; three analysts may specialize in risk arbitrage (see Chapter 10); and one analyst may do nothing but highly leveraged fixed income trading (see Chapter 11 for more on leverage). The goal of all involved is to post as great a return as possible, given the amount of money allocated. (You can find out more about the different jobs of hedge fund staff members in Chapter 1.)

Managers usually assign risk-management responsibilities to those who determine the investment strategies. Someone at the top needs to make sure that the strategies mesh and that the fund takes on only as much risk as its investors want and its prime broker is prepared to accept. If a fund has too much risk, it may not be able to borrow money for leverage strategies, borrow securities for short-selling, or even get its trades executed (see Chapter 11 for more information).

What does this mean for you? In a situation where a fund has too much risk, it may take money away from a trader who's doing well because his or her success may be increasing the fund's exposure to one specific strategy.

Scoping the pitfalls of working with a broad portfolio

A multi-strategy fund is often a very large hedge fund — one with a few billion dollars under management; after all, it's expensive to do the research and have the staff members execute a variety of strategies well. A small hedge fund would have a hard time justifying the costs of managing different investment styles under one roof. Some trading strategies utilized by a multi-strategy fund require large commitments of the firm's capital as collateral, which alone may limit the number of strategies that a small hedge fund can try.

Multi-strategy funds face another interesting problem: keeping top employees happy. All hedge funds — actually, all employers — have this problem, but a multi-strategy fund has some unique issues. If the fund as a whole doesn't do well one year, for instance, it may not be able to collect the performance fee (see Chapter 2). No performance fee means the fund may not have money to pay bonuses, even to employees who had great performances in their parts of the portfolio. And, with so many people in the firm, it may be tough for anyone to be a star.

People in the investment business make a lot of money, but that doesn't mean they don't want more! In 2005, the CFA Institute — the trade organization for investment analysts and money managers — reported that the median compensation for members working at hedge funds was $250,000.

So, what happens to the disgruntled fund workers? An analyst with a good track record for her part of the fund will quit, possibly starting her own hedge fund that focuses only on her chosen investment technique. The multi-strategy fund then has to replace her, with the fund's performance suffering during the transition.

Funds of Funds: Investing in a Variety of Hedge Funds

An alternative to traditional hedge funds is a *fund of funds,* which is an investment that pools money from several different investors — who may be individuals or institutions like pensions, foundations, or endowments — and puts it into a handful of different hedge funds.

A fund of funds is usually set up as an investment pool registered with the U.S. Securities and Exchange Commission (SEC; see Chapter 3 for more information on registration), although it doesn't necessarily have to be registered. The process for buying into most funds of funds is the same as for other hedge funds (see Chapter 4).

A registered hedge fund, including a registered fund of funds, may offer the people or institutions that invest more protections if the fund turns out to be mismanaged or a fraud, but registration is no assurance that the hedge fund or fund of funds is a good one.

Funds of funds have unique characteristics you need to consider. Not only do you have to decide if a hedge fund is the right investment for you (see the chapters of Part II) and what kinds of hedge funds are the right investments for you (see the chapters of Part III), but also whether a fund of funds is the right way for you to buy into a hedge fund.

In the following sections, we outline different types of funds of funds, list the advantages and disadvantages of funds of funds, and enter the realm of funds of funds of funds (not a typo!).

Surveying fund of funds types

Hedge funds themselves fall into many different categories. Some funds invest in growth equities, almost the same way that a mutual fund might. Others do some very fancy risk arbitrage transactions involving emerging country debt. (The chapters of Part III describe the different strategies that funds follow.) When it comes to funds of funds, some are diversified across many investment styles, and others are designed to capture the best hedge funds working in a specific investment style.

But, although funds of funds may follow different strategies, they fall into only two distinct types: multi-manager and multi-strategy.

Multi-strategy funds of funds

Like a multi-strategy hedge fund (see the first section of this chapter), a multi-strategy fund of funds pursues different investment strategies to achieve the goal of increased return for a given level of risk. The fund of funds manager chooses funds that complement each other and that usually have a directional market return (in other words, they have some market risk, unlike a traditional hedge fund, which is designed to remove market exposure; see Chapter 6). The goal is to give investors diversified exposure to an array of hedge funds in order to generate a steady annual return.

Multi-manager funds of funds

A multi-manager fund of funds puts its money into several hedge funds that follow a similar strategy. The manager may look for absolute-return funds, which are hedge funds that follow a traditional strategy with no market exposure (see Chapter 1), or he may concentrate on a single aggressive strategy. Investing in several funds within the same strategy eliminates the manager risk, which is the value that the manager adds or subtracts (also called *alpha;* see Chapter 6). After all, in any strategy and in any year, some people do a lot better than others. The goal of the multi-manager fund is to combine the expertise of many different money managers following the same strategy in order to get a more consistent return for investors than they may get by investing in just one fund.

Highlighting the advantages of funds of funds

Funds of funds have some neat benefits for investors, hedge fund managers, and the banks, brokers, and consultants who put hedge funds together.

First off, no matter who's investing, funds of funds have two distinct advantages you can take to the bank:

- ✔ **Relatively low minimum investment.** A fund of funds doesn't have to limit itself to accredited investors, or people with a net worth of more than $1 million or an annual income of at least $200,000 ($300,000 with a spouse; see Chapter 2). (Some funds of funds may set net-worth requirements anyway in order to help comply with suitability rules.) Funds of funds are designed to have relatively low minimum investments. Many traditional hedge fund managers, by contrast, would rather have a few large investors than many small ones, so they may set minimum investments out of the range of even the most accredited investors. Instead of having to come up with $250,000 or more to put into a hedge fund, a fund of funds may call for you to buy in for $25,000 or less.

  Just because you can afford an investment doesn't mean that the investment is right for you. The National Association of Securities Dealers requires member firms to determine if investments are suitable for their clients before they sign on the dotted line. Chapters 7 and 8 cover some of the features of hedge funds that may affect your investment objectives.

- ✔ **Easy diversification.** The high minimum investments for many hedge funds prevent even people who can afford to buy into them from diversifying among investment strategies. Diversification is one of the easiest ways to reduce risk in an investment portfolio (you can see the math in

Chapter 6). With a fund of funds, the pooled money goes into different hedge funds, which may lead to a broader range of holdings that increase returns and reduce risk.

✔ **Better due diligence.** The manager of a fund of funds has resources to run background checks on hedge fund managers, and he may uncover potential problems or conflicts of interest. See Chapter 18 for more information on due diligence.

Beyond those distinct and attractive advantages, the following considerations are unique to people involved in a fund of funds:

✔ **For the hedge fund manager:** One challenge for many hedge fund managers is attracting enough money to get the funds going. Hedge fund investment strategies often require big commitments of capital, and the high expenses are better covered over large asset bases. At the same time, few hedge funds are set up to deal with many investors, and unregistered hedge funds simply can't have many people (see Chapter 3). The fund of funds counts as a single investor, so it's a great way for a hedge fund to get plenty of money without running against regulatory limits on the number of investors that the fund may have.

✔ **For the fund of funds organizer:** The bank, broker, or consultant who organizes a fund of funds has one big incentive — the big fees involved. But what's good for the fund of funds organizer isn't necessarily good for you! This can be an expensive way to invest in hedge funds.

Acknowledging the problems with funds of funds

Although a fund of funds may make it easier for you to enter a hedge fund, it can't solve some of the problems inherent in the hedge fund structure — problems that make them unappealing to many investors:

✔ **Limited redemption rights.** A fund of funds investor has few redemption rights, so you may not be able to get your money out when you need it. Many traditional hedge funds limit how often withdrawals can be made (see Chapter 7), and they place the same limits on any funds of funds that invest with them. Therefore, a fund of funds has to place limits on how often its investors can withdraw money.

Some funds of funds allow investors to sell their shares as new investors come in. With this loophole, investors can get money out, but only if they wait until others want to come in, and only if the fund of fund's performance is good enough to attract new buyers.

✔ **Complicated tax structure.** Hedge funds are set up as partnerships, and each investor is a limited partner in the fund (see Chapter 2). Come April 15, tax day bloody tax day, each partner is responsible for a proportionate share of the fund's expenses and profits. The partners have to pay taxes on gains, even if they won't receive any cash until they exit the fund (see Chapter 8 for more on tax considerations).

A fund of funds adds another layer. Each fund in the portfolio reports to the fund of funds manager, who aggregates the expenses and profits and reports them to each investor. At a minimum, the extra step means you'll probably have to file for an extension of the Internal Revenue Service's deadline.

✔ **Excessive diversification.** Diversification is great in and of itself, but too much or poorly handled diversification can make investors worse off. If you eliminate all risk with diversification, you may eliminate all return, and if you don't match the funds so that their risks offset, you may find yourself taking on too much volatility in certain market conditions. Funds of funds that invest in more than 25 hedge funds may be excessively diversified; on the other hand, those with less than 5 may not be diversified enough.

The Modern (Markowitz) Portfolio Theory (MPT; see Chapter 6) says that each additional asset added to a portfolio increases its diversification by reducing some of the unique risk of the asset. When a portfolio features 30 items, unique risk is statistically close to zero, meaning that the expected return of the portfolio is the expected return of the market.

✔ **High fees.** You get an introduction to this in the previous section when I present an advantage for funds of funds organizers: the high fees they receive. For more a more detailed discussion, check out the following section (and Chapters 2 and 4).

Multiple funds, multiple fees

Funds of funds are expensive — so much so that some observers call them "fees of fees funds." First, the managers of all the hedge funds in the fund of funds portfolio charge their fees. On top of those fees, the fund of fund manager charges an additional fee for his or her services. In some cases, an investor may be better off in a traditional investment with poorer absolute performance but better results after the fees.

Table 15-1 shows how layers of fees can erode investment return. For this example, assume that a fund of funds placed $5 million in three different hedge funds. Each fund charged a management fee equal to 2 percent of beginning-of-year assets as well as a performance fee of 20 percent of investment profits. At that point, the fund of funds charged a fee equal to 1 percent of beginning-of-year assets and a performance fee of 10 percent of the invest-ment return. The result? A return of 19.3 percent before the fees chop the return almost in half, to 10.5 percent. (See Chapter 2 for more on the fees associated with hedge funds.)

Table 15-1		How Fund of Funds Fees Can Cut into Return			
	Assets	Asset Management Fee	Investment Return	Performance Dollars	
Fund A	$5,000,000	$100,000	8%	$400,000	
Fund B	$5,000,000	$100,000	15%	$750,000	
Fund C	$5,000,000	$100,000	35%	$1,750,000	
Total	$15,000,000	$300,000		$2,900,000	
Performance in Percentage Terms					19.3%

	Performance Fee	Ending Assets	Fund of Funds Management Fee	Fund of Funds Performance Fee	Ending Assets
Fund A	$80,000	$5,220,000			
Fund B	$150,000	$5,500,000			
Fund C	$350,000	$6,300,000			
Total	$580,000	$17,020,000	$150,000	$290,000	$16,580,000
Net Percentage Return					10.5%

Some funds of funds, mindful of the burden of the fees, are trying alternative fee structures. Be sure to ask when you look into funds of funds.

Graduated performance fees

A hedge fund charges its performance fee on its first positive dollar. To prove that they're adding value with their fund manager selection, some funds of funds managers charge performance fees only on the performance increase over some reasonable return, like 8 percent or 10 percent. Unless the fund of funds returns at least that much, the fund of funds manager charges no fee. (Remember, the hedge fund manager already took out a cut.) The reason for a graduated performance fee is that otherwise, after you take all the fees into account, the fund of funds may have a performance that's average or even below average relative to the performance of the market or simpler investments, like index mutual funds (mutual funds that invest in the same stocks as a market index, like the S&P 500, in order to return approximately the same amount). The graduated performance fee helps ensure that the fund of funds manager adds value when selecting hedge funds for the fund of funds.

Negotiating with the hedge fund manager

Many hedge funds want to attract money. Funds of funds offer them large pools of money in the control of sophisticated investors. Even though his or her money may come from individual investors, the fund of funds manager should understand the investment business well enough not to need much hand-holding. The fund of funds won't be looking to make big withdrawals, either, because it won't have the distribution requirements that some pension or endowment funds may have. Because of this, many hedge fund managers are willing to offer funds of funds discounts off of management fees and performance fees.

The big pot of money a fund of funds offers can be both a blessing and a curse to a hedge fund manager. An investment from a big fund of funds can help launch a hedge fund, but if the fund of funds pulls out the money, it can destroy the hedge fund. Not all hedge fund managers welcome investments from funds of funds.

Advancing to funds of funds of funds (I'm not making this up!)

The truly daring may be interested in another level of hedge-fund investing: the so-called *F3s*, or "funds of funds of funds." At first, people thought the title was a joke, but it turns out that these investments are real. An F3 pools investors' money to put into funds of funds (see the previous sections). In some cases, a financial advisor takes money from a handful of small clients and pools the money to meet the minimum investment in a fund of funds (which is almost always lower than the minimum investment in a hedge fund). Naturally, the person forming the F3 charges a fee for this — usually about 1 percent per year. This may sound cheap, but you need to account for the additional 1 percent taken out of the investment return.

Some investors are interested in funds of funds of funds because they want to be in hedge funds, without regard for whether this is an appropriate investment. Others are interested because a broker or other financial advisor is pushing an F3 in order to get a commission, not because it's a great investment.

Before you take on the fees of a fund of fund of funds, think long and hard about whether you want your portfolio in hedge funds right now. Small investors can get many of the same benefits through other investments, which I cover in Chapter 16. And if you still want to inform people at a cocktail party that you're in an F3, you can always lie. The lack of transparency in hedge funds means that your nosy neighbor won't be able to check up on you (see Chapter 8).

Many hedge fund managers are already joking about the next investment level: the F4, or the fund of funds of funds of funds. By the time you read this, the F4 may be a reality, but it still won't be a sign of progress for investors!

Hedge Funds by Any Other Name

A hedge fund can be pretty much anything you want it to be. It can be a relatively low-risk, low-return investment that uses conventional investment techniques, or it can be a high-risk endeavor that uses exotic strategies. It's simply a lightly regulated private investment partnership that removes market risk, leaving only the value added by the manager's skill — the so-called alpha (see Chapter 6).

And guess what? Many investments are managed the same ways, even though the managers don't call them hedge funds. No rule states that a private investment account can't use short-selling, leverage, and other hedging techniques in order to generate greater than expected return for a given level of risk (see Chapter 11 for more on these techniques).

A hedge fund that solicits investors has to deal with only accredited investors (see Chapter 2). But no rule can stop an investor with fewer assets, or more assets, from hiring someone to manage an account. Some brokers and financial planners like to develop and recommend aggressive hedge-fund strategies if they're appropriate for their clients, and many money-management firms take individual accounts of $100,000 or so. Your blowhard brother-in-law may not be impressed that your financial planner put together an individually managed beta-neutral portfolio for you (see Chapter 9 for more information), but do you really need to impress him? However, it won't be impressive if the strategy isn't appropriate for you, or if you pay more than you can afford to make the investment.

If you're an accredited investor, but you need more flexibility than a hedge fund offers, an individually managed account may be for you. To get involved, contact a brokerage firm, private bank, or wealth-management firm. However, you need to keep an eye on the expenses and taxes incurred in an individually managed account. Great returns have a way of disappearing after you pay all the commissions and fees. (See Chapter 2 for more on this topic.)

Hedging into a family office

Many wealthy families, especially those that have had money for several generations, operate investment pools solely for their own benefit. They hire personal portfolio managers who may use the same techniques as hedge fund managers to control the risk in the portfolios. In essence, such family funds are private hedge funds that you must be born into or — depending on the pre-nup — marry into. This is called a *family office*. Of course, if you build a vast fortune for yourself, you may end up starting your own! (Chapter 2 has more on this topic.)

Entering Mutual Funds That Hedge

In recent years, many mutual fund companies have formed several mutual funds to follow some of the same investment strategies that hedge funds do. (A *mutual fund* is a publicly traded investment that pools money from different investors. They're regulated under the Investment Company Act of 1940, and they're mostly formed by companies that do this as their primary business.) The mutual funds are late to the hedge fund party (sounds like a blast!), and for good reason: For many years, securities laws forbid mutual funds from short-selling or from using leverage (borrowing money; see Chapter 11 for more on both topics) when investing. Changes to the laws in 1997 expanded the list of investment techniques that mutual funds can use.

If you're not an accredited investor (see Chapter 2) but still want some exposure to hedge fund investing techniques, you can now identify a handful of mutual funds that pursue short-selling strategies, offering many of the risk-management benefits of hedge funds to mutual fund investors, and more are scheduled for introduction. These hedging mutual funds fall into two categories:

- ✔ *Bear funds*, which short-sell stocks that the managers believe are too expensive
- ✔ *Long-short funds*, which try to manage market risk by buying shares in stocks that appear to be inexpensive and short-selling stocks that appear to be overpriced

You can discover more about mutual funds that follow some of the same strategies as hedge funds in Chapter 16.

Quiz: Having fun with unique hedge funds

Can you categorize and recall all the funds I mention in this chapter? Take the following quiz before you get hit with double or trouble fees:

1. A hedge fund is

a. A lightly-registered, private investment partnership.

b. An investment pool that's likely to use aggressive hedging techniques.

c. Just about anything it wants to be, really.

d. All of the above.

2. A fund of funds is

a. A single hedge fund that uses many different strategies.

b. A low-cost way to get money to put into a hedge fund.

c. An investment that pools money to buy into different hedge funds.

d. Illegal.

3. "Fees on fees" means that

a. Funds of funds rebate money to the investors.

b. Funds of funds save investors money through reduced fees.

c. Funds of funds charge fees on top of the fees charged by the hedge funds.

d. The power of compound interest is working for the investor.

4. An F3 is

a. A fund of funds of funds.

b. A new Navy bomber.

c. A new Air Force transport plane.

d. Food, fun, and frolic.

5. Which of the following is a good reason to own a fund of funds?

a. You like paying extra fees.

b. You've determined that you can benefit from a diversified portfolio of hedged assets, but you don't have the assets to do it on your own.

c. It will impress the ladies.

d. It will impress the fellows.

6. A family office

a. Is the room off the kitchen where you keep the computer and pay the bills.

b. Won't increase the market value of your house as much as a master suite with a steam shower will.

c. Is irrelevant to a discussion of hedge funds.

d. Is an investment pool for people in the same family, usually of inherited money, that may be run similarly to a hedge fund.

7. Mutual funds

a. Now can pursue some of the same strategies that hedge funds do.

b. Are forbidden from following the strategies that hedge funds do.

c. Are irrelevant to a discussion of hedge funds.

d. Are bad investments.

Answers: 1) d 2) c 3) c 4) a 5) b 6) d 7) a

Chapter 16

Using Hedge-Fund Strategies without Hedge Funds

In This Chapter

▶ Hedging through the diversification of your portfolio

▶ Expanding your assets

▶ Exploring margin and leverage techniques

A full-fledged hedge fund may not be appropriate for you for a variety of reasons. You may not be an accredited investor (see Chapter 2). You may not be able to lock up your money for long periods of time (see Chapter 7). Or you may not be able to buy into a fund that seems suitable for you. However, these obstacles don't prevent you from taking advantage of hedge-fund strategies to protect your other investments in all types of market conditions.

Investors of all shapes and sizes can (and should) use diversification to reduce risk and increase return — a staple of the hedge-fund strategy. Some investors may also want to try their hands at more aggressive techniques, like leverage (investing with borrowed money; see Chapter 11), short-selling (selling borrowed shares of stocks expected to fall in price; see Chapter 11), and using derivatives (options, futures, and so on; see Chapter 5). You can diversify your investments to take advantage of natural hedges, which are offsetting risk and return relationships between asset classes. And, you can enter mutual funds that follow certain hedge-fund investment styles without the accredited-investor requirements. This chapter shows you how to make these hedge-fund strategies and more work for you.

A Diversified Portfolio Is a Hedged Portfolio

You have a choice of different investment assets: stocks, bonds, cash, real estate, and precious metals, to name a few. These assets all perform differently at different times over an economic or business cycle, which is why long-term investors usually hold a mix of assets, figuring that some years will bring fruitful returns and others will be down years. The process of mixing the assets that investors hold is known as *diversification.*

Because different assets have different risk-and-return profiles, they offset each other to generate smoother long-term performance. Some years, bonds will be great performers but stocks will be disappointing. Other years, bonds will be not-so-hot and stocks will be burning up the charts. That's why investors should buy some of each. Some people work with a mutual fund or investment manager who promises a diversified portfolio, and others simply buy a mix of assets to create diversification on their own.

Diversification is a long-run strategy, although it can have short-term benefits. Over the long run, the performance of the different asset classes, working together, should lead to a solid long-run total return. In the short term, you'll have a little exposure to everything, meaning that you won't miss out when one asset class shows spectacular performance.

Many investors think that instead of diversifying, they should simply move around their assets so that they're always invested in the top-performing asset. This strategy, however, requires clairvoyance, something that few people have without a 900 number attached. I've never met someone who enjoyed success with this strategy, although that could be because they're living in their beachfront houses on Maui rather than making mortgage payments in the Midwest. But beware: Following this strategy means you run the risk of constantly selling at the bottom and buying at the top, a sure-fire way to lose money (see Chapter 11 for info on buying low and selling high).

A slow-and-steady strategy works over the long run . . .

A diversified portfolio may not have stellar performance in any one year, but in exchange, you get consistent performance over the long run. Not convinced? Here's an example: Say that you had $2,000 to invest at the beginning of 1996. You put $1,000 in the S&P 500 (an index prepared by the Standard and Poor's Corporation that tracks the performance of 500 large American companies) and another $1,000 in an absolute-return investment (see Chapter 1) designed to generate a 10-percent return, year in and year out. Table 16-1 shows what would've happened to your investments.

Table 16-1	Comparing the Total Return on the S&P 500 with a Steady 10-Percent Return			
Date	S&P 500 Total Return	Value of Investment in the S&P 500	Absolute-Return Investment Total Return	Value of the Absolute-Return Investment
Initial Investment		$1,000		$1,000
12/31/1996	22.96%	$1,230	10%	$1,100
12/31/1997	33.36%	$1,640	10%	$1,199
12/31/1998	28.58%	$2,108	10%	$1,307
12/31/1999	21.04%	$2,552	10%	$1,425
12/29/2000	−9.10%	$2,320	10%	$1,553
12/31/2001	−11.89%	$2,044	10%	$1,692
12/31/2002	−22.10%	$1,592	10%	$1,845
12/31/2003	28.69%	$2,049	10%	$2,011
12/31/2004	10.88%	$2,272	10%	$2,192
12/31/2005	4.91%	$2,384	10%	$2,389

At the end of the 10 years, you would've been better off in the absolute-return investment, but you would've sat with an investment that underperformed in the early years. Many investors would've thrown their hands up in 1998 and moved their money out of the absolute-return fund and into the S&P 500, just in time for a big move up — followed by a long slide down.

A diversified portfolio requires some patience, just as any long-run investment strategy does. Diversification eliminates the problem of predicting which assets will do best in which years, but it means that your portfolio won't do as well in years when a single asset class shows unprecedented, high rates of return. When thinking about what investment style is right for you, you have to decide if you'd rather have a steady return and give up the excitement of the up years, or if you'd rather ride the roller coaster and end up in the same place.

...But some investors want to hit a home run NOW

Many investors — professional and amateur alike — claim to invest for the long run, but the reality is that they track the prices of their investments daily. When you follow your investments like your fantasy sports teams, it can be painful to sit with a portfolio designed for long-run, steady return during a period when less-diversified portfolios are showing fabulous growth.

And maybe you don't want to be in hedge funds to get a steady, low-risk 8-percent or 10-percent return. Maybe you want to double your money this year. Well, don't we all? If doubling your money were easy, we would all move to Las Vegas.

Some hedge funds have had long stretches of abnormally strong performance, so such success is possible. Can you do it by yourself, on occasion? Maybe. Here are two strategies that can help:

- ✔ Take on more risk by reducing the amount of diversification in your portfolio.
- ✔ Continue diversifying by adding riskier assets than those already in your portfolio.

The following sections explore these two approaches in more detail.

Reducing your diversification

If you're after return, and you can live with some risk, a solution for you may be to concentrate your investments into riskier assets. Investors often take undiversified bets in one asset class (see Chapter 5 for more on asset classes). Young investors tend to buy more stock than older investors because they can accept more risk. Entrepreneurs may have almost all their assets in their businesses, but they can live with that risk because they believe in what they're doing. You may not be hedging, technically, but remember: Not many of what people call "hedge funds" are hedging, either.

Suppose you just barely have enough money to invest in a hedge fund, but you still want to invest in one. So, you decide to sell all your stock and some of your bonds and put all that money into a macro fund that invests in currencies and commodities outside the United States (see Chapter 13 for more information on macro funds). In effect, you've reduced the amount of diversification in your portfolio by taking a large bet in one sector.

Diversification into riskier assets

Ah, you say, you've read Chapter 6, and one of the points I make there is that diversification can actually increase return while reducing risk. So how do you do that?

Well, you diversify into riskier assets! Here are some examples of this strategy:

- If you hold mostly cash, you can buy bonds.
- If you hold cash and bonds, you can buy stock.
- If you hold mostly U.S. assets, you can buy in markets outside the United States.

These assets you diversify with may have the same or greater risk on a stand-alone basis as the assets you already have, but if the new assets don't correlate with the old assets — in other words, if they don't move up and down in the same direction at the same time — you can improve your overall return while reducing risk.

Diversification into riskier assets is the reason that big institutional investors like pensions and endowments put money in risky, directional hedge funds (see Chapter 1). Their small positions in aggressive commodities-trading funds or highly leveraged global macro funds not only increase returns in the years that those strategies do well, but also offset the risk in other parts of the portfolios.

To a finance professor, *risk* is the likelihood of getting any return other than the return you expect to get. In these terms, if your investment does better than expected, you took on risk. In the real world, most investors don't see getting more money than expected to be a risky proposition, which is why you need to think about downside risk, not total risk. See Chapter 6 for more information.

Exploring Your Expanding Asset Universe

Hedge fund managers invest in a huge range of assets. If you look through most of the chapters in Part III, you discover the many ways that a hedge fund manager can make money. Currency. Commodities. Private equity. Common stock. Options. Warrants. Convertibles. Plain-vanilla bonds. Selling ice cream on eBay. (Just wanted to make sure that you're still paying attention.) The list is long, and that's the point: The easiest way for you to hedge risk is to diversify holdings among your different assets with different risk and return characteristics. You can do that without a net worth of a million dollars and without paying a hedge fund manager a 20-percent performance fee. After you develop a core portfolio of stocks, bonds, and cash, you can think about adding positions in other assets. This section explores the asset alternatives that you can explore, at least until you get that million dollars (and even long after).

Individual investors should keep an emergency fund of cash equal to about six months' worth of expenses. Pension funds and endowments keep some of their holdings in cash to meet their obligations, and so should you.

Rounding up the usual asset alternatives

If you're interested in hedge-fund strategies and want to be involved with a fund at some point, you're probably familiar with stocks, bonds, and cash as asset classes. However, at this stage in your investment career, you may not be as familiar with some alternative investments that could help you round out your investment portfolio. I dive into some alternatives in the pages that follow.

International stock

The U.S. economy has a direct effect on the U.S. stock market. Other stock markets don't feel the same effect, or at least not to the same extent, which is why one way to diversify your portfolio is to add international stock. You can buy stock directly or through mutual funds — some of which buy shares in companies all over the world, and some of which concentrate on certain markets. Which strategy is right for you depends in large part on what risks you want to manage and what other assets you hold in your portfolio.

Table 16-2 shows what happens to an investor's portfolio if he puts half the money he allocates to U.S. equities into an international fund with a lower beta but the same expected total return (you can find out about beta in Chapter 6). The result? The same performance with less risk.

Table 16-2	Reducing Mutual Fund Risk, but Not Return, through Diversification				
	Mutual Fund	*Expected Return*	*Beta*	*Portfolio Percentage*	*Weighted Beta*
Original Portfolio	Domestic growth	15%	1.60	50%	0.80
	Bond	6%	0.80	30%	0.24
	Money market	1%	—	20%	=
				100%	1.04
Expected Portfolio Return		10%			
Revised Portfolio	Domestic growth	15%	1.60	25%	0.40
	International growth	15%	1.10	25%	0.28

Mutual Fund	Expected Return	Beta	Portfolio Percentage	Weighted Beta
Bond	6%	0.80	30%	0.24
Money market	1%	—	20%	=
			100%	0.92
Expected Portfolio Return	10%			

Now, you may be thinking, why not just put all the money in the international fund? After all, it has a lower risk for the same return. You need to remember that beta is calculated relative to the U.S. stock market. You choose the international fund because it has less correlation with the U.S. market, not necessarily less total risk.

Foreign currencies

Want to hedge against volatility in the U.S. dollar? One easy way to combat the dollar is to buy other currencies, like the euro or the yen. You could go to the bank, exchange your bills, and then put them under a mattress, but then you lose out on the interest you could earn on that money. A better tactic is to put the money in a foreign currency certificate of deposit. One bank that offers certificates is EverBank (www.everbank.com).

Another alternative is currency *exchange-traded funds,* which are investment pools that trade on the stock exchanges. Exchange-traded funds that invest in currencies hold cash in whatever currency that they're designed to track — like euros, British pounds, Mexican pesos, and so on — so their performance matches the change in the price of the currency. If the currency increases in value, so does the exchange-traded fund.

Commodities

Commodities are the raw materials of life: metals, minerals, agricultural products, and so on. You have four ways to add commodities to your diversified portfolio:

- ✔ **Buy the commodity outright.** This strategy may not be practical — who wants barrels of oil in the garage and wheat in the shed? — but it is possible, especially for some types of commodities that you can keep on hand. For example, some coin dealers sell silver, gold, and platinum coins and ingots.

- ✔ **Increase your commodity exposure through exchange-traded futures and options.** These allow you to speculate on future price changes, although trading can be complicated.

- ✔ **Buy a commodity exchange-traded fund.** This is an investment pool that trades on the stock exchanges. It invests money in futures contracts or in physical commodities so that the price of the exchange-traded fund changes with the price of the commodities themselves.

- ✔ **Buy stock in companies that operate in the commodities business.** This is the way to go if you don't want to deal with storage and you don't want to trade derivatives. Oil companies have exposure to petroleum prices, mining company shares go up with metals prices, and the prices of winter wheat and pork bellies profoundly affect food processors, for example.

Other assets you may not have considered

One of the reasons academic models often don't describe what actually happens in the markets is that in financial theory, a *market* is defined as every possible asset that one could hold. In practice, that definition is way too broad, so the models test by using market indexes or stock-exchange data that exclude huge categories of assets.

You don't want to make that mistake with your personal investments! When you think about how to best diversify your portfolio in the interest of reducing risk, mimicking the investment strategy of a hedge fund, think about every asset you have. The two easiest assets to overlook are your own earning capacity, or your *human capital,* and your house.

Your human capital

Investors often overlook their greatest asset: their *human capital.* The ability to go out and make a living often trumps the ability to get an unusually large return on investable assets, which is a good thing. If your retirement savings fall short, you can always work a year or two longer. You may not want to, but at least your ability to work cushions your risk.

However, you have heavy exposure to the industry in which you ply your trade, so keep that in mind when you choose your investments. Many companies offer their employees good deals on company stock, and some companies even use the stock to match employee retirement contributions. These perks are great when your employer is doing well, but if your employer isn't enjoying much success, you could lose both your job and your life's savings (Enron, anyone?). To reduce your risk, you should consider diversifying your holdings away from your industry and your employer.

Institutional investors don't have human capital to fall back on if they have a bad year or two. As an individual, you have that key advantage.

Separating luxuries and investments

People sometimes justify frivolous purchases by thinking of them as investments. Calling many items "investments" makes them sound necessary, but face it, most of them are not. Most cars go down in value. Diamonds are expensive mostly because a cartel controls their sale — ask any jilted bride what she got when she tried to return her ring. An expensive suit may help you get a job or win a client, but it will ultimately end up at the thrift shop. Art sometimes goes up in value, but not always. And can you really get someone to buy your stuffed-animal collection? Go ahead and spend your money if you want, but don't confuse luxuries with investments.

Residential real estate

Your personal residence may be an investment, or it may be insurance against risk. Its label depends in part on your personal preference and in part on your investment strategy. If your place is completely paid for, you have a place to live regardless of what happens to your job and the markets. Even if the value of your house declines, you won't need to move. For this reason, many corporations and almost all universities own their land and buildings outright instead of financing them.

For the most part, land is a store of value. It increases in price at about the same rate as inflation, so you can sell it and get back the same purchasing power that you put into it. Land isn't so much an investment as a safety net. In some cases, it appreciates faster than inflation, especially if an area becomes more desirable.

Despite conventional wisdom and your real-estate agent's advice, real estate doesn't always go up in value, especially when you take inflation into account. Real estate can be a risky investment. One way that people increase their risk is by borrowing money to buy property. (Unfortunately, that's also the only way that many people can afford their primary residences!) By taking out a mortgage, you make a bet that the price will increase faster than inflation or that the interest rate will soon be less than inflation. If either of those situations comes to fruition, you'll post a real return greater than inflation.

No matter how you finance it and no matter what your philosophy toward risk, residential real estate doesn't perform exactly like other investments. By including it in your portfolio, you offset some of the risk of your other investments, which is what hedging is all about.

Structuring a Hedge-Filled Portfolio

You have several ways to structure a hedge in order to reduce risk without necessarily reducing return. You can use complex computer programming to make the hedge perfect, or you can do it yourself and get most of the way there.

Most brokers, financial planners, and investment consultants have access to programs that can help you find offsets for some of the risks in your portfolio. Even if these gurus don't recommend a hedge fund — and even if a hedge fund isn't suitable for you — they can still help you use some hedging techniques.

Recognizing natural hedges

A *natural hedge* is a built-in protection that already exists in your business or personal life. For example, if a business has both revenue and expenses in the same foreign currency, it has a natural hedge against the fluctuation of that currency relative to the U.S. dollar. If you work in technology and your spouse works in social services, you have a natural hedge in your family's human capital because the chances are low that you would both be out of work at the same time.

When you examine your investment portfolio, be sure to define it broadly enough to think about where you may have natural hedges. If you own a lot of bonds, for example, you have a lot of exposure to inflation, but if you have a fixed-rate mortgage on your house and have recently inherited a rare-coin collection, you have some natural hedges against deterioration in the price of the bonds.

When you're looking at the natural hedges in your accounts, sit and think: What could go wrong? How can you insure against these events? How much are you willing to pay to insure against something going wrong, like interest rates going up or the stock market going down or the dollar changing in value?

The natural hedges you find may not be in your portfolio, but rather in your lifestyle. If you own your house outright, you can afford more variability in your retirement investments than if you expect to be making house payments while you're collecting Social Security. If a university can cover its basic operating expenses through tuition, its endowment fund can take more risk than if its income is vital to the short-term survival of the institution.

There's no such thing as a free lunch when investing. Investment return is a function of risk. If you give up all risk, you give up all potential for return.

When you understand your risk, you can start to think about what you need to hedge. Do you need to hedge your earnings power for next year (possibly with disability insurance)? Hedge the value of your portfolio against huge swings in value (possibly by using options and futures)? Lock in the return on company stock that you can't sell for six more years? With a sense of the dollars and time involved, you can take a more quantitative approach.

Doing the math

A qualitative analysis of your holdings and your risk levels can get you pretty far (see the previous section), but you may want to go further in order to more precisely hedge your portfolio by crunching some numbers. Two alternatives include matching your cash flow obligations and portfolio optimization.

Matching cash flows

If you examine your finances for several years, you can see some of the different payments that become due:

> **For an individual:** Mortgage, college tuitions, new cars, retirement spending, and so on

> **For an institution:** New dorms, scholarships, expanded laboratories, pensions, and so on

With a list in hand, you can structure an investment to match the cash flow needs of each situation. For example, if you have ongoing mortgage payments that you must fund, one solution is a bond or other fixed-income investment that generates interest payments equal to the mortgage payments. Also, if you don't need your retirement money for 40 years, you can invest it more aggressively to generate maximum capital gains — and re-adjust your investing as needed before the 40 years are up.

Portfolio-management tactics can help you separate how much money you can put into risky, illiquid investments and how much money you need to keep safe. In other words, you figure out how much return you need and when (see Chapter 7).

And yes, hedge fund managers use the same tactics. If they allow investors to make withdrawals, they need to make sure that they have enough cash on hand to meet the withdrawals. They also need to generate cash for the management and performance fees (see Chapter 2). The managers can keep the rest of their portfolios in longer-term investments.

Portfolio optimization

Portfolio optimization is a mathematical process that attempts to maximize portfolio return and minimize risk, given whatever measure of risk you choose (see Chapter 6). The risk measure may be *beta,* or the correlation of a security with the market under the Capital Assets Pricing Model (which I also discuss in Chapter 6), or it may be *value at risk* (see Chapter 14), the maximum dollar loss expected in a time period with a specified confidence level — say, 95 percent.

For the most part, you have to purchase the software required to do an optimization, or you have to access it through a broker or financial advisor. It's difficult, but not impossible, to do a good optimization on your own. If you want to try, go to `www.spreadsheetmodeling.com/free_samples.htm` to see a portfolio optimization spreadsheet created by Craig Holden, author of *Excel Modeling* (Prentice Hall), a textbook on portfolio optimization.

You (and hedge fund managers) measure risk and return historically. No matter the quality of the optimization software you purchase and the data that you put into it, the results won't be perfect because the future will never be exactly like the past.

Utilizing Margin and Leverage in Your Accounts

Not all hedge fund managers structure their funds to reduce risk. Some take on huge risks, with the goal of generating huge returns in the process. The expected returns may be greater than anticipated for the amount of risk taken, but take note: Risk is taken. An easy way for you to follow this hedge-fund strategy and increase risk is through *leverage* — the use of borrowed funds to make an investment.

Chapter 11 covers how hedge funds use leverage to increase return. The same techniques are available to you. However, you have to meet necessary net-worth requirements and intermediate payments while you wait for your investment to work out, which can put pressure on your portfolio. And if your leveraged investment fails, you still have to repay the loan.

Hedge funds also borrow money to make trades. You can follow this strategy, too, through a margin account (see Chapter 11). You can open a margin account at almost any brokerage firm through an application called a *margin agreement.* After the agreement is in place, you can borrow up to 50 percent of your investment — a rate set by the Federal Reserve Bank to ensure that markets function even if a crash occurs.

Here's an example. Say you want to purchase 400 shares of a stock at a price of $25.00. Your total investment is $10,000, and you borrow $5,000 at an interest rate of 10 percent. Table 16-3 shows you how the margin works and what you can expect in terms of return.

Table 16-3				An Example Return from a Margin Account			
Ending Price per Share	Ending Position Value	Loan Value	Net Equity	Maintenance Margin	Change in Stock Price	Interest Charged	Rate of Return
$40.00	$16,000	$5,000	$11,000	69%	60%	$500	110%
$25.00	$10,000	$5,000	$5,000	50%	0%	$500	–10%
$15.00	$6,000	$5,000	$1,000	17%	–40%	$500	–90%

The $5,000 loan you take out to buy the stock leads to a huge return if the stock price goes up (to $40.00). However, because you have to pay interest, the margin trade loses money if the stock stays flat or goes down. If the stock price declines, you may have to put more money in your account, too. The tradeoff for the increased return is increased risk.

The following sections discuss leverage and how you can use margin and derivatives to manage risk in investment portfolios. Hedge fund managers use these techniques, and you can, too. (I introduce derivatives, which are contracts that draw their value from the price of a different security, in Chapter 5.)

Derivatives for leverage and hedging

You can use *derivatives* — or options and futures (see Chapter 5) — both to protect your investment positions and to generate high levels of return. Derivatives transactions have built-in leverage because you put up only a small amount of money to buy exposure to a security's price.

For example, a call option gives the owner the right to buy a stock at a set price in the future. If the stock goes up in price, the option has a lot of value, especially relative to the price the owner paid for it.

Allow me to illustrate my point. Say a stock has a current price of $61.00. The strike price (which is the price where the option can be executed) is $65.00, and the option price is $0.85. If you purchase options on 100 shares, your total price is $85. You're out that money no matter what happens. Tables 16-4 and 16-5 use this information to show you how derivatives add leverage to a portfolio and may generate a big return for a relatively small initial purchase.

Option contracts are priced on a per-share basis and issued to cover a lot of 100 shares, so you would need one contract for each 100 shares.

Table 16-4	Return to the Buyer of the Call Option	
Share Price at Expiration	**Dollar Return**	**Percentage Return**
$65.00 or less	$(85.00)	–100%
$66.00	$15.00	18%
$67.00	$115.00	135%
$68.00	$215.00	253%
$69.00	$315.00	371%
$70.00	$415.00	488%

Table 16-5	Return to the Seller of the Call Option	
Share Price at Expiration	**Dollar Return**	**Percentage Return**
$65.00 or less	$85.00	Infinite
$66.00	$(15.00)	–18%
$67.00	$(115.00)	–135%
$68.00	$(215.00)	–253%
$69.00	$(315.00)	–371%
$70.00	$(415.00)	–488%

You may have noticed that every dollar the option buyer makes, the option seller ends up losing. Options are a *zero sum game*. Every winner creates an equal loser. Value is traded, not created.

Sure, you can use derivatives to add risk and return to your portfolio, but you can also use them to hedge risk. Many hedge fund managers rely on derivatives to minimize risk and maximize return. The following sections dive deeper into this topic.

The information in this chapter isn't enough to get you started in derivatives trading. If you want to discover more, check out the courses offered by the Chicago Board Options Exchange (www.cboe.com/LearnCenter) and the Chicago Mercantile Exchange (www.cme.com/edu). And, of course, you can pick up *Futures and Options For Dummies* (Wiley), by Joe Duarte, MD.

Derivatives make brokers rich, but they don't always do the same for clients. The commissions to small investors can be high, and because options and futures expire on a regular basis, folks who invest in them have to trade constantly. Derivatives may be right for you, but do your homework to make sure that your financial broker is acting in your best interest and not in his.

Options

An *option* gives you the right to buy or sell an asset in the future at a price set in the present. But an option doesn't require you to buy or sell; you use the option only if you can use it to your advantage. For example, if you buy an option that allows you to buy shares of stock at $65 per share in three months, and in three months the stock is trading at $50, you wouldn't exercise the option. You'd be out whatever you paid for it, but no more.

A *call option* gives you the right to buy, and a *put option* gives you the right to sell. How might you use these options to hedge?

- ✔ If you want to protect a *long position* — that is, the price of securities that you own — you should buy a put. If the price goes down, you have the right to sell at a set price.

- ✔ If you want to protect a *short position* — that is, borrowed stock you sell in hopes of repaying when the stock goes down in price — you should buy a call. At that point, you have the right to repurchase the stock at a set price.

Suppose you own 20,000 shares in your company's stock (at an initial price per share of $50), in total currently worth $1,000,000, but you can't sell any shares right now. In six months you plan to retire and be able to sell, and you want to use that money to buy a condo in Florida. To ensure that the money stays put, you use a strategy known as a *straddle* that expires in six months; in other words, you sell a call option and use the proceeds to buy a put. If the stock price goes up, you'll have to sell it, but you'll lock in the value of your holding. If the stock price goes down, you can put the stock to the seller of the option (which means that you'll force the seller of the option to buy the stock from you), also locking in your value.

Table 16-6 shows you the breakdowns for selling a call option and buying a put option. Table 16-7 shows you what happens with the return to the buyer of the call option.

Table 16-6		Hedging with a Straddle		
	Strike Price	Option Price per Share	Option Contracts Traded	Purchase Price
Sell a Call Option	$65.00	$0.75	200	$15,000.00
Buy a Put Option	$35.00	$0.75	200	$15,000.00

Table 16-7	Return to the Buyer of the Call Option
Share Price at Expiration	Portfolio Value
$30.00	$700,000
$35.00	$700,000
$40.00	$800,000
$45.00	$900,000
$50.00	$1,000,000
$55.00	$1,100,000
$60.00	$1,200,000
$65.00	$1,300,000
$70.00	$1,300,000

The put and the call have the same price, so the straddle has no upfront cost. You're now guaranteed a value of at least $700,000 in six months, and it can go up to a maximum value of $1,300,000. What happens if another business takes over your company and the stock doubles or even triples? You have $1,300,000. Don't laugh — it happened to Ted Turner when AOL acquired Time-Warner. Experts estimate that a straddle he had in place caused him to give up $190 million. He had a lot of Time-Warner stock that he picked up when he sold CNN to the company, and he was not allowed to sell it right away. To protect his portfolio from the possibility of the stock going down in price, he bought puts; to cover the cost of the puts, he sold calls. He had no idea of knowing that the stock would go up as much as it did, because not every Ted Turner is clairvoyant. Return is compensation for taking risk, so keep in mind that if you give up some risk, you may also give up some return.

Futures

A *futures* contract lets you lock in a price for an asset or a market index. Unlike an option (see the previous section), you commit to a futures contract: You have the obligation to pay up. Almost all investors settle futures with cash, not with their underlying assets. So, if you agree to sell corn at a specified future price, you don't have to go out and find a farmer to deliver the product.

You buy a future if you want to add a type of risk to your portfolio, either to speculate or to diversify, and you sell a future if you want to remove a risk — and removing a risk is the same as hedging. Futures have a finite life, so you have to close out the transactions at some point. Here are a few examples of where futures may be the way to go:

- ✔ If you want to add exposure to pork bellies
- ✔ If you want to sell off your interest-rate risk
- ✔ If you want to lock in the yen/euro exchange rate

Here's an illustration of the second bullet: You have a large bond portfolio that you plan to use to pay for your son's college education. He's a high-school junior, so you don't want to put any money into the stock market or other assets. However, you're concerned that if interest rates go up, the value of your portfolio will go down. To reduce your interest-rate risk, you sell interest-rate futures. (See Chapters 10 and 11 for more info on futures strategies.)

Short-selling as a hedging and leverage strategy

Short-selling is the process of borrowing a security, selling it, and then hoping that the price declines so that you can buy the security back at a lower price in order to repay the loan. Short-selling is a popular tactic with hedge fund managers, because it allows their funds to make money even when the markets are going down. (See Chapter 11 for some of the different short-selling strategies that hedge funds use.)

Short-selling is also a form of leverage. Not only do you borrow the shares you sell, but also you can invest the proceeds of your sales into other securities. The risk? You need to cover the short at some point, an expensive proposition if the security goes up in price rather than down. And yes, if the security more than doubles in price, you can lose more than 100 percent of your original investment.

I see no reason why you can't use short-selling as a strategy as well. Just keep in mind that whenever you borrow, you increase your risk. And, in the long run, markets have an upward bias as long as the economy is growing, so short-selling goes against that trend. I'm not saying you can't make money, but you need to do very careful research on the securities that you plan to sell short.

More leverage! Other sources of borrowed funds

You can add leverage to your portfolio by borrowing money from other sources to invest, thereby increasing the risk, and the potential return, in your overall investment portfolio. Options include the following:

- ✔ Taking a home equity line of credit
- ✔ Borrowing against a retirement plan or life-insurance policy
- ✔ Taking out a personal loan to fund an investment account

Just because you *can* add leverage doesn't mean you *should*. Few individual investors should take on more leverage than they can with a margin account. In only a very few cases is borrowing against home equity a suitable way to fund an investment account; for instance, if you know that a payment like a bonus from work is coming to you very soon, interest rates are low, and you have a need to make an investment now and not when the bonus arrives.

Think long and hard about adding leverage, and make sure you consult with your spouse or other co-owner of your property. Your spouse may not know much about leverage, but you don't want to see the look on his/her face when you explain that you have lost everything and still owe money.

Hedge Fund Strategies in Mutual Funds

Mutual funds are publicly traded investment pools. Investors buy shares in them and use the money to buy securities. For decades, laws prohibited mutual funds from tactics such as short-selling, but a specific law, the so-called "short-short rule," was repealed in 1997. Now, you can find a handful of mutual funds that offer the hedging of a traditional hedge fund without the accredited-investor requirement, long lockup, or high minimum investment (see Chapters 1 and 2).

Hedge-fund style mutual funds fall into three categories:

- ✔ Bear funds
- ✔ Long-short funds
- ✔ Funds of funds

You should keep these funds in mind if you aren't sure hedge funds are right for you or if you can't meet the accredited-investor requirement but you still want to search for suitable investments for your portfolio.

Bear funds

Bear funds are mutual funds that are invested under the assumption that the stock market is going to go down. Bear funds are designed to make money in bad markets. In order to make money in bad markets, the fund managers use a combination of short-selling (see Chapter 11), hedging, and investments in assets that tend to have low or negative correlations with the market — that is, they're likely to perform better when the market is down. If you're feeling negative about the market, a bear fund may help you profit from your pessimism. If you simply have no idea what the market will do, including a bear fund among your other holdings can reduce the risk associated with getting your expected average return.

Experts aren't exactly sure why or when markets became categorized as bear markets (down) or bull markets (up). Folks who are optimistic about the market are called *bulls,* and the pessimists are known as *bears.* Some think the terms developed because when attacked, bulls charge and bears retreat.

Long-short mutual funds

A *long-short mutual fund* is designed to be market-neutral. In theory, its performance should be consistent no matter what the market does. The manager of a long-short fund buys shares (*goes long*) in the best companies in an industry and then sells borrowed shares (*goes short*) for the worst companies. The idea is that no matter what the market does, winners and losers will emerge in every market sector. By matching pairs of stocks, fund managers cancel out much of the market risk.

Some long-short managers look for good and bad stocks, regardless of industry. Others prefer to be mostly long when they expect the market to do well and mostly short when they expect it to do poorly.

Mutual fund of funds

A *mutual fund of funds* is a mutual fund that takes shares in different mutual funds to build a balanced portfolio. Some people design funds of funds with time targets or risk levels in mind, and others simply want to diversify. The key is to know what funds the fund of funds invests in and to make sure that your portfolio needs this level of diversification. If you already own a mix of stocks and bonds, you don't need a stock-and-bond fund to help you diversify; you may need a bear fund, an international fund, or a currency fund, however.

Chapter 17

Hiring a Consultant to Help You with Hedge Funds

*T*he decision to invest in a hedge fund is a big one — especially considering it often involves a large investment that could be locked up for years. Funds are structured as private partnerships, so a person buying into a hedge fund needs to know whom he or she will be going into partnership with, and that partner is the hedge fund manager. Investors want advice that helps them make good decisions, and fund workers who have to report their decisions to a board of directors or a regulatory agency want assurance that they've acted prudently and appropriately.

For all these reasons and more, hedge fund investors often work through consultants — people who sort through the available funds to make recommendations to their clients. In this chapter, I give you the rundown on consultants. I let you in on what consultants do. I give you everything you need but a map to find the right consultant for you. You find out how consultants structure their pay. Finally, I help you avoid conflicts of interest. Not all consultants are neutral parties, so you need to find a good one before making the leap into a fund.

Who Consultants Work For

Investment consulting is a big business, and the services of consultants are in demand for pensions, endowments, foundations, and other investors who are accountable to others. The staff and trustees at investment organizations often need more information than they can gather on their own, and they need to prove that they performed an objective analysis when they made decisions about how to invest their money (see Chapter 8 for more).

Most consultants work only with institutional investors, but some may provide services to high-net-worth individuals — the kind who often look to invest in hedge funds.

Smaller accredited investors — people who don't have millions of dollars to put into hedge funds — may be able to get some of the services that investment consultants provide from other professionals, like lawyers, accountants, or financial planners.

What Do Consultants Do (Besides Consult)?

What do these consultants do for an investor, and how can they help in the hedge-fund decision process? Well, they do the following jobs that I cover in greater detail throughout the rest of this section:

- ✔ Offer an analysis of the investor's investment objectives.
- ✔ Make recommendations about asset allocation to optimize performance.
- ✔ Collect information on the risk-and-return performance of different asset managers.
- ✔ Introduce suitable investors to hedge fund managers who may be able to improve their overall investment performance.

Analyzing performance

A key task for a consultant is to analyze performance. Many consultants maintain their own performance databases or subscribe to detailed information collected by other services. They perform detailed statistical analysis to determine the following:

- ✔ How well funds performed relative to the risks that they took
- ✔ What risks the funds actually took
- ✔ How you may expect the funds to perform in different market conditions

I bet I know what you're asking right now: Just whose performance do these consultants analyze? Well, they analyze performance both for the investor and for the funds that the investor may consider:

- **Performance analysis for the investor:** For the investor, the consultant looks at how the individual's or organization's investments performed over the last quarter and the last year. He should include a look at risk, return, and investment objectives. At that point, the consultant makes recommendations for *portfolio rebalancing* (adjustments that will bring the portfolio back into compliance with its risk, return, and other objectives) based on how the client's investments performed and how the objectives have changed since the last period.

- **Performance analysis for the funds:** Many consultants compile databases of hedge funds and funds of funds (see Chapter 15), including detailed analysis of fees, risk, and return. Research often includes the use of statistical and technical measures like the Sharpe measure, which I discuss in Chapter 14.

Some consultants have collected years of data on different funds, and this archive of information can help an investor thinking about a hedge fund understand what may happen in different market scenarios and how different fund strategies can pay off. The store of info can also help an investor discover more about a person who starts a new hedge fund; if the person worked for a different fund in the past, that fund's performance may offer clues to how he may do now that he's on his own.

Determining your investment objectives

A consultant can help you determine what investment objectives you should implement and how you can manage your money to achieve and stay true to your objectives. For an institutional investor like a pension, a foundation, or an endowment, this process may involve interviews with stakeholders, research into the history of the organization, and strategic planning.

If the organization is a pension or other type of fund that has to meet a series of future payments, it can hire a consultant to determine how well its current investment assets will meet those liabilities. The consultant may help put together an investment policy that guides the fund's investment choices based on its investment objectives, and he or she may provide education to show everyone in the organization how they can best meet their obligations for investing the money.

Putting a hedge fund manager under the microscope

Investigating a fund manager is difficult but necessary work. After all, your investment is probably a big one, and your money may be locked away for many years. Even if the fund you're interested in is registered with the U.S. Securities and Exchange Commission (see Chapter 3), it isn't subject to a lot of regulatory oversight, so you better feel confident about your decision. In Chapter 18, you discover more about how you should perform due diligence on a fund. What you need to know now is that the process is a lot of work, and it's the kind of work that consultants often do for their clients.

What are the advantages of relying on a consultant to check out a fund? Consultants have an advantage in due diligence because they may already have some information collected on different funds, making the process go faster. As intermediaries, they're also more willing to ask tough questions than their clients themselves would be comfortable with.

Consultants may have huge conflicts of interest. Investors often hire them to recommend specific hedge funds based on analysis of their needs, information about the hedge funds' performance, and due diligence that the consultants perform. The problem is that hedge funds may hire consultants to do performance analysis, and the consultants may receive commissions or fees from the hedge funds when their clients make investments. Or, the consultants may be employed by the hedge funds' prime brokers, which are the brokerage firms that handle most of the funds' trades; that means the consultants would be more interested in generating money for the funds than in looking out for investors. A consultant receiving money from a hedge fund may have a hard time making an unbiased recommendation to a hedge fund investor.

Optimizing your portfolio

The topic of portfolio optimization comes up elsewhere in this book (see Chapter 16 for an example). When you optimize your portfolio, you figure out how to diversify it in order to maximize your return and minimize your risk, given your set of investment objectives (see the section "Determining your investment objectives"). The process is technical, involving statistical know-how and computing power — two areas of expertise best left to professionals. Consultants, to the rescue!

Managing a Request for Proposal (RFP)

Many organizations and some wealthy individual investors looking to invest in hedge funds start by sending out a *Request for Proposal* (RFP) — sometimes called a *Request for Quote* (RFQ). This document outlines exactly what the investor wants, and it poses a set of questions to the hedge fund manager to find out what the fund can do. Many investors hire consultants to help manage the RFP process, so many consulting firms offer the service upfront.

RFPs are as different as the clients and consultants who put them together, but the issuing consulting firm usually starts by listing the minimum requirements of a winning bid so that unqualified investors don't spend time putting together a proposal.

Along with any applicable deadlines and information on what the finished bid should look like, the RFP lists the following items that the bidder — in this case, an investment firm — must provide:

- ✓ Firm name, address, and contact information

- ✓ A history of the firm

- ✓ Résumés or biographies of key employees

- ✓ A list of the fund's accountant firm, prime broker, and other professional service providers

- ✓ Copies of any U.S. Securities and Exchange Commission (see Chapter 3), National Association of Securities Dealers, or Commodity Futures Trading Commission filings

- ✓ Explanations of any regulatory sanctions, disciplinary investigations, or recent litigation

- ✓ Clients whom the investor can contact for reference

- ✓ A description of the hedge fund's investment objectives and the strategies that it will use to meet them

- ✓ Historical risk-and-return data, with an explanation of how the fund calculated the numbers

- ✓ The fund's fee structure

Consultants and funds of funds

Because investment consultants often know so much about the structures and investment styles of different hedge funds, some parlay their knowledge into success in the fund of funds business, although some prefer the term "manager of managers." *Funds of funds* are investment pools that invest in several different hedge funds in an attempt to maximize the potential return and diversify (or reduce) some of the risk. (Chapter 15 has more information on funds of funds.)

A fund of funds is a great way for the consultant to put his big database to work. The consultant's interest becomes closely allied with the interests of his clients. Most fund of funds managers receive a cut of the performance, so they make the most money when their clients do well. That's pretty good, right?

Yep, you guessed it . . . here's the catch. The fund of funds manager usually charges an asset-management fee for services. If the same consulting firm charging you good money for its advice recommends that you invest in its fund of funds, well, you just may have to deal with a conflict of interest.

Your consultant's fund of funds may be a good investment for you, or it may not be. The best way to know whether the consultant is looking out for your best interests is to do your homework first. Know what your investment objectives are and what the fund of fund's performance and investment restrictions are.

Hunting for the Hedge-Fund Grail: A Qualified Consultant

The good news is that finding a consultant who fits your needs is easier than finding a hedge fund that does the same (or is that bad news?). Consultants are out there talking to investors. They advertise in places where investors can find them, attend investor conferences, and feature Web sites and listed phone numbers — a tactic some hedge funds are loath to employ for fear of accidentally marketing to non-accredited investors (people without a net worth of $1 million or a yearly income of $200,000 [$300,000 with a spouse]; see Chapter 2). Many funds prefer to have consultants serve as go-betweens rather than deal with investors directly.

So, to aid in your search and to appease the paranoid hedge funds, I provide the following sections full of detailed information on how to pick the right consultant for you.

Following recommendations and referrals

The best way to find an investment consultant is the best way to find any professional service provider: Ask for recommendations and referrals from people you trust who have similar situations (in this case, similar investment situations). For example, if you're a board member on a charitable endowment that's considering a hedge-fund investment, talk to board members or staffers at similar charities that have already worked with consultants. If you're an individual investor, you can talk to your lawyer, accountant, or another advisor for referrals.

Many investment consultants are active in trade organizations for nonprofit organizations, pensions, and endowments. You may know people, or know of them, who work in these environments. Don't be shy about contacting multiple sources and building a potential consultant list. At that point, you can pick up the phone and start the next step: meeting the consultant and checking her out.

Some consultants lock down clients by wining and dining them. If you're in a position of fiduciary responsibility (see Chapter 8 for more information about this topic), make sure you choose your consultant for valid business reasons that benefit the owner(s) of the money that you're investing. Otherwise, you may be breaking the law.

Performing another round of due diligence

Naturally, you should check out the consultant who piques your interest before you hire him. You wouldn't hire a nanny to watch your kids just because she seems sweet, right? (And maybe your money is your baby!) Here are some ways you can check up on your potential consultant:

- ✔ Call up other clients for references (see the previous section).
- ✔ Search online databases to see what you can find out (see Chapter 18 for some that are useful).
- ✔ Verify any U.S. Securities and Exchange Commission registrations the consultant may hold at www.sec.gov.
- ✔ Check with trade organizations like the CFA Institute to make sure the consultant has the credentials he claims to have. You can look up contact information for issuing organizations online and then call up the organization and ask if the consultant really holds the claimed credential.

Most consultants, like most professional service providers, have nothing to hide, so your search shouldn't turn up anything interesting. But if you do find something unusual that involves the consultant or his firm, wouldn't you like to know before signing a contract?

Managing Conflicts of Interest

Face it: The hedge fund investor hires the consultant, but that doesn't mean that the consultant is completely objective. Some consultants have very serious conflicts of interest. You need to ask some questions to make sure that the person you hire is working *for you*. After all, this is your money. You're using your money to make an investment, and you're using your money to pay for the consultant's services.

The biggest conflict is that the consulting firm may be receiving compensation from the hedge fund for finding investors. That means that the consultant has an incentive to put you in a fund that's almost, but not quite, right for you. If the consultant's firm puts together fund of funds products, it may also have an incentive to recommend that investment option, whether or not it's ideal for you.

Other conflicts are more subtle. The consultant may want access to the hedge fund manager for other clients, so he recommends the fund to you in order to keep up his relationship with the fund. Maintaining access may be on the consultant's mind even if the consulting firm wants performance information only for the firm's analysis products.

So, what do you do? Your first option is to ask consultants about compensation and business arrangements that may create conflicts of interest. After you identify possible conflicts, you can figure out if you can live with them or not. If you decide that you can accept them, see if you can set up offsetting fee arrangements (in other words, paying the consultant the equivalent of a commission for choosing a non-commission fund) or the use of additional research sources.

The consultants aren't the only ones who may have conflicts of interest. If you're working for a pension plan, endowment, or trust, you have to make sure that you represent the best interests of the people who depend on that money. In some cases, those interests may be different from what's best for you as an individual. Consultants and investment managers sometimes throw lavish parties, send out hard-to-get sports tickets, and pick up the tabs at fancy restaurants for their clients. Don't let those actions cloud your judgment.

Questions to ask a consultant

Before you hire a consultant, here are a few questions to ask about the consultant's background and services:

✔ What's the background of your staff members? Who will be working on my account?

✔ How do you get paid for services? Do you accept soft dollars (see the section "Compensating Consultants for Their Services")?

✔ Do you prefer to work on retainer or on a fee-for-service basis? What services are included in the retainer?

✔ What types of clients do you work with? Can you give me the names of clients who have similar accounts?

✔ How do you work with hedge funds? Do you offer them services on a fee basis? Do they pay you for referrals?

✔ Do you offer investor conferences? Who underwrites them?

✔ Do you offer any fund of funds' or manager of managers' services?

Compensating Consultants for Their Services

Consultants can get paid in many different ways. Some pay arrangements can save you money, but others can create conflicts of interest. Many consultants work on a *retainer* basis: You pay a monthly fee that goes toward the consultant's time and materials. In exchange, you receive ongoing services. Some consultants work on a *fee-for-service* basis, sending you a bill for each service that you need. Some consulting firms offer alternatives to the fee-based model, and a few collect both fees from investors and other types of compensation from hedge funds. The fee structure affects the price you'll pay and the service you'll receive.

In the investment business, most folks group the many payout options into two sectors: hard dollars and soft dollars. *Hard dollars* are cash expenditures — what you usually spend when you need to pay for something. *Soft dollars* are commission credits. Soft dollars give an investment fund or money manager a way to pay for consulting and other services without writing a big check. However, not all consultants accept soft dollars. I jump headfirst into these topics in the following sections.

If you're a political junky, you may know that soft dollars of another type are a controversial form of campaign finance. In politics, soft dollars are contributions to specific candidates made through third parties, like party organizations, in order to circumvent legal limits on the size of donations.

Hard-dollar consultants

Hard dollar is another term for cash. Some hard-dollar consultants work on a strict fee-for-service basis. They pride themselves on not taking any money from hedge fund managers or others who invest money. This policy reduces conflicts of interest, but it can be expensive. The process is simple: The consultant performs the service and sends the client a bill. The client writes a check and pays the bill. Other consultants prefer to work on retainer. I cover both options in the sections that follow.

A la carte consulting

If your consultant bills you each time you use her service, she's billing you for an *a la carte* service. You pay only for the services you need as you need them. For example, the consultant may write a Request for Proposal for you (see the section "Managing a Request for Proposal [RFP]") and then send you a bill for the work.

You need to be on the lookout for two potential pitfalls in the a la carte system:

- ✔ The consultant has an incentive to push you to buy additional services that you may not need. Your consultant could turn into the fast-food clerk who asks if you want fries with your burger.

- ✔ You may become too conscious of what you're spending and turn down services that you could benefit from buying.

Retainers

Many hard-dollar consultants prefer to work on a *retainer* basis: You agree to pay a fixed amount per month or per year, and in exchange you can rely on the consultant for regular reports, updates, and research projects. Unless an unusual project crops up in the middle of the year (such as a corporate takeover that may affect the management of a pension fund), your retainer covers the costs of all the services you need.

Paying on retainer is an expensive way to go, because you pay for the consultant's time whether or not you need it. However, it may be the best option for you, especially if you don't have the benefit of a large in-house staff (true for many institutional investors and most individual investors).

Soft-dollar consultants

Soft dollars are credits generated by brokerage commissions that money managers or investors can use to pay for a range of investment services. For example, a brokerage firm may agree to give a money manager research reports as long as the money manager generates $50,000 per year in commissions. Otherwise, the money manager has to pay a hard-dollar fee of $25,000 (that is, the manager has to write a check on the firm's account; see the previous section).

Legally, soft dollars belong to the person whose money is used to generate the trade, not to the money manager. Many institutional investors, like university endowments, ask the money manager to use soft dollars to pay for consulting services that benefit the endowment fund itself. Instead of writing a check, the money manager, under instruction from the endowment, directs trades to a brokerage firm that in turn writes a check to the consultant.

The main problem with a soft-dollar setup is that the commissions may be inflated, or the brokerage firm offering the arrangement may not have the best traders. A second problem is that some folks try to use soft dollars for everything, including rent on office space and leases on computers, even when the use of soft dollars adds little or no value to the investment process. That's simply not appropriate and possibly illegal.

Just as you have soft dollars to spend on services, a hedge fund manager has plenty of soft dollars to spend, too. Because hedge funds are lightly regulated (by the SEC; see Chapter 3), the hedge fund manager has much more freedom to spend soft dollars than a mutual fund or pension fund manager. This soft-dollar propensity means that you, the hedge fund investor, may not be getting the best possible return on your investment. If soft dollars enter into the equation when you interview prospective consultants and funds, you need to ask some tough questions of the consultants and spend some time monitoring the situations.

Some consultants accept brokerage soft dollars in exchange for their services. They may go this route through their own brokerage subsidiaries, or they may have contracts with outside brokerage firms. For a large pension or endowment fund that wants to make some investment decisions internally, using soft dollars is one way to pay for services. After all, if the fund is trading, it's generating commissions anyway, so why not put the commissions to use? As long as the value of the services provided by the consultant is in line with the cost, using soft dollars is a legitimate practice.

The United States Department of Labor has made it clear that for pension funds regulated by the Employee Retirement Income Security Act of 1972 (ERISA), commissions generated belong to the plan beneficiaries. Unless the value of the soft dollars will benefit the people who will receive the pension, soft dollars are prohibited. Some other regulators have been following suit.

Before entering into a soft-dollar contract with a consultant or other service provider, be sure that laws allow you to do so and that the service you require is worth it. You'll only know that if you do your research and know what the hard-dollar price is for the services that you're buying.

Hedge Funds Pay the Consultants, Too

Many hedge funds need investors (good news for you, I hope!). The fund managers need more money than they have to follow the investment strategies that they've put in place. Because most funds charge an annual fee of a few percent of their assets, a larger asset base means more revenue. Therefore, in order to encourage consultants to recommend their hedge funds to clients, some managers pay commissions. This may not be a bad thing if the fund you choose is right for you. A problem occurs only when the consultant recommends a less-than-ideal fund just to get his or her commission.

Some consultants reduce their fees by the amount of any commissions they receive in order to minimize the conflict of interest on their end. But remember: If you're making an investment decision on behalf of someone else — say, the beneficiaries of a pension fund or trust account — you need to make sure that you choose a fund because it's the best overall, not because it results in lower fees.

Hedge funds pay consultants for many different reasons, some of which may create a conflict of interest for you:

- **"Pay to play."** Some consultants get hard-dollar payments from hedge funds and other money managers. They may not do this directly, because that could be construed as extortion. Instead, they may accept payments for performance reporting and analysis services, or they may organize investment conferences and ask hedge fund managers to help sponsor them.

- **Shares in hedge funds.** Instead of paying commissions, some hedge fund managers give consultants and other investment advisors shares in their funds in exchange for recommending them to others. These shares have real value, especially if the funds go up! As with an outright cash commission, though, giving out shares creates a conflict of interest for the consultants. Just because a hedge fund offers this type of compensation doesn't make it a bad fund, but it does mean that you as a client need to watch out to make sure that your interests are met.

Chapter 18

Doing Due Diligence
on a Hedge Fund

· ·

In This Chapter

▶ Making peace with the need for due diligence

▶ Knowing what (and who) you need to check on

▶ Carrying out your due diligence

▶ Preparing for when the microscope falls on you

▶ Abiding by the limits of due diligence

· ·

*I*f your mother says she loves you, check it out." Harsh, maybe, but that
was the motto of Chicago's now-defunct City News Bureau, a cooperative
news agency that spread reporters over the major news sources of the city.
The lesson for Bureau reporters was that no matter what a source told them,
they needed to find a way to verify their information. Due diligence was the
key, and it's also the key to hedge funds.

Due diligence is the process of ensuring that a hedge fund is what it claims to
be. You and any lawyers, consultants, or accountants that you hire to assist
you perform a series of interviews, reference checks, and background checks
to ensure that the fund manager runs the fund well, that its investment style
meets your investment objectives (see Chapters 7 and 9), and that the people
working the fund have had few problems in their past. Doing due diligence is
in your best interest, and this chapter gives you information on how to go
about the process.

Why Do Due Diligence?

People often do business on trust. You're pretty sure the realtor or car dealer on the other side of the table is a straight shooter, and he or she is sure that you are, too. Heck, most people are basically good, and you've always done well with your other investments, so why not just write the check, sign the papers, and be done with it? Why do you have to take the time to do due diligence when everything is most likely on the up-and-up? Because sometimes, people and business transactions are not on the up-and-up.

Face it: People lie. Every day, all the time. And people exaggerate just as frequently. But that doesn't make it right. What this means is that before you commit your money to a hedge fund, you need to do some homework.

I've included the stories of some recent hedge-fund frauds in a sidebar in this chapter, "Hedge fund horror stories." Trust me, it's scary stuff.

Hedge funds are private partnerships (see Chapter 2 for more about hedge fund structure), and hedge fund managers don't always have to report everything that they do. Many investors, after looking at the stellar performances that some funds have, don't want to ask too many questions; they just want to get a piece of the action.

I can give you many specific reasons to do your due diligence, like the following:

- **Because it's your money!** The most important reason to do due diligence is that you're investing *your* money, the result of hard work and calculated risk taking. If you feel that you can just sign your money away to a hedge fund that you know little about . . . well, I hate to stop you, but why would you do that? Part of being a good investor is asking questions and understanding what you're doing. If you can't handle the basic responsibilities of investing, hedge funds just aren't right for you. Hedge funds are designed for sophisticated investors, and sophisticated investors do their homework (see Chapter 1 for more on the basics of hedge funds).

- **Meeting fiduciary responsibilities.** If you're selecting hedge-fund investments for a pension, an endowment, or a trust, or you're otherwise handling someone else's money, you have fiduciary responsibilities to uphold. (See Chapter 8 for a detailed discussion of the requirements that go with being in a fiduciary position.) You have to make sure that you have a reasonable and adequate basis for your investment decisions. In other words, you have to do your due diligence, documenting every step you take.

In fiduciary positions, due diligence forms what's known as an *affirmative defense against malpractice*. If the pension or endowment's beneficiaries decide to sue you because the hedge fund you chose turned out to be a bad choice, you can show that you made the decision carefully and that you knew as much as you could've known about the fund and the people who ran it. What's more, you'll have the documentation to prove it. A due-diligence report shows that you took your responsibilities seriously and helps you avoid being found guilty of violating your fiduciary duties.

Becoming Your Own Magnum, 1.1.: Investment Investigator

Because hedge funds are structured as partnerships (see Chapter 2), you enter into a relatively intimate business relationship with the fund manager when you buy into the fund. The better prepared you are, the better the relationship will be. If you do the work necessary to know that the fund manager is who he says he is, you'll have a greater level of trust. If you understand the hedge fund manager's attitudes about managing risk and generating return (see Chapter 6), you'll feel more comfortable with the results that the fund posts. If you know who handles the fund's cash, you can rest easier despite having few opportunities to make withdrawals (see Chapter 7).

Likewise, the hedge fund manager should know that you'll be doing your research. He should expect it, in fact. Good hedge fund managers know that if their partners do their homework, they'll be happier with their investments. Although a consultant may help you evaluate a fund manager (see Chapter 17), you still need to do your own due diligence. Fortunately, you have public databases and other resources at your disposal to help you rule out managers with a history of problems and to give you a better understanding of how the managers run the hedge funds and how they'll invest your money.

Don't judge a hedge fund by its cover (or a fund manager by his or her suit). Sure, successful people in the investment business have money to spend on designer clothes, overpriced watches, and high-end interior design. But a lavish style doesn't always indicate success. Some investors enjoy success because they're cheap; they would no more buy new cars than pay a penny over their buy prices on stocks. Others are absent-minded professor types who care only for their elaborate new futures strategies, not whether their socks match their suits. Still others go out and lease Hummers, buy expensive suits on credit cards, and dodge phone calls from collections bureaus that represent art galleries. A hedge fund manager may have the trappings of success, but that doesn't mean he's successful. You have to do your research.

First things first: Knowing what to ask

One of the first steps in determining if a particular hedge fund makes sense for you is to ask a lot of questions. After you assure the hedge fund manager that you're a serious investor (both accredited and able to invest in the fund now; see Chapter 2), you'll probably receive an offering document that answers some of your questions — and raises others that don't appear on the list. No matter how thorough the offering document is, you'll have to sit down for an interview with the fund manager or submit a list of questions to the fund's staff. And be sure to look for ways to verify the answers with outside sources (I cover how to do this next) — this is part of your due diligence.

Here's a list of questions to get you started. Your offering document will cover some; some you'll ask in an interview; and some you may have to find answers to on your own. You probably want to get an answer for each one, and you may well come up with other questions to ask.

- ✔ **Investment strategy (see Chapters 10, 11, 12, and 13):**

  - What's your investment objective? How do you achieve alpha (see Chapter 6)?

  - How did you construct your portfolio? How and why is it rebalanced?

  - What's your analysis and investment style? What would cause you to deviate from your style?

  - If you use computer models, do you ever override them? Do you change the models?

  - What's the average number of positions your fund holds? How long do you hold a typical position? What's the level of portfolio turnover?

  - Do you use sub-advisors? (*Sub-advisors* are money managers who handle a portion of the portfolio.) When and why? How do you compensate them?

  - Do you see yourself as a trader, an investor, or an analyst?

  - Why is your fund different from others with the same investment style? What edge do you have over other managers?

  - Is your fund more suitable for taxable investors or for tax-exempt ones (see Chapter 8)?

  - How does your fund keep enough liquidity to meet allowed withdrawals (see Chapter 7)?

✔ **Performance (see Chapter 14):**

- What have been your worst months? Your best months? Why?

- Did you earn your performance evenly in the past year, or did you have one or two really good months? If so, what made those months so good for your strategy?

- What was the time (the *peak-to-trough range*) between your best month and your worst month?

- What holdings have worked out the best for you? Which one was your worst ever? Why?

- Who calculates your fund's returns? How often? Where does this person get his/her data: from the prime broker or from the fund manager?

- How do you value the portfolio? When do you price it? How do you handle illiquid securities?

- Is your performance GIPS compliant? If not, why not? Do you report your performance to Morningstar or other tracking services?

✔ **Risk management (see Chapters 6 and 14):**

- How does your fund use leverage (see Chapter 11)? What's the average leverage? What's the maximum leverage allowed? How often are you near those limits?

- Does your fund always have some leverage?

- Does your fund borrow from one bank or broker, or from several?

- What's your maximum exposure to any one security? Any one market? How often are you near those limits?

- How much of your borrowing is overnight? Short-term? Long-term? How has that changed over time?

- How do you define risk? What's your firm's attitude toward risk?

- What risks have you identified? What are your strategies for managing them?

- What happens if a trader exceeds his or her limits?

- What are your long-tail risk scenarios (see Chapter 6)?

- Do you use derivatives to hedge? To speculate?

- Do you try to profit from, or hedge against, interest-rate risk? Currency risk? Market risk?

✔ **Fund operations (see Chapter 2):**

- Who are your fund's founders? Are they still with you? If they've left, why did they leave and where did they go?

- How do you compensate your traders? What's the turnover of your investment staff? Of your total staff?

- How much do the fund principals have invested in the fund? Is this a good portion of their net worth?

- How do you keep the front and back office separated?

- Who is the asset custodian?

- What are your data-backup and disaster-recovery plans? How quickly could you get back into business if your building shut down?

- Who takes over if the fund manager is incapacitated or dies? What is the key person risk?

- What are your data-security practices?

- Is the fund audited annually? If not, why not? If yours is a new fund, have you lined up an auditor to do an audit at the end of the year?

- What's your accounting firm? Your law firm? Your prime broker? Your administrative-services firm?

✔ **Compliance and transparency (see Chapters 3, 8, and 9):**

- What are your compliance policies and procedures? May I see them?

- Are you registered with the Securities and Exchange Commission? With the Commodity Futures Trading Commission? Why or why not?

- How much disclosure and reporting can I expect? How much transparency should any hedge fund investor expect?

Interviewing the hedge fund manager

Getting to know the hedge fund manager on the other side of the table is a good idea. When you talk to a fund manager, you get a sense of what it will be like doing business with this person. Is she someone who will take your calls and be patient with your questions? Does she seem to have the nerves to handle volatile markets? Does her fund's investment strategy require strong nerves and a stronger stomach? Does she like to invest? Like to make money?

Like to spend money? You want to make sure that the fund fits your needs, and that you're comfortable with the fund's strategy and the fund manager's personality.

The hedge fund manager probably won't tell you everything. For example, she probably won't discuss the fund's short positions (securities that the fund borrows from others and then sells in hopes that they'll go down in price; see Chapter 11) or even its long positions. She should, however, tell you about the following:

- ✔ How the fund goes about getting its return
- ✔ How she manages risk
- ✔ What types of securities she invests in
- ✔ How fund operations are handled

With this information, you'll know if the fund's investment strategies, risk-and-return parameters, and administration situation are logical and if they fit your investment needs.

Due diligence is as much about making sure that the hedge fund makes sense for you as an investment as it is about checking up on the fund manager.

Poring over fund literature

After you arm yourself with the right questions, and hopefully get some answers, your next step is to start checking up on the information you receive. One way to do this is by reviewing the firm's literature. A hedge fund manager will give a prospective investor thick legal documents after he or she is satisfied that the investor is accredited and serious about investing in the fund now. The documents lay out the investment policies that govern the fund and its operations. The hedge fund manager may also hand accredited and interested prospective investors glossy decks of PowerPoint slides or other sales materials that explain the fund's investment policies and operations with less "legalese."

The information in these legal documents and glossy marketing materials includes the fund's investment strategy and fees as well as biographical information on the people who run the fund. You can use these resources to make a list of information you want to verify elsewhere and to come up with questions that you still consider unanswered.

Picking up the phone

Another important step in the due-diligence process is to call former employers of the fund you're interested in and others to verify the information you've received through interviews and literature and that appears on the hedge fund manager's résumé.

The fund manager should give you reference names and contact information for the resources you want to investigate. Even if the list has a former employee's or current investor's direct line or personal cell phone, you should go through the organization's main switchboard and ask to be connected. In the unlikely event that a fraud is hot on your trail, you can catch it faster this way. Sometimes, criminals hire an accomplice and give the person a cell phone and a script to use when the phone rings. You're doing due diligence to catch an unlikely but devastating fraud.

Here's a list of people you should call:

- **Former employees.** They may restrict their details to only dates of hire and positions held, but that information is useful — especially if it doesn't match with what the hedge fund manager tells you. If you can talk to a former fund colleague in depth, consider asking about the following topics:

  - How the fund manager researched and made trades
  - How the manager worked with others on staff
  - How the manager worked with clients
  - How the fund manager affected the performance at his old position at his old firm

- **Universities and colleges.** Be sure to call the colleges listed on the hedge fund manager's résumé. Many folks have an unfortunate habit of lying about their educational backgrounds, so you should verify the degrees that the hedge fund manager claims from the schools that he says he attended. Many Wall Streeters have taken night-school classes through Harvard University's extension program and promoted them to MBAs at Harvard Business School at their own discretion.

- **Associated firms.** While you're smiling and dialing, be sure to call the law firm that the hedge fund lists as its counsel, as well as the hedge fund's accounting firm, prime broker, and administrative-services firm. You want to make sure that these firms are providing the services that the manager says they do, and you want to make sure that the relationships are good ones. After all, you'll be dealing with these people, too. (Read the rest of this chapter and Chapter 2 for more information.)

✔ **Current investors.** You may also be able to talk to current investors in the hedge fund. If so, you should ask them for the following information:

• Why they chose this fund

• If the fund's performance has met their expectations

• What type of communication they've received from the hedge fund manager

Don't be impressed by famous names or affiliations. You want to find out about the fund's operations, not the celebrities in the fund manager's social circuit.

Searching Internet databases

An easy due-diligence step is to see if the folks in charge of the hedge fund are who they say they are. One way to find out is to do some simple Internet searches and look beyond the first pages of results you see. Most likely, your search will turn up nothing interesting, but that's the point (I hope). A basic Web search can also help you grow comfortable with a fund manager by showing you the following (be on the lookout for these):

✔ Articles that the fund manager may have written

✔ Speeches that he/she may have given

✔ News stories about him/her that give you more information about the fund manager's investment philosophy

Internet databases sometimes have incorrect information, and they can be thrown off if the person that you're looking for has a common name or relatives who share the same name. Consider any information that you find to be a point for further questioning and research, not an automatic reason to accept or reject the fund. Also, some of the sites that show up may be products of the hedge fund manager herself; what you want are sites that objective outsiders have prepared.

Here are some recommended database sites:

✔ **Pretrieve** (www.pretrieve.com): Offers free searches of property records, court records, and other databases. You can see if the hedge fund's principals have had run-ins with regulators before. Pretrieve isn't as powerful as LexisNexis, but it's a good first stop.

✔ **LexisNexis** (www.lexisnexis.com): A huge database of court records, public records, and news stories. Law firms rely on it heavily because it includes more information than any free service. Unlimited access is expensive, but an a la carte service allows you to search for free and then buy the documents you need at about $3.00 each.

✔ **NASD BrokerCheck** (The National Association of Securities Dealers; www.nasdbrokercheck.com): Has an online service that lets investors check on brokers. Many people in the securities industry hold brokers' licenses, not just folks holding sales jobs. Some hedge fund managers may be registered with the NASD now, or they may have been in earlier jobs. You can find the employment and disciplinary history of managers who are registered at this site.

✔ **U.S. Securities and Exchange Commission** (SEC; www.sec.gov): Many hedge funds are registered with the U.S. Securities and Exchange Commission, so you can do research on the funds through the commission's Web site. You can also search for enforcement records (www.sec.gov/divisions/enforce.shtml) to see if a registered fund has had problems or to find out if the fund manager ran into trouble while at another job.

✔ **National Futures Association** (www.nfa.futures.org/basicnet): Many hedge funds are registered as commodities trading accounts, which the Commodity Futures Trading Commission oversees. The National Futures Association maintains a database of people and funds registered with the Commodity Futures Trading Commission, and you can look up information about the people and funds at the Web site I list here.

Given the amount of academic research that goes into finance and that hedge fund managers have absorbed, you may think that academic research can help you with your due diligence. Although many professors are researching hedge funds, and university research centers are set up to look into the market, almost all of them concentrate on historical prices. Their studies can tell you if reported macro-fund alpha was predominantly positive or negative from 2000 to 2005, for example, but they can't tell you if sharp people who will generate a positive return this year run a given fund.

Seeking help from service providers

Many hedge funds are small organizations, showing that a small number of people can manage a lot of money! However, most hedge funds rely heavily on outside service organizations, and you should check out these firms as part of your due diligence. The following list breaks down the firms that should be on *your* list:

✔ **The prime broker:** The brokerage firm that handles most of the securities trades that the fund makes. The prime broker may also handle administrative services, such as taking in new investments, dispersing any funds withdrawn, and sending out periodic statements (a dedicated administrative-services provider can also handle these functions).

The folks who actually handle the fund's cash, taking in investments and disbursing withdrawals, should be part of an outside organization. So many great administrative-services firms work with hedge funds that a fund doesn't need to manage money on its own, nor should it try. Consider it a red flag if the hedge fund you're investigating does its own administrative work, even if the fund is part of a brand-name broker, and especially if it isn't. At a minimum, separate legal subsidiaries that have guidelines to ensure that transactions happen at arm's length should provide the fund's administrative services.

✔ **A law firm:** Assists with the fund's regulatory compliance activities; even an unregistered fund has laws that govern its activities (see Chapter 3).

✔ **An accounting firm:** Assists with the fund's valuation of assets, calculation of returns, and preparation of tax forms.

✔ **Sub-advisors:** Manage certain types of assets.

✔ **An actuary or other risk-management consultant:** Helps the fund calculate the risk it takes.

You, the prospective hedge fund investor, should know who the people in these firms are and what they do. The hedge fund manager should give you a list of the fund's service providers, and you should call at least a few to verify the services provided.

More assistance with due diligence

If you represent a pension or endowment firm, you probably won't want to do all the due-diligence work on your own. You may have a lawyer or investment consultant (see Chapter 17) shoulder much of the legwork. If another person is checking on a fund, make sure you see the checklist that the person is using (see the previous sections of this chapter). And make sure to ask for a report that shows the findings of your aide's investigation, as well as any questions that remain unanswered.

If you're committing large dollars to a relatively unknown entity on your own, you may want to hire a private investigator to do some due diligence. This tactic isn't unheard of. Remember, many outstanding hedge fund managers prefer to stay out of the limelight, so it may be difficult to do research on them.

One good reason to invest in a fund of funds, an investment pool that invests in several hedge funds (see Chapter 15), is because the fund of funds organizer does the due diligence for you. However, you should still make sure that due diligence has taken place. Ask to see the organizer's reports, and ask about the methods he or she used to research the funds chosen.

What Are You Gonna Do When the Hedge Fund Does Due Diligence on YOU!

Hedge funds can't take money from anyone off the street (even if it is Wall Street); they can deal only with *accredited investors,* or people who have at least $1 million in assets or an annual income of $200,000 ($300,000 with a spouse; see Chapter 2). Securities laws also require that hedge funds ensure that their investment options are suitable for their investors (see Chapter 3).

Hedge funds operate on what's sometimes called the *Know Your Customer rule.* The fund needs to verify that you're accredited, possibly by seeing any of the following:

- ✔ Account statements
- ✔ Pay stubs
- ✔ Past tax returns

The fund manager should also ensure that the fund is suitable for your investment goals (see Chapters 7 and 9); just because you're accredited doesn't mean an investment is right for you.

Because of Federal anti-terrorism and anti-money laundering laws, a hedge fund manager may want to verify that you are who you say you are and that the money for your investment came from a legitimate source. If you don't like it, complain to your elected officials, not to the fund manager.

The fund manager may ask for certification of your accredited status before anyone on staff will talk to you. You may not need to show other information until you write the check to make the investment. And, truth be told, some smaller hedge funds don't do the work on their customers, so they may never ask you for anything but your cash.

Knowing the Limits of Due Diligence

Due diligence is a necessary process that helps you better understand the investment you're making and its ability to assist you in meeting your investment goals. The process may even stop you from investing with a fund manager who has a history of trouble with investors or who's perpetrating a fraud.

But due diligence has its limits. Good people go bad. Bad people sometimes hide problems for a while and then run out of ways to cover them up. One of the hallmarks of a really good fraud is that it has a strong foundation that stays hidden for a long time. Due diligence reduces the likelihood of fraud and gives you a defense for your fiduciary duties if a fraud occurs (see the section "Why Do Due Diligence?"), but it can't prevent every problem.

You should review your due diligence work on a regular basis to discover information that a manager may hide and to stay up to speed on current events. For example, a fund manager may not tell you about sanctions by the Securities and Exchange Commission or the National Association of Securities Dealers, even though this information is public information. An easy way to keep tabs on breaking events is by setting up a personalized news section on the Google News Web page (`news.google.com`) or by subscribing to Google's Alerts (`www.google.com/alerts`), both of which are free.

A hedge fund and its manager may check out, but that doesn't mean you'll make money. You can find plenty of honest ways to lose vast fortunes, and past performance is no assurance of future results. Keep this info in mind when you write a check.

Hedge fund horror stories

Here's the bottom line: Hedge fund managers tend to be secretive about the specifics of their trades, and hedge funds don't have to register with the U.S. Securities and Exchange Commission (see Chapter 3). Many investors are so blinded by greed that they don't ask the tough questions. And what can result from this negligence? Outright fraud. It doesn't happen often, but it does happen. Here are some recent spectacular cases of fraud:

✔ **Bayou Management.** Bayou Management operated a series of hedge funds that took in a total of $450 million from investors after the firm's inception in 1996. It seems that Bayou started as a legitimate business, but the fund had some big losses starting in 1997. The Securities and Exchange Commission alleges that rather than admit the losses to investors, the fund's managers

made up performance numbers and then used the receipts from new investors to meet withdrawal requests. It also seems that the managers pursued some extremely risky investments in hopes of making up the funds, but these risks caused them to lose more money. In the meantime, the fund's executives collected commissions from trades and took incentive payments based on allegedly phony performance.

Among the warning signs of potential problems was that Samuel Israel III, the founder of the fund, claimed to have been the head trader at Omega Advisors, a successful New York hedge fund, when he actually worked as an order taker. Bayou also operated its own brokerage firm, which made it easier to conceal wrongdoing than if it had used an outside broker to handle its trades.

(continued)

(continued)

✔ **GLT Venture Fund.** Keith Gilabert, who operated the Capital Management Group Holding Company — which managed a hedge fund, the GLT Venture Fund — raised $14.1 million from 38 investors beginning in September of 2001. The fund posted losses almost from the beginning, but it reported gains to its investors. Gilabert charged his management fees based on the phony profits, and he received commission kickbacks from one of the brokers with whom he did business. When investors made withdrawals, they received money from new investors coming in, not from the fund's assets. Federal agents also have evidence that Gilabert mass-marketed the fund, a violation of the rules requiring unregistered funds to deal only with accredited investors (see Chapter 2).

Due diligence could have uncovered two warning signs: The fund wasn't formed until 2000, but it claimed performance dating back to 1997, and in 2003, the California Department of Corporations revoked Gilabert's investment adviser registration.

✔ **International Management Associates.** In February 2006, a group of current and former NFL players filed suit against a hedge fund that they invested in, accusing the general partners of stealing their money. The Securities and Exchange Commission filed its own suit shortly thereafter. The firm involved was International Management Associates, which ran seven hedge funds but hadn't verified or audited its returns for two years. The manager, Kirk Wright, had taken in $185 million from more than 500 investors beginning in 1997. He lost money during much of that time period but sent investors statements showing big gains.

Due diligence could've shown several hints of trouble. First, the firm had no auditor. Second, instead of using a prime broker that specialized in work for hedge funds, the fund kept its accounts at E*Trade, AmeriTrade, and other online brokerage firms that usually deal with individual investors. Finally, the fund's COO and CFO were both anesthesiologists. Doctors are smart people, but medical school isn't adequate training for investment jobs.

✔ **KL Group.** KL Group started a series of hedge funds in 1999. Between 1999 and 2005, the fund managers collected $81 million in assets from investors and lost all but $11 million of that to trading losses and management fees. However, the fund reported incredible returns of over 125 percent a year. In early 2005, investors trying to withdraw found out that all their money was gone and that two of the fund's managers, Won Sok Lee and Yung Bae Kim, had fled the country. The third manager, John Lee, cooperated with investigators.

Three things could've tipped off potential investors. The first is that KL Group's principals refused to discuss the fund's strategy, holdings, or risk levels, arguing that they were entirely proprietary. You're entitled to some information about what's going on in a fund and what kind of risk the fund has. Second, a 125-percent return isn't sustainable over the long run; it's possible to make that much money, but only with large risks. That fabulous claim alone should've raised some questions, especially because the managers made the claim back to 1997 for a fund that didn't begin operations until 1999. Finally, the fund made trades through an in-house brokerage firm, Shoreland Trading — simply not a good practice. Hedge funds should use outside brokers.

✔ **Wood River Capital Management.** In October 2005, Lehman Brothers, a major investment banking and prime brokerage firm, sued Wood River Capital Management, a hedge fund that claimed to have a diversified investment style. The fund owed Lehman $20 million. It turns out that 68 percent of the fund's assets sat in a single stock, EndWave Communications, which declined in price. This went against Wood River's marketing materials, which promised investors that the fund would hold a variety of securities. Also, the fund's management had never filed statements with the Securities and Exchange Commission showing that it owned 45 percent of EndWave. Any shareholder with more than a 5-percent stake in a company must notify the Securities and Exchange Commission.

Wood River's investors had two warning signs that should've sent off bells and whistles. The first was that in 2002, the landlord of Wood River's San Francisco office sued the company for non-payment of rent. The second is that the fund's executives never presented audited financial statements, despite saying that they would — and despite that being a good practice. Wood River claimed in its offering memorandum that its audit firm was American Express Tax and Business Services. A phone call to that company would've revealed that it doesn't provide business-audit services for hedge funds or anyone else.

Part V
The Part of Tens

The 5th Wave   By Rich Tennant

"I sense you're in a hurry, so I'll be brief."

In this part . . .

The chapters in Part V contain some lists of quick information about hedge funds: myths associated with hedge funds, good reasons to invest in them, and good reasons to avoid them. The lists here help you gauge your interest and point you toward information you need to know to make good decisions with your money.

Chapter 19

Ten (Plus One) Big Myths about Hedge Funds

In This Chapter

▶ Recognizing the differences between hedge funds and other funds

▶ Figuring out the true amount of risk that comes with funds

▶ Determining who can and can't (and should and shouldn't) use hedge funds

*H*edge funds are big, glamorous, secretive, moneymaking machines. These are the facts! Unfortunately, myths fuel the media headlines, the market commentaries, and the rumors as much as reality. So, before you invest your money in a big and glamorous hedge fund, a little skepticism is in order. This chapter helps by covering myths that you're most likely to hear.

A Hedge Fund Is Like a Mutual Fund with Better Returns

A hedge fund is an investment partnership with relatively little regulatory oversight that can invest in a wide range of assets and follow a wide range of aggressive strategies. A mutual fund, on the other hand, is a heavily regulated public company that can't invest in some assets or pursue some trading strategies.

"Sign me up!" is what the hedge funds want you to say after reading these descriptions. Not so fast. The flip side of the coin is that hedge funds can lose money. Many post mediocre performances, especially after you take the fees into consideration (see Chapters 2 and 4). On the other hand, some mutual funds have great performances with relatively low fees. Just because an investment is structured as a hedge fund doesn't mean its performance is any good.

Hedge funds are great investments for investors who have a lot of money and who need the risk and return benefits that hedge funds offer. Because a hedge fund has a very different structure than a mutual fund, an average investor may have a difficult time getting into one, regardless of the performance. It's like the difference between a private club and the YMCA. You may not be able to get into the private club or afford its membership fees, but you can still get a great workout and meet plenty of interesting people at the Y.

Hedge Funds Are Asset Classes That Should Be in Diversified Portfolios

Hedge funds are *not* asset classes. That is, they're not distinct securities with distinct risk and return profiles. (You can read more about asset classes in Chapter 5.) A hedge fund is a lightly regulated private investment partnership. The hedge fund's manager probably charges a management fee of 2 percent of the assets, as well as a performance bonus of 20 percent of the profits. Saying that you want to diversify into hedge funds may be like saying, "I'm tired of shopping at stores with a 100-percent markup; I want to start shopping at places with a 150-percent markup."

Now, among the thousands of private investment partnerships that charge the *2 and 20* combination (a 2 percent or more management fee and a 20 percent performance bonus) are some that may fit your investment objectives and help you diversify your overall portfolio (see Chapters 7 and 9 to find out more about these goals). But these benefits aren't results of the fund structure; they come from the fund manager's skill and choice of assets. Look for these two characteristics when searching for a suitable hedge fund.

Alpha Is Real and Easy to Find

Ask a hedge fund manager how she plans to earn her fees, and she'll start raving about alpha like a sorority or fraternity member. Managers draw the term from the Capital Assets Pricing Model (CAPM), an academic attempt to explain how securities are valued (see Chapter 6). Alpha is performance added from the portfolio manager's skills (in other words, the performance that the manager adds or subtracts from her intellectual ability, her ability to time the market and make decisions, and her ability to come up with new investing strategies). Each hedge fund has its own way of achieving alpha, and fund managers love to talk about it.

In theory, alpha is zero. The market is so huge and so efficient that no fund can get a consistent advantage over it. If alpha does exist, it can be positive or negative. In other words, the fund manager could be subtracting value from the fund. Yowsa!

The fact is positive alpha isn't as common as most hedge fund investors would like to think. I'm not saying it *doesn't* exist, or that some fund managers haven't figured out a way to beat the market consistently. Just remember: Anyone who has really figured out alpha isn't getting up and going to work every day.

A Fund That Identifies an Exotic and Effective Strategy Is Set Forever

Assuming that some kind of alpha does exist (see the previous section), and that a hedge fund manager finds a way to get it, will the great excess performance of the fund last? Probably not.

Markets may not be perfectly efficient, but they're close (sounds like a bad sales pitch for an air conditioner, right?). Thousands of traders all over the world are connected to electronic information networks. They work for hedge funds, brokerage firms, mutual-fund companies, and other financial institutions. And while these pros are connected, they're looking to make money from aberrations in prices and patterns. One trader may find an unusual strategy that makes a ton of money. Eventually, other traders will notice the strategy and try the same thing. Either that, or market conditions will fluctuate, regulations will change, or economies will move, making the strategy obsolete.

 As much as hedge fund managers and investors want to believe that alpha can be achieved, thrive, and generate consistent profits, the success is probably a short-term opportunity. Good fund managers know this and adapt to changing markets.

Hedge Funds Are Risky

Hedge fund traders, the people who trade securities for hedge funds, are go-go people. They make crazy trades in exotic securities; they often drive fancy cars; and they have mouths that need washed out with soap. Their goal is to get extra return so that they can collect their bonuses. When they succeed, they sometimes tick off people on the other side of the trade — people including national leaders, corporate executives, and stock-exchange officials. These unhappy folks badmouth hedge funds and leave the casual observer with the idea that hedge funds are wild and crazy investments.

Some managers run hedge funds to maximize investment return relative to market performance, but others design funds to generate returns within a narrow band — say 7 percent to 9 percent — by eliminating market risk (see Chapter 6 for more on returns). The traders on these funds may be just as crazy, but they trade to insure their funds' returns to capture big profits.

Hedge Funds Hedge Risk

Not all hedge funds are risky, but not all hedge funds hedge, either. You can't make the assumption that an investment partnership called a "hedge fund" actually hedges. The first fund, set up by Alfred Winslow Jones (see Chapter 1), was a private partnership that charged a management fee and a 20-percent bonus paid out of performance. It also hedged risk by buying securities it expected to go up and selling short shares it expected to go down (see Chapter 11). In other words, Jones had a unique business structure and a unique investment strategy in his hedge fund. Nowadays, investment partnerships that call themselves "hedge funds" keep the business structure but not necessarily the hedging strategy.

Recently, I heard of a manager who claims that he's running a hedge fund. His strategy? Borrowing plenty of money and using it to buy shares in the 10 largest technology companies. If technology performs well, he'll make a fortune for himself and his investors. If tech stocks go down, though, he still has to repay his loans, which will magnify his losses. His strategy carries astronomical risk without hedging in any sense of the word.

The Hedge-Fund Industry Is Secretive and Mysterious

Hedge fund managers often shun the press, have unlisted phone numbers, and refuse to send out information to potential investors. Because these managers don't talk, they leave the outside world to assume that they have almost magical ways of making money that they can't discuss or disclose to the uninitiated.

The reality is this: In exchange for their relatively light regulation, hedge funds agree to market only to accredited investors, which are people who have at least $1 million in assets or who earn at least $200,000 per year ($300,000 with a spouse; see Chapters 1 and 2). Any activity that resembles marketing to unaccredited investors could bring a fund major trouble with the U.S. Securities and Exchange Commission, whether or not the fund is registered (see Chapter 3).

Now, if you *are* an accredited investor, a hedge fund manager who's looking for new investors should talk to you, answer your questions, and be able to explain the fund's investment strategy. You don't have to pledge allegiance, prick your finger, or learn secret passwords; you just have to invest money! (See Chapter 8 for more on transparency.)

The Hedge-Fund Industry Loves Exotic Securities

In their quest for alpha (see Chapter 6) and in their desire for big profits, hedge fund managers often invest in offbeat securities that most investors won't touch. But not all hedge funds follow this strategy. Many invest in traditional assets, like common stocks of large companies and U.S. treasury bonds — the same assets that an average mutual fund or average trust fund will focus on. The fund managers may trade differently, especially because you can't make withdrawals at any time (see Chapter 7), but the securities involved are often quite ordinary.

Hedge Funds Are Sure-Fire Ways to Make Money

Many investors want to get into hedge funds because they think they can make big bucks. Many money managers want to start hedge funds for the same reason. The idea of a flexible investment policy that can profit from markets, whether they go up or down, is mighty appealing to investors who want returns and fund managers who want to collect annual bonuses.

The stark reality is that many hedge funds don't perform well. You don't hear about these funds, because hedge funds don't have to report their results. And when a fund does perform well, the fund manager's cut of the profits may bring the returns down to the same levels that mutual fund investors receive.

Hedge funds are like any other type of investment: Some do well, and some don't. The label of the investment has nothing to do with its performance.

Hedge Funds Are Only for the "Big Guys"

Hedge funds are open only to accredited investors — people who have $1 million in assets or who earn at least $200,000 per year ($300,000 with a spouse; see Chapters 1 and 2). That's a big nut! But that requirement doesn't have to leave you out in the cold if you're a smaller investor. You can learn a trick or two from hedge fund managers:

- ✔ You can look into *funds of funds,* which have lower investor requirements that allow smaller investors to buy into a portfolio of several hedge funds (see Chapter 15).

- ✔ You can join mutual funds that sell stocks short to benefit from down markets, just as traditional hedge funds do (see Chapters 15 and 16).

- ✔ You can carefully diversify your current investment portfolio to take advantage of natural hedges that can increase return for a given level of risk — and you don't have to give up 20 percent of your profits (see Chapter 16)!

All Hedge Fund Managers Are Brilliant

Many hedge fund managers have PhDs in finance or physics, have top grades from top schools, and can solve even the toughest Sudoku puzzles in minutes. But that doesn't mean that all hedge fund managers are brilliant. Some developed a reputation for being good investors because they had one or two really good years (the result of luck); others are very good at promoting their funds, creating an aura of success even though their skills are mediocre.

Chapter 20

Ten Good Reasons to Invest in a Hedge Fund

Some hedge funds live up to the hype you've undoubtedly heard by generating great returns to help investors meet their investment objectives. Unlike in Chapter 21, I'm here to present 10 really good reasons for you to consider hedge funds for your portfolio. Want one right off the bat? Hedge funds can reduce risk and increase return, and the fund manager doesn't get paid unless he or she makes money for you. Talk about eliminating a conflict of interest! Without further ado, let me show you want funds *can* do. This chapter explores how hedge funds live up to the hype and why you should consider them.

Helping You Reduce Risk

In their purest forms, hedge funds are about reducing risk. In investing, a *hedge* is a form of insurance against an asset price decline. A hedge fund is structured to reduce the risk of the portfolio without sacrificing return. Financial research has shown that investment return is closely related to the risk that an investor takes. For example, in a traditional stock investment (see Chapter 5), the investor takes on the risk of the stock market. The more risk the investor is willing to accept, the greater his or her potential for return (and for loss). But by matching that investor's market investment with offsetting futures positions (see Chapter 5), a hedge fund can remove the market risk and isolate only the extra performance.

Because hedge funds generally have high minimum investments, they appeal most to high-net-worth individuals and to larger pension and endowment funds. In most cases, a hedge fund investor has other investments outside of the fund that carry market risk. The different risk-and-return profile of the hedge fund can offset the risk in the other investments, making the investor, as a whole, better off.

Helping You Weather Market Conditions

Markets change as quickly as the weather in Chicago. Political turmoil, natural disasters, and economic upheaval, for example, all are reflected in the daily machinations of stocks, bonds, currencies, and commodities. Hedge funds are set up to work through this upheaval for two reasons:

- They have access to a wide array of risk-management techniques that can help limit the effects of market downturns.
- They have less oversight and more freedom in their operations, which allows them to move quickly to profit from the wild swings in markets.

If you want to learn more about hedge funds and what they do, read Chapter 1. Better yet, read the rest of this book! A mutual fund manager, by contrast, would be held to the investment strategy in the prospectus, which is the offering document that it must make available to all potential investors, and would probably have to sit through hours of investment committee meetings to make any major structural changes in the portfolio. A hedge fund manager simply makes a trade when the time is right.

Increasing Your Total Diversification

Diversifying your portfolio is an easy way of hedging. Buy one stock, and you're stuck if it goes down in price. Buy two, and you can be confident that both won't go down at the same time. Buy three, and the risk of all three going down together is even smaller. Add some bonds, and the risk of your total portfolio crashing and burning is smaller still. Each of these aforementioned investments has a slightly different risk-and-return profile (see Chapters 5 and 6).

A hedge fund increases the amount of diversification in a portfolio because it has a different risk-and-return profile than other investments you may have. A fund also has more freedom to invest in other types of assets. A good hedge fund manager stays plugged into the market, maintaining access to currency swaps, commodity pools, private offerings, and other types of investments that may be hard to own otherwise. A hedge fund manager can generally use investments and investment techniques that would be impossible for individuals to try.

Increasing Your Absolute Return

If you remove market risk, which is the goal of many hedge funds, you still need some return, which is why hedge fund managers look for investments that can bring them alpha. In their search, they may find offbeat investments that can generate a greater return than what they have available from other types of investments. In financial theory, *alpha* is the excess return to an investment, a return that market performance can't explain (see Chapter 6). Performance is a simple equation:

$$\text{Exposure to Market Return} + \text{Alpha} = \text{Total Performance}$$

A stock market index fund has no alpha, because it buys all the stocks in an index in the same proportion to achieve the same performance. The return on investment is pure market, with no addition or subtraction for the manager's skill (or lack thereof).

Hedge funds also increase potential return by using leverage. In other words, they can borrow money to take greater positions in their investments (see Chapter 11). If you own a house, for example, you probably used leverage in the purchasing process. Say you put $50,000 down on a $250,000 house — a 20-percent down payment. You take a $200,000 mortgage at 5-percent interest. In a year, the house appreciates 10 percent to $275,000, and your gain on the $50,000 down payment is even greater. If you subtract the $10,000 or so that you paid in interest that year, your gain is $15,000 — a 30-percent increase.

A hedge fund uses the same process. Because a fund can borrow money in ways that other types of investments can't, it can look for an asset with a relatively low return and relatively little risk that can become an asset that offers a much higher return.

Increasing Returns for Tax-Exempt Investors

Hedge fund managers often invest without concern for the tax implications of its investment positions. That's perfectly fine for major hedge fund investors, because they don't pay taxes. These tax-exempt investors are pension funds, university and institutional endowments, and charitable foundations. For them, the aggressive and offbeat investment techniques that some hedge funds use are a perfect fit, because they don't have to worry about the friendly revenue collector taking the profits away.

If you're working for a large tax-exempt investor, it makes sense for you to investigate hedge funds as a way to increase your portfolio's overall rate of return. (See Chapter 8 for more on tax considerations and fiduciary responsibility.)

Helping Smooth Out Returns

With its emphasis on risk reduction, a hedge fund may offer a more predictable investment performance. A fund may not go up as much as the stock market during a year when the market is unusually strong, but the fund shouldn't perform as badly as the market during years when the market isn't so hot. This baseline may make returns more predictable.

Predictability is especially important to pensions and endowments. Pension funds have to pay out money to retirees every month, so the fund administrators need to know that the money is available. Endowments generate income to fund the operations of charities or educational institutions, and the beneficiaries want some assurance that money will be there to pay the bills. No student wants to lose his scholarship because his endowment lost money during the year. (See Chapter 8 for more on fiduciary responsibility.)

An investment in fixed-income securities, like U.S. government bonds, generates a predictable return, albeit a relatively low return. Therefore, such an investment won't help a pension reduce its ongoing funding costs, and it won't help with the expansion of a charity or college. Many hedge funds can offer increased predictability at higher rates of return.

Giving You Access to Broad Asset Categories

Most investment pools have specific investment objectives and specific lists of investments. They invest in only certain types of assets, and they have regular reviews. A portfolio manager may set asset classes in a prospectus or other offering document, so the manager can't make a change without having a regulatory compliance problem. In addition, outside consultants may be on hand to carefully scrutinize the portfolio manager, looking with suspicion for changes in investment style.

Hedge funds have a broader charter. The fund manager doesn't need approval to try a new investment strategy. She doesn't have to report to fund investors daily, weekly, or even monthly, so she doesn't have to worry about how an investment will look on some report card (see Chapters 8 and 9 for more on transparency). Private equity deals, complicated currency hedges, and strange commodity plays all have time to work, free of the messy oversight of people who aren't intimate with the market's machinations (see Chapter 5 for more information on different types of assets).

Exploiting Market Inefficiencies Quickly

Hedge funds have the ability to move quickly in changing markets. If a fund manager sees an investment opportunity but doesn't have the necessary cash on hand to make a transaction, he can borrow money from a bank, a brokerage firm, or even a loan shark to make the purchase (see Chapter 11). Few other types of investments have the power to use leverage the way that hedge funds do.

Hedge funds are also free to sell short. In other words, a fund can borrow an asset, sell it in hopes that it goes down in price, and then buy it back at the lower price to repay the original loan, pocketing the difference. The ability to sell short increases the opportunities to make money, even in a down market. Few other investment managers have the same freedom and the expertise to sell short. (See Chapter 11 for more info on short-selling.)

Another opportunity for hedge funds is merger and acquisition financing. The private-partnership structure limits the number of people who have to approve a capital commitment. A hedge fund can move quickly to make money on even a small difference between the market price of a company's bonds and the price that an acquirer is willing to pay. By the time other investors see the price discrepancy and put themselves in a position to act, the opportunity may be gone. (See Chapter 12 for more information on corporate considerations.)

Fund Managers Tend to Be the Savviest Investors on the Street

Allow me to give you some insight on the characteristics of a hedge fund manager. Hedge fund managers

- ✔ Tend to be really smart
- ✔ Are passionate about investing
- ✔ Care about making money, period

Making you (and themselves, of course) money is their drive, meaning they don't show interest in

- ✔ Sales and marketing
- ✔ Management
- ✔ The niceties of business etiquette

Want to make a fund manager happy? Put him in front of a quote machine.

Many of the brightest people on Wall Street run hedge funds. A good portion of them have PhDs in math or have spent time as actuaries. Fund managers don't want to deal with the overhead and the business obligations of a larger organization. When you invest in a hedge fund, you're more likely to have a sharp manager than if you choose another vehicle for your money.

Of course, brainpower is no guarantee of great results. Long-Term Capital Management had two Nobel Prize–winning economists among its general partners (see Chapter 1 for more on this fund). But smarts are a good start!

Incentives for Hedge Fund Managers Are Aligned with Your Needs

Investing in a hedge fund is a great way to ensure that your interests are taken as seriously as the fund manager's. Hedge fund managers eat what they kill, as the saying goes. Although they take a hefty cut of the fund's profits, usually 20 percent, they receive that money only if the fund sees profits. If the fund has a losing year, a fund manager can't collect a performance fee until the fund gets back to the level it enjoyed before the losses occurred, a level called the *high water mark*. This requirement gives the fund manager a huge incentive to make money for his or her investors. A mutual fund manager, by contrast, takes home a nice salary even if the fund's performance is poor.

In addition to adhering to the pay-for-performance policy, hedge fund managers often manage money for themselves and their families. Talk about pressure!

Index

BUSINESS, CAREERS & PERSONAL FINANCE

0-7645-5307-0

0-7645-5331-3 *†

Also available:
- Accounting For Dummies †
  0-7645-5314-3
- Business Plans Kit For Dummies †
  0-7645-5365-8
- Cover Letters For Dummies
  0-7645-5224-4
- Frugal Living For Dummies
  0-7645-5403-4
- Leadership For Dummies
  0-7645-5176-0
- Managing For Dummies
  0-7645-1771-6

- Marketing For Dummies
  0-7645-5600-2
- Personal Finance For Dummies *
  0-7645-2590-5
- Project Management For Dummies
  0-7645-5283-X
- Resumes For Dummies †
  0-7645-5471-9
- Selling For Dummies
  0-7645-5363-1
- Small Business Kit For Dummies *†
  0-7645-5093-4

HOME & BUSINESS COMPUTER BASICS

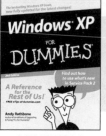

0-7645-4074-2

0-7645-3758-X

Also available:
- ACT! 6 For Dummies
  0-7645-2645-6
- iLife '04 All-in-One Desk Reference
  For Dummies
  0-7645-7347-0
- iPAQ For Dummies
  0-7645-6769-1
- Mac OS X Panther Timesaving
  Techniques For Dummies
  0-7645-5812-9
- Macs For Dummies
  0-7645-5656-8

- Microsoft Money 2004 For Dummies
  0-7645-4195-1
- Office 2003 All-in-One Desk Reference
  For Dummies
  0-7645-3883-7
- Outlook 2003 For Dummies
  0-7645-3759-8
- PCs For Dummies
  0-7645-4074-2
- TiVo For Dummies
  0-7645-6923-6
- Upgrading and Fixing PCs For Dummies
  0-7645-1665-5
- Windows XP Timesaving Techniques
  For Dummies
  0-7645-3748-2

FOOD, HOME, GARDEN, HOBBIES, MUSIC & PETS

0-7645-5295-3

0-7645-5232-5

Also available:
- Bass Guitar For Dummies
  0-7645-2487-9
- Diabetes Cookbook For Dummies
  0-7645-5230-9
- Gardening For Dummies *
  0-7645-5130-2
- Guitar For Dummies
  0-7645-5106-X
- Holiday Decorating For Dummies
  0-7645-2570-0
- Home Improvement All-in-One
  For Dummies
  0-7645-5680-0

- Knitting For Dummies
  0-7645-5395-X
- Piano For Dummies
  0-7645-5105-1
- Puppies For Dummies
  0-7645-5255-4
- Scrapbooking For Dummies
  0-7645-7208-3
- Senior Dogs For Dummies
  0-7645-5818-8
- Singing For Dummies
  0-7645-2475-5
- 30-Minute Meals For Dummies
  0-7645-2589-1

INTERNET & DIGITAL MEDIA

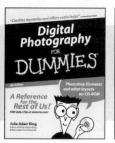

0-7645-1664-7

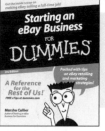

0-7645-6924-4

Also available:
- 2005 Online Shopping Directory
  For Dummies
  0-7645-7495-7
- CD & DVD Recording For Dummies
  0-7645-5956-7
- eBay For Dummies
  0-7645-5654-1
- Fighting Spam For Dummies
  0-7645-5965-6
- Genealogy Online For Dummies
  0-7645-5964-8
- Google For Dummies
  0-7645-4420-9

- Home Recording For Musicians
  For Dummies
  0-7645-1634-5
- The Internet For Dummies
  0-7645-4173-0
- iPod & iTunes For Dummies
  0-7645-7772-7
- Preventing Identity Theft For Dummies
  0-7645-7336-5
- Pro Tools All-in-One Desk Reference
  For Dummies
  0-7645-5714-9
- Roxio Easy Media Creator For Dummies
  0-7645-7131-1

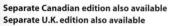

SPORTS, FITNESS, PARENTING, RELIGION & SPIRITUALITY

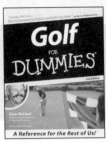

0-7645-5146-9

0-7645-5418-2

Also available:

- Adoption For Dummies
  0-7645-5488-3
- Basketball For Dummies
  0-7645-5248-1
- The Bible For Dummies
  0-7645-5296-1
- Buddhism For Dummies
  0-7645-5359-3
- Catholicism For Dummies
  0-7645-5391-7
- Hockey For Dummies
  0-7645-5228-7

- Judaism For Dummies
  0-7645-5299-6
- Martial Arts For Dummies
  0-7645-5358-5
- Pilates For Dummies
  0-7645-5397-6
- Religion For Dummies
  0-7645-5264-3
- Teaching Kids to Read For Dummies
  0-7645-4043-2
- Weight Training For Dummies
  0-7645-5168-X
- Yoga For Dummies
  0-7645-5117-5

TRAVEL

0-7645-5438-7

0-7645-5453-0

Also available:

- Alaska For Dummies
  0-7645-1761-9
- Arizona For Dummies
  0-7645-6938-4
- Cancún and the Yucatán For Dummies
  0-7645-2437-2
- Cruise Vacations For Dummies
  0-7645-6941-4
- Europe For Dummies
  0-7645-5456-5
- Ireland For Dummies
  0-7645-5455-7

- Las Vegas For Dummies
  0-7645-5448-4
- London For Dummies
  0-7645-4277-X
- New York City For Dummies
  0-7645-6945-7
- Paris For Dummies
  0-7645-5494-8
- RV Vacations For Dummies
  0-7645-5443-3
- Walt Disney World & Orlando For Dummies
  0-7645-6943-0

GRAPHICS, DESIGN & WEB DEVELOPMENT

0-7645-4345-8

0-7645-5589-8

Also available:

- Adobe Acrobat 6 PDF For Dummies
  0-7645-3760-1
- Building a Web Site For Dummies
  0-7645-7144-3
- Dreamweaver MX 2004 For Dummies
  0-7645-4342-3
- FrontPage 2003 For Dummies
  0-7645-3882-9
- HTML 4 For Dummies
  0-7645-1995-6
- Illustrator CS For Dummies
  0-7645-4084-X

- Macromedia Flash MX 2004 For Dummies
  0-7645-4358-X
- Photoshop 7 All-in-One Desk Reference For Dummies
  0-7645-1667-1
- Photoshop CS Timesaving Techniques For Dummies
  0-7645-6782-9
- PHP 5 For Dummies
  0-7645-4166-8
- PowerPoint 2003 For Dummies
  0-7645-3908-6
- QuarkXPress 6 For Dummies
  0-7645-2593-X

NETWORKING, SECURITY, PROGRAMMING & DATABASES

0-7645-6852-3

0-7645-5784-X

Also available:

- A+ Certification For Dummies
  0-7645-4187-0
- Access 2003 All-in-One Desk Reference For Dummies
  0-7645-3988-4
- Beginning Programming For Dummies
  0-7645-4997-9
- C For Dummies
  0-7645-7068-4
- Firewalls For Dummies
  0-7645-4048-3
- Home Networking For Dummies
  0-7645-42796

- Network Security For Dummies
  0-7645-1679-5
- Networking For Dummies
  0-7645-1677-9
- TCP/IP For Dummies
  0-7645-1760-0
- VBA For Dummies
  0-7645-3989-2
- Wireless All-In-One Desk Reference For Dummies
  0-7645-7496-5
- Wireless Home Networking For Dummies
  0-7645-3910-8